W9-CEG-061

The Rise of Nationalism
in Vietnam, 1900–1941

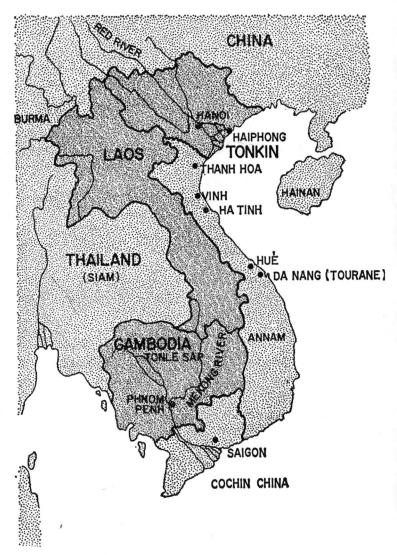

CHINA

RED RIVER

BURMA

LAOS

HANOI

HAIPHONG

TONKIN

THANH HOA

HAINAN

VINH

HA TINH

THAILAND
(SIAM)

HUẾ

DA NANG (TOURANE)

CAMBODIA
TONLE SAP

ANNAM

MEKONG RIVER

PHNOM
PENH

SAIGON

COCHIN CHINA

Map 1. Indochina

The Rise of Nationalism
in Vietnam, 1900–1941

WILLIAM J. DUIKER

Cornell University Press

ITHACA AND LONDON

First published 1976 by Cornell University Press.
Published in the United Kingdom by Cornell University Press Ltd., 2-4 Brook Street, London W1Y 1AA.

International Standard Book Number 0-8014-0951-9
Library of Congress Catalog Card Number 75-18723
Printed in the United States of America by York Composition Co., Inc.

To my wife, Yvonne

Contents

Maps

Preface

For many observers, one of the most puzzling questions raised by the conflict in Vietnam has been why the communists seem to fight so much better than their opponents. What force gives the communists the ability to maintain their determination, sometimes in the face of great odds? Why were the noncommunist elites in South Vietnam unable to unite against what was obviously a major threat to their security and their survival? As a foreign service officer with the American Embassy in Saigon during the mid-1960s, I was struck by these questions. After my resignation from government service I decided to investigate Vietnam's recent past in an attempt to find some answers to the confusing political realities of today. This work describes the reaction of the Vietnamese people to the conquest of their land by the French and traces the rise of Vietnamese nationalism from 1900 to the beginning of World War II.

Despite the intense interest in Vietnam in recent years, relatively little has been written in English about the growth of Vietnamese nationalism before World War II, probably because until recently there were few scholars capable of undertaking serious research in the Vietnamese language, and few archives from which to do research. Now the situation is changing. Historical materials relating to the period from 1900 to World War II are being uncovered and made available to scholars, particularly in France. More scholars are beginning to show an interest in the colonial period of Vietnamese history. We are now at a point where the Vietnamese response to the French conquest is subject to serious historical analysis. It is hoped that this work will make a contribution to our growing knowledge of Vietnamese history.

A number of problems afflict the English-speaking student of Vietnamese history. Not the least troublesome is the handling of proper names. The Vietnamese usually refer to themselves by their given names rather than their surnames (that is, by the last part of the name rather than the first, as it is written). In the case of prominent personalities, however, often only the surname is used, as a measure of respect. Because it is impossible to do justice to this Vietnamese custom without utterly confusing the reader, I have referred in all cases to individuals by their surnames even though, strictly speaking, this does not conform to common usage in Vietnam.

Another problem that frequently creates confusion is the labeling of geographic areas. Upon conquering Vietnam, the French divided the country into three separate administrative areas, Tonkin (along the Red River Valley and extending to the Sino-Vietnamese frontier), Annam (along the central coast), and Cochin China (the area of the Mekong Delta and south to the Ca Mau peninsula). The Vietnamese referred to the three regions as Bac bo (North Vietnam), Trung bo (Central Vietnam), and Nam bo (South Vietnam). The two designations will be used interchangeably.

I am indebted to a number of people for their kind assistance to me during the course of my research. Certainly a major source of information has been the newly opened archives relating to the period 1920–1941 at the Archives Nationales de France, Section Outre-Mer. I am especially grateful to director Marie-Antoinette Menier and her staff for helping me to obtain the full benefit of this rich source of documentary materials. Also helpful in locating sources have been Cecil Hobbes, former director of the Orientalia Division of the Library of Congress, and Abdul Rony, currently connected with the Division's South Asia Section. Giok Po Oey of the Cornell University Libraries has assisted me on a number of occasions to locate Vietnamese works not available elsewhere. I would also like to thank Ilene Glenn for her editorial assistance and for her help in typing the manuscript. Others who have been helpful in various ways have been John Balaban, Michel Borri, Mark Pratt, David Marr, Daniel Hemery, Peter White, Hoang Tan Tran, Joseph Zasloff, Vo Lang, Milton Osborne, Peter Baugher and, in particular, Tran Van Dinh, with whom I have had the pleasure of many long and fascinating conversations on the nature of modern nationalism in Vietnam. Financial assistance from the Institute for the Arts and Humanistic Studies, from the Central Fund for Research in the College of Liberal Arts at The Pennsylvania State University, and from the National Endowment for the Humanities helped in bringing this work to completion, and I am grateful for their aid.

Parts of my articles "The Revolutionary Youth League: Cradle of Communism in Vietnam," *China Quarterly,* no. 51 (July–Sept. 1972), "The Red Soviets of Nghe-Tinh: An Early Communist Rebellion in Vietnam," *Journal of Southeast Asian Studies,* 4 (Sept. 1973), and "Phan Boi Chau: Asian Revolutionary in a Changing World," *Journal of Asian Studies,* 31 (Nov. 1971), are reprinted with the permission of these journals.

Finally, I would like to express my appreciation to my wife, Yvonne, who for so many years has given me help and encouragement in writing this book.

WILLIAM J. DUIKER

State College, Pennsylvania

Abbreviations and Shortened Titles

(of works to which frequent reference is made)

AF   *Asie Française*

AOM   Archives Nationales de France, Section Outre-Mer

Buoc Ngoat   *Buoc Ngoat Vi Dai Cua Lich Su Cach Mang Viet Nam*. Hanoi, no date.

Contribution   *Contribution à l'histoire des mouvements politiques de l'Indochine Française*. Hanoi, 1930–1933.

Giai Cap   Tran Van Giau. *Giai Cap Cong Nhan Viet Nam*. Hanoi, 1961.

Giai Cap (1930–1935)   Tran Van Giau. *Giai Cap Cong Nhan Viet Nam, 1930–1935*. Hanoi, 1962.

Giai Cap (1936–1939)   Tran Van Giau. *Giai Cap Cong Nhan Viet Nam, 1936–1939*. Hanoi, 1962.

Lich Su   Tran Huy Lieu et al. *Lich Su Tam Muoi Nam Chong Phap*. Hanoi, 1958.

NCLS   *Nghien Cuu Lich Su*

Nien Bieu   Phan Boi Chau. *Phan Boi Chau Nien Bieu*. Hanoi, 1957.

NTT   Phan Boi Chau. *Nguc Trung Thu*. Saigon, no date.

TLTK   Tran Huy Lieu. *Tai Lieu Tham Khao Lich Su Cach Mang Can Dai Viet Nam*. Hanoi, 1958.

SLOTFOM   Service de Liaison avec les Originaires de Territoires de la France Outre-Mer

Introduction

As these lines are being written, the communists are just beginning to consolidate their power in Saigon, apparently putting an
end to a civil struggle that has lasted three decades. The disintegration of the Thieu government ends an era, and a dream. For
with the communist victory comes the final collapse of an American illusion that, with the help of the United States, a noncommunist society could be built in South Vietnam.

The most basic miscalculation made by the United States, however, was its misreading of history. In committing its influence
and its power in the defense of the noncommunist forces in Vietnam, the United States was attempting to reverse the trend of history. As recent events in South Vietnam have confirmed, the noncommunist forces in Vietnam never possessed the organization or
the will to guarantee the survival of a noncommunist state in
Vietnam. The American presence, like that of the French before
Geneva, obscured the fact that the communists had already won
the civil war in Vietnam at the close of World War II, and that
foreign power alone had prevented them from consolidating their
victory.

What has been happening in Vietnam in recent years can be
viewed as simply one way—the Vietnamese way—in which a nation of Southeast Asia has attempted to come to terms with the
Western world. In the simplest terms, the Vietnamese conflict rep-
resents a struggle between two divergent approaches—capitalist
and communist—to the problems of social and political change in
Vietnam. What is unique about the Vietnamese experience has
been the strength of the communists in the postwar period. In
Vietnam, alone in Southeast Asia, the communist movement be-

came the major political force within the indigenous nationalist movement. For this reason, it was Vietnam that became a pawn in the ideological cold war between East and West. In 1954, when the French finally relinquished their hold on Indochina, the power of communism in Vietnam persuaded the United States to step in to fill the gap. For while the United States did not object to the establishment of Vietnam as a modern nation-state, it saw the potential victory of communism as an indicator of the dominance of the Kremlin in Southeast Asia, and thus as a development to be opposed at virtually any cost.

Why was Marxism able to obtain such a strong foothold in Vietnam and not elsewhere in Southeast Asia? Or, to put the question another way, what factors in Vietnam prevented the rise of a mass nationalist movement similar to Nehru's Congress Party in India, or Sukarno's Nationalist Party in Indonesia? These questions are of more than mere historical interest, for answers to them might lead to tentative answers to broader questions: under what conditions does communism prosper in a developing society; are there more "Vietnams" in our future, or was the conflict in Vietnam a product of the convergence of unique circumstances? While concrete answers to these questions will not emerge from a work primarily concerned with prewar Vietnam, much can be learned from a history of the Vietnamese nationalist movement that will help us toward a greater understanding of the nature of changes taking place in Asia.

Students of modern nationalism are faced with many problems, not least of which is disagreement about the very meaning of "nationalism." Some maintain, for example, that true nationalism can exist only in the form of a mass nationalist movement led by men with a sophisticated awareness of the concept of the nation-state. For this reason, some who have written about the history of modern Vietnam hesitate to apply the term "nationalist" to many of the anticolonial groups in the twentieth century.[1] Others take a broader view, and contend that the anti-French resistance movement of the late nineteenth century was already nationalist in na-

1. David Marr, *Vietnamese Anticolonialism, 1885–1925* (Berkeley, 1971), p. 6.

ture, because of the peculiarly well-developed Vietnamese sense of
self-awareness.[2]

I do not intend to engage here in a lengthy theoretical discussion of the nature of nationalism. Indeed, nationalism is a word
widely used but poorly defined, and it would be unwise to attempt
a definition in a work of this nature. Since this is a study of the
emergence of national consciousness in a particular society, however, an explanation of the working definition used here may clear
up some potential disagreement. I am inclined to take a rather
broad view of nationalism. Like most manifestations of group
feeling, nationalism is the result of a gradual process which begins
with a primitive awareness of shared destiny and of ethnic or cultural distinctiveness. Only gradually does national consciousness
expand into an awareness of the modern concept of nationhood,
rooted in the mass of the population.

Nationalism, then, is not a phenomenon that appears suddenly.
It is the result of a *process* by which a people become conscious of
themselves as a separate national entity in the modern world, a
process by which they become willing to transfer their primary
loyalty from the village, or the region, or the monarch, to the
nation-state. In the early stages, the sense of nationality is often
primitive, and patriotic movements might be labeled protonational-
ist. As the elite leadership of such movements becomes increasingly sophisticated about the nature of the world beyond the
borders, however, it might be said that modern nationalism begins.
Mature nationalism makes its appearance when a substantial portion of the local community begins to be aware of its society as a
definable national community in the world, as a body of citizens
linked together by a common destiny, and not simply as the patrimony of a ruler or of an aristocratic class.

As defined here, therefore, nationalism will refer not solely to
the finished product, the mass nationalist movement, but to the
stages by which the Vietnamese people developed a modern sense
of nationhood. One of the problems involved in analyzing Vietnamese nationalism is the fact that during the traditional period

2. Truong Buu Lam, *Patterns of Vietnamese Response to Foreign Intervention, 1858–1900* (New Haven, 1967), p. 29.

the Vietnamese already possessed a rudimentary sense of nationalism. Two millennia of struggle for survival against the political and cultural domination of China had created in Vietnam a distinctly "national" ethnic spirit, more self-conscious, and more passionate, than that found virtually anywhere else in Southeast Asia. To a degree, this emotional commitment could be simply described as loyalty to the reigning monarchy. It was characteristic of the Vietnamese, however, to make a clear distinction between the ruler and the community and, where a distinction had to be made, to place the latter at a higher level of importance. This unique sense of ethnic awareness was subsumed in a phrase loaded with emotional overtones—the *dan toc* (roughly, "the people").[3] In view of the relatively primitive level of this awareness, and its frequent identification with the Vietnamese monarch, it is probably advisable to consider this phenomenon an example of proto-nationalism.

Any conceptual discussion of modern nationalism inevitably leads to specific questions of classification. Can moderate reformist groups who are willing to tolerate a temporary continuation of colonial rule be considered nationalists? Or are nationalists only those who strive for immediate and full independence? At what point does a moderate nationalist become simply a collaborator? The view here again will be fairly broad, for I am not inclined to deny the label of nationalist to groups who were willing to compromise their desire for national independence with an acceptance of the necessity of foreign influence on native soil. Many groups shared a sincere desire for independence with a belief that *early* independence would be a disaster. In some cases, however, tolerance of colonial rule seems to have merged into a total willingness to collaborate with the foreign authority. To such groups, perhaps, we should deny the label of nationalist. Where appropriate, however, they will be discussed here in order to determine the far boundaries of nationalism in Vietnam.

The student of Vietnamese nationalism must at some point come to terms with communism. Some scholars maintain that communism, by definition, cannot be an element within a nationalist movement. I contend that such is not the case. Communists, like

3. For a comment, see Marr, p. 6.

other nationalist groups that receive mention in this work, wanted above all to find a solution to the *national* problem, to establish Vietnam as a proud member of the world family of nations, and to render Vietnam capable of meeting the challenges of modern civilization. Marxism, like democracy or fascism, was a tool in this process.

Vietnamese nationalists, then, often differed in their solutions to the problems affecting Vietnam in the modern world. In some cases they seemed more hostile toward their rivals within the movement than toward the French, their common enemy. With all of their differences in political viewpoint and in emotional makeup, however, they shared one ultimate concern—the future survival and prosperity of the nation of Vietnam.

PART I

SCHOLAR-PATRIOTS

Chapter 1

For King and Country

One of the misfortunes of the Vietnamese has been their consistent ambivalence toward the Western challenge. It seems strange to talk about ambivalence when discussing Vietnamese history, for since early times the Vietnamese have been aware of themselves as a distinct people, inhabiting a particular area. Although their historical origin is still obscure, they initially appear in the first millennium before the Christian era as an agricultural people living mainly by the cultivation of wet rice in the region of the Red River Delta in the northeastern corner of Southeast Asia. They were culturally as well as politically distinguishable from the Chinese to the north as well as from the Chams and Khmer to the south.

Exposed to increasing pressure from the north as Chinese civilization gradually expanded into the area south of the Yangtse River, the Vietnamese were finally conquered by their larger neighbor in the second century B.C. and were then subjected to nearly one thousand years of cultural Sinicization. These centuries of Chinese control provided an avenue for the entry of Chinese culture, ranging from Confucian ethics and political institutions to the Chinese written language and artistic forms, into Vietnamese society. The cultural Sinicization of Vietnam did not, however, assimilate the Red River Valley into the Chinese political orbit. The Vietnamese retained an awareness of themselves as a separate people, and when opportunity beckoned with the decline and fall of the T'ang dynasty in China in the tenth century, Vietnam rebelled against Chinese rule and restored its independence. Yet the years of Chinese domination had left their mark, and although the Vietnamese fought off sporadic invasions from the north, they had already become more tolerant of Chinese cultural forms. The local leadership deliberately retained Chinese institutions and values in Vietnam, to the extent of creating in the Red River Valley a nation built on the model of the great empire to the north. Vietnamese political institutions, from the local administration to the imperial court itself, were consciously patterned on equivalents in China; the Chinese civil service examination system was developed, and aspiring Vietnamese bureaucrats were trained in the same Confucian classics as their young Chinese counterparts in Peking and in the Yangtse Valley. Certainly, Chinese influence had not erased all native Southeast Asian elements from Vietnamese society, but the cultural influence of China continued.[1] Vietnam's isolation from the remainder of Southeast Asia, already ordained by the chain of mountains stretching down the spine of Southeast Asia from the Chinese border to the South China Sea, was intensified as she became ever more closely attached to the cultural world revolving about China. As a political confirmation of this symbolic relationship, Vietnam periodically paid formal tribute to her more powerful neighbor to the north.

Despite their subordination to a kind of Chinese cultural imperialism (maintained by their own elites), the Vietnamese did not lose their proud sense of self-awareness as a separate people and a separate civilization in Asia. A tradition of resisting Chinese efforts at conquest became deeply imbedded in the national consciousness, not only among the scholar-gentry elite but among the peasants as well. As Vietnamese history unfolded, most of the great heroes of the Vietnamese state—the Trung sisters, Tran Hung Dao, Le Loi, Nguyen Hué—made their mark by resolutely defending Vietnamese soil against invasion from beyond the Chinese frontier, sometimes against overwhelming odds. Behind these national heroes stood nameless thousands of ordinary peasants.

Vietnamese expansion from the Red River Delta southward to the Ca Mau peninsula on the Gulf of Siam—a march that took the better part of several hundred years (from about 1000 A.D. to 1757)—led to problems of unity. The government of a nation 1,300 miles long and often less than 100 miles wide proved difficult. A civil war between political forces in the Red River Delta in

1. See Alexander Woodside, *Vietnam and the Chinese Model* (Cambridge, 1971), especially pp. 7–60.

the North and newly conquered areas in the Mekong region in the South began in the early seventeenth century and lasted for two hundred years. The country was finally reunited in 1802 by the Nguyen dynasty from the South, with the founder of the new ruling house taking as his reign name the symbolic title Gia Long (standing for the unity of the separate parts of Vietnam, Gia Dinh in the South and Thanh Long in the North).[2] Separate cultural and political traditions had developed during the long years of division, and the Nguyen dynasty was never quite recognized as fully legitimate among the majority of the population living in the Red River Region. Also, Gia Long's successors in the nineteenth century permitted the growth of a number of problems serious enough to create the constant threat of rebellion throughout the country.

These strains in Vietnamese society during the rise of the Nguyen dynasty help to explain the lack of determination with which the Vietnamese state responded to a new challenge in the middle of the nineteenth century. Gia Long had originally come to power with the assistance of the French, who had hoped to win commercial privileges and permission to propagate Christianity in the newly united kingdom. As it turned out, however, Gia Long granted only minimum advantages to his erstwhile allies, and his successors—Minh Mang, Thieu Tri, and Tu Duc—nourished a growing hostility to European influence in Vietnam. By the late 1850's, the French emperor Napoleon III had begun to exert military pressure on Vietnam to increase French influence in Southeast Asia. Beginning with an attack at Da Nang harbor on the central coast in 1858, the French shifted their focus the following year to Gia Dinh near the site of present-day Saigon, and over a period of several years gradually conquered the entire southern portion of the country from Saigon down to the Gulf of Siam. Later attacks in the next two decades consolidated France's conquest of the remainder of the country. By treaty in 1884, the monarchy was permitted to retain a modicum of authority along the central coast (now to be called Annam by the French) and in the Red River region to the north (now labeled Tonkin). Cochin China, the area

2. Gia Dinh was the name of a Cambodian village near the site of the modern capital of Saigon. Thanh Long is an historic term for Hanoi.

first conquered to the north and south of the Mekong Delta in the South, remained a French colony.[3]

Vietnam's inability to stem the tide of French advance has no simple explanation. One obvious reason was French military superiority. For this superiority, the Vietnamese had no one to blame but themselves. With the presence of the French in Vietnam during the early years of the nineteenth century, Western technological advances had become available to the Vietnamese; but the court and the military establishment, hindered by a sense of cultural superiority and a Confucian fear of outside ideas that was reminiscent of attitudes in the Manchu court in Peking, failed to take advantage of the opportunity. They made virtually no attempt to learn the secrets of French military success. When the crisis came, the Vietnamese were militarily unprepared to eject the invaders.

The above suggests, of course, that the problem was deeper than simply a question of weaponry, and that a fair share of the responsibility must be assigned to the attitude of the ruler himself and his closest advisers. Emperor Tu Duc, though an educated and apparently intelligent man, was plagued with indecision about what action to take, and his inability to lead was apparently compounded by inveterate ill health. In fairness to the emperor, there was a wide discrepancy in the advice he was receiving from his advisers at court. Some were cautious and counseled negotiations and compromise, particularly after a disastrous defeat at Ky Hoa near Gia Dinh in 1861 which demonstrated the superiority of French arms. In the view of such men, the wisest course was to make peace in order to gain time to modernize the military and civilian apparatus.[4] Such figures as Nguyen Lo Trach, Bui Vien and Nguyen Truong To were strongly critical of the army and felt that it needed to be modernized before effective resistance could

3. For an explanation of the use of geographic terms here, see the preface.

4. For a discussion of these proposals, see Dang Huy Van, "Cuoc dau tranh giua phai 'chu chien' va nhung phai 'chu hoa' trong cuoc khang chien chong Phap o cuoi the ky XIX" [The struggle between the 'hawk' and 'dove' factions in the anti-French war at the end of the nineteenth century], *Nghien Cuu Lich Su* [Historical Research], no. 94 (Jan. 1967), pp. 29–40. This journal will hereafter be cited as *NCLS*.

be raised. Indeed, it was the French invasion that sparked the first serious proposals for internal reform in Vietnamese society.

Nguyen Truong To, a Roman Catholic from Nghe An province and a Confucian scholar, issued a series of memorials to the emperor suggesting major reforms in Vietnamese society. Unlike some advisers who felt that improvement in the army alone was required, Nguyen, who had studied with a French missionary in Saigon and later spent two years in France, concluded that only a thoroughgoing reform of Vietnamese society would be sufficient to strengthen her defenses against the tide of Western advance in Southeast Asia. Nguyen had nothing but scorn for Confucian purists; he laughed at the idea that one word from the Confucian classics was worth one thousand troops and contended that the classics would not make the enemy soldiers retreat in fright. In his view, Vietnam should devote itself to the study of science and other practical matters, to develop commerce, exploit natural resources, initiate administrative and financial changes, reform the land tax, and so forth. To learn new ways, young Vietnamese should be sent abroad to study. The army should be modernized and improved and a Vietnamese mission should be sent to Europe to seek diplomatic and political support from other nations, such as Great Britain and Germany. In the meantime, he advocated a policy of negotiations with the French until the Vietnamese were in a position to match their strength with the enemy. In Nguyen's view, fighting now was like putting oil on a fire.[5]

Such views were vigorously criticized by proponents of a more active strategy of resistance. These advocates of resistance considered negotiations as the path of cowardice, and contended that the only proper course of action was retreat to the hills and the development of a guerrilla struggle against the French. Only war could settle the conflict, not peace.[6]

In the long run, Emperor Tu Duc did not really take the advice of either faction, and it might be said that his policy combined the worst of both possible worlds. He rejected suggestions for waging a

5. *Ibid.*, p. 33, citing Nguyen Truong To, *Thien Ha Dai The Luan*. For additional information on Nguyen Truong To, consult Van Tan, "Nguyen Truong To va nhung de nghi cai cach cua ong" [Nguyen Truong To and his reform proposals], *NCLS*, no. 23 (Feb. 1961), pp. 19–26.
6. Dang Huy Van, pp. 34–35.

war of guerilla resistance against the French.[7] At the same time, proposals for internal reform submitted by such scholars as Nguyen Truong To were given only perfunctory imperial consideration, were turned over to the bureaucracy, and then promptly forgotten. With a lifeless and vacillating policy at court, and a near-total failure of leadership from the emperor, it was only a matter of time before even the small numbers of French were able to complete their conquest of Vietnam.

If the emperor and the court in Hué were not doing justice to Vietnam's glorious history of resistance, tradition was being better served in the countryside. In countless villages and district towns, the local gentry and low-level military officers, steeped in the proud tradition, responded to the national crisis by attempting to organize local defense forces against the foreign invader. First to react to the challenge was Truong Dinh, son of a military officer who had settled in the Gia Dinh area. When the French opened their attacks in that part of the country in 1859 he organized a local military force to cooperate with imperial forces under the direction of Nguyen Tri Phuong. The imperial troops were badly beaten at the battle of Ky Hoa in early 1861, however, and Truong Dinh took his own forces into the northern Mekong Delta and attempted to maintain a war of attrition against the superior forces of the French. Internal factionalism and a failure to obtain support from the court at Hué hindered his movement, and defeat came in 1864.[8]

Not until 1885 did a relatively organized outbreak of violence against French rule begin. Having completed their conquest of the entire country and established a protectorate over the Center and the North by 1884, the French imposed a child-emperor on the throne. This action sparked a reaction at the court, as regent Ton That Tuyet fled from Hué with the young emperor Ham Nghi in an effort to stimulate a war of national resistance. Seeking refuge in the nearby mountains, the royalist elements issued an edict (the famous Can Vuong or "loyalty to the king" edict) formally calling

7. Marr hypothesizes that Tu Duc would have been reluctant to take to the hills, for that would have made him more dependent on the masses. David Marr, *Vietnamese Anticolonialism, 1885–1925* (Berkeley, 1971), p. 28.

8. For a discussion, see *ibid.*, pp. 30–34.

on all patriotic elements to rise in support of the king in defense
of his patrimony.[9] The message was highly traditional in content,
relying on Confucian symbols of righteousness and duty to the
appointed monarch. The emperor reminded his subjects of their
duty to follow the path of loyalty, and invoked examples of virtuous officials in the past. Ironically, the edict neglected the rich
tradition of Vietnamese resistance to the Chinese, and was limited
to citing examples of loyalty and sacrifice from the history of China.

The Can Vuong edict elicited a response from scholar-gentry
and peasants in various parts of Vietnam, and a resistance movement by the same name arose throughout the country. The most
determined reaction, however, came in the Center, where the
prominent mandarin Phan Dinh Phung created a guerrilla force
which withdrew into the tangle of mountains in the provinces of
Nghe An, Ha Tinh, and Thanh Hoa. His headquarters was at Vu
Quang, directly west of the coastal city of Vinh. After Emperor
Ham Nghi was captured by the French in 1888 and deported (the
French had already replaced him on the throne with his more
docile brother, Dong Khanh), Phan continued his resistance, although perfectly aware that the chances for victory were minimal.
The French relentlessly tracked down his forces, however, and
the movement finally collapsed in 1896, when Phan Dinh Phung
died of dysentery. With his death and the disintegration of his
forces, the momentum had gone out of the traditionalist movement.

The failure of the Can Vuong and related resistance movements
can only be explained as a consequence of several factors. Certainly a major cause of their lack of success was the absence of real
coordination among the various rebel elements. Despite laudable
attempts by Ton That Tuyet and Phan Dinh Phung to formulate
a truly national strategy, anti-French uprisings as a rule were
sporadic and poorly organized. In the end, each isolated group
continued the resistance more out of loyalty and pride than out of
any real hope of victory. The problem was complicated by the
ambiguous position of the monarchy. While Ham Nghi was in hiding and his own rebellion against the French was still active, resistance elements could claim to be fighting out of loyalty to the
dynasty. Once he was captured and placed in exile, however, there

9. The edict is located in English translation in *ibid.*, pp. 49–51.

was only one emperor in Vietnam, and he was an obedient subject of the French in Hué. Hesitant elements could thus excuse their own inaction on the grounds that the imperial dynasty itself had accepted the situation.

The betrayal of the cause by the dynasty did not necessarily deprive resistance elements of their historical justification for revolt, however. Resolute patriots could cite countless examples of ordinary citizens or lowly officials like Le Loi and Tran Hung Dao rising up to defend the homeland against the northern invader, sometimes even against the wishes of the incumbent ruler. Confucian tradition, ever practical, had made provision for this type of situation, and was capable of drawing a delicate distinction between the needs of society and the person of the ruler. A king who did not live up to the sacred duty of protecting the homeland against an outside force could simply be considered to have failed in his duty to the people, and in such a case, the Mandate of Heaven would pass into new hands. Throughout Vietnamese history, this transferral of the Heavenly Mandate had taken place more than once. In effect, it was the *symbolic* importance of the ruler as the embodiment of the sacred obligation of defending society that was important.

In consequence, the refusal of the court to mount full-scale resistance against the French did not pose an insuperable theoretical obstacle to rebel movements. If the Can Vuong needed a symbolic focus for their cause, they could call upon their forces to rise up "for king and country." And if the king in fact did not lead the resistance, the monarchy could be viewed as an abstraction, to be filled ultimately with another, more appropriate, leader of the Vietnamese people.[10] Had Phan Dinh Phung's movement successfully repulsed the invading forces, it would not have been surprising to see the rebel leader himself ascend the throne as the founder of a new ruling dynasty.

Of course Phan's movement did not win in its struggle against France. By the time the Can Vuong leaders had begun to buckle on their swords, a substantial proportion of the Vietnamese elite was beginning to conclude, for a variety of reasons, that French rule in Vietnam was tolerable. For some, the dynasty had long

10. *Ibid.*, p. 22.

been discredited and was simply not worth saving. For others the *attentiste* attitude of the court was decisive. Now that the emperor and his court were themselves collaborating, cooperation with the French became more socially acceptable. As the letters written by Hoang Cao Khai to his old friend Phan Dinh Phung attest, more than a few at court felt that further resistance was futile and could only lead to useless bloodshed.[11] Without decisive and inspired leadership from the court and the literati, nationwide resistance never materialized. Many peasants did heed Phan Dinh Phung's appeal for resistance, but by then it was too little and too late.[12]

It might be said with some justice that the feeble Vietnamese response to the French invasion was in part determined by the particular conditions in mid-nineteenth century Vietnam: a weak ruler, a divided and demoralized literati class, and a relatively unpopular dynasty. The Western challenge had come at a time when indigenous forces were not in a position to make a united stand in defense of king and country.

This can be only a partial explanation of the Vietnamese defeat, however, for the Can Vuong movement was caught in the familiar whipsaw that has rendered traditionalism so ineffective when faced with the challenge of the West. It was strictly traditionalist in nature; its potential power was based on appeals to old loyalties and beliefs. The traditional approach had often worked in the past. With leadership from the court it might have worked against the French. In the long run, however, the old ways could not win in a changing world. And yet a program of reforms, which was the only real alternative, could not easily be combined with a resistance movement based on traditional appeals. The scholar-gentry, with the notable exception of reformers such as Nguyen Truong To, were not intellectually or emotionally prepared to combine the appeal to tradition with an effective program of social and political change. Vietnamese patriots of this period, then, were the inevi-

---

11. Examples of these letters are given in Truong Buu Lam, *Patterns of Vietnamese Response to Foreign Aggression, 1858–1900* (New Haven, 1967).

12. For an assertion that the Can Vuong was a peasant uprising, see Suren A. Mkhitarian, *Rabochii Klass i Natsional'no-Osvoboditel'noe Dvizhenie vo Vietname* [The Working Class and the National Liberation Movement in Vietnam] (Moscow, 1967), p. 56.

table first sacrifice on the altar of historical evolution. And it would require another half a century before new men could attempt more successfully to combine the appeal of history with that of modernity.

Can the traditionalist resistance movement be called "nationalist," as Truong Buu Lam contends in his study of the period? By his definition, nationalism is "a sense of ultimate loyalty to, or inclusion in, a community of people."[13] The Can Vuong, and indeed their predecessors who had fought against invasion from China for centuries, might qualify for nationalist status, because they were conscious of themselves as a distinct community, and not simply as the subjects of a king. Yet in a broader sense, it is doubtful whether these early resistance movements should be classified as "nationalist." Their leaders were only dimly aware of the nation-state system as it existed in the West, and did not clearly distinguish between the concept of nation and that of monarchy. At best, they were protonationalists.

With the defeat of the Can Vuong in 1896, the first stage of Vietnamese resistance against French control had come to an end. The nationwide response the rebel leaders had hoped for was not realized, and their desperate movement was easily crushed. As Vietnam itself was conquered, so too were the forces of traditional society in retreat—the monarchy discredited, the scholar-gentry divided and in disarray, the literati decimated and discouraged. The corrosive power of French culture had already begun to undermine the cultural foundations of Vietnamese society. The emotions and sacrifice that had gone into the traditionalist movement were not totally wasted, however. For man lives by his myths as much as by reality, and the courageous chapter of the Can Vuong was destined to live on as a symbol of Vietnamese resistance to outside control that would nurture the patriots of the future. As the century closed, the Can Vuong movement, the last best hope of traditional society in Vietnam, had clearly failed. It was time for new men, with new ideas, to come to the fore.

13. Truong Buu Lam, p. 29.

Chapter 2

The Age of Phan Boi Chau

As the twentieth century dawned, Vietnamese society began to enter a new era. Exposed to the harsh glare of modern culture from the West, to French education, French political institutions and commercial practices, the traditional Sino-Vietnamese civilization could not be maintained for much longer.

The old Can Vuong remnants had not all been captured or killed. The surviving leaders, in the aftermath of defeat, simply retreated back to their native villages. Their peasant followers scattered or drifted back to their paddy fields. A new generation of patriots was beginning to mature, and with the memories of the heroic deeds of Truong Dinh and Phan Dinh Phung before it, was preparing to renew the battle. This new generation represented the period of transition between traditional and modern Vietnam. Reared under the Confucian system and educated in Confucian values, the new patriots reflected many of the assumptions and values of their forefathers. To a considerable degree, they were a product of the scholar-gentry class. They were often sons or younger brothers of the followers of Ham Nghi and Phan Dinh Phung, and many were, at some time of their lives, civil servants. At the same time, they were becoming gradually exposed to Western ideas, either through direct contact with the French administration or through the works of reformist writers in China. Forced to reevaluate their predicament because of the disastrous defeat of the traditionalists, the new patriots were the first to look abroad for solutions to Vietnamese problems. For a quarter of a century, it was this transitional general of scholar-patriots that kept alive the tradition of resistance to foreign rule, and which laid the basis for the foundation of a modern nationalist movement in Vietnam.

This new generation can be called the age of Phan Boi Chau, after the recognized leader of the anticolonial movement during the first decades of the twentieth century. For it was Phan Boi Chau who attempted to reorganize the remnants of the Can Vuong into a modern anticolonialist organization, and it was his arrest and exile in 1925 that for all practical purposes brought to a close the age of scholar-patriots. This chapter focuses primarily on that remarkable man in tracing the first vital stage in the evolution of twentieth-century nationalism in Vietnam.

In Defense of Tradition

In 1867, when Phan Boi Chau was born, the French conquest of Vietnam had already been in process for nearly a decade. The French had not yet penetrated to Nghe An, the central coastal province where Phan was born, but that hard, austere land—traditional home of heroes and rebels—would, in the 1870s and 1880s, become the target of French conquerers. Eventually, it would spawn the most determined opponents of foreign rule in Vietnam, including not only Phan Boi Chau and Phan Dinh Phung, but later Ho Chi Minh and much of the leadership of the Communist Party.

Phan Boi Chau was born in Sa Nam village, Nam Dan district.[1] Phan's father was a scholar who had earned the *tu tai* (the first level in the civil service examinations) but who had refused to serve in the bureaucracy and had become instead a village school teacher. Although the father had little money, he was determined to give Phan a traditional education. The boy was exposed to the Confucian classics, and at thirteen began to study with a local scholar. Phan enjoyed reading about the drama of Vietnamese history, and about the great heroes of the past. When in 1874 local disturbances arose against the peace policies being followed in the imperial capital of Hué, he attempted to organize his fellow students into a military unit, armed with weapons fash-

1. For information on his name, see David Marr, *Vietnamese Anticolonialism, 1885–1925* (Berkeley, 1971), p. 83, and Joseph Buttinger, *Vietnam: A Dragon Embattled* (New York, 1967), I, 144.

ioned from bamboo. He was promptly chastised by his father for this childish indiscretion, and returned to his studies for the next ten years. His concern for the fate of his country continued to grow, however, and in 1885, when Ham Nghi abandoned the capital and issued the Can Vuong edict, Phan answered the appeal by organizing sixty fellow students into an "exam candidacy army" and formulated a plan to seize public buildings in the province capital.[2] Once again his plans proved abortive, however, and after troops came and punished his village, he returned, sadder and wiser, to his family responsibilities. When his father became ill the same year he took over teaching duties, earning the respect of the village population. Having decided that no one would listen to his pleas for action until he had achieved status in the traditional way, he began to subject himself to the grueling experience of preparing for the civil service examinations. After failing several times, he finally passed the regional examinations as a valedictorian.[3]

By 1900, Phan had achieved some local renown as a promising young scholar, and was now ready to move actively against the French. He began to travel in search of allies and conceived a simple plan for evicting the enemy: (1) unite the scattered resis-

2. Phan Boi Chau, *Nguc Trung Thu* [A Letter from Prison], published by Dao Trinh Nhat under the title *Doi Cach Menh Phan Boi Chau* [The Revolutionary Career of Phan Boi Chau] (Saigon, n. d.), p. 11. Much of the information about Phan's life comes from his two autobiographies, the above and *Phan Boi Chau Nien Bieu* [A Chronological Biography of Phan Boi Chau] (Hanoi, 1957), written by Phan under the title *Tu Phe Phan* [A Self-criticism] at the end of his life. A French-language version of the latter has recently been published by Georges Boudarel in *France-Asie,* 3d and 4th trimesters, 1968. There are only minor discrepancies between the two versions, but *Phan Boi Chau Nien Bieu* includes coverage up to his arrest in 1925. For a discussion of the accuracy of the two versions, see Tran Minh Thu, "Tu *Nguc Trung Thu* den *Phan Boi Chau Nien Bieu*" [From Nguc Trung Thu to Phan Boi Chau Nien Bieu], in *NCLS,* no. 69 (Dec. 1964), pp. 46–51; and Chuong Thau, "Ve hai tap tu chuyen cua Sao Nam: *Nguc Trung Thu* va *Phan Boi Chau Nien Bieu*" [Concerning the two autobiographies of Sao Nam: Nguc Trung Thu and Phan Boi Chau], in *NCLS,* no. 75 (June 1965), pp. 37–45. Hereafter the two autobiographies will be referred to as *NTT* and *Nien Bieu.*
3. There is some contradictory information concerning how many times Phan took the examinations, although it appears that he did take them several times. See Marr, p. 132. In 1904 he tried the metropolitan examinations in Hué but failed. *Nien Bieu,* pp. 40–41.

tance elements throughout the country, (2) seek support in the imperial family and the bureaucracy, and (3) obtain foreign aid, if necessary.[4] In support of the first goal he spent the next three years of his life traveling from north to south to make contact with former Can Vuong elements and any others who would join him in the struggle to restore Vietnamese independence. In the process he made the acquaintance of a number of patriots who would be comrades in arms for the next few years—including Dang Thai Than and Nguyen Thuong Hien.[5]

It is noteworthy that although not all of the early supporters of Phan Boi Chau were degree-holders themselves, virtually all had come from scholar-gentry families and most had spent time in preparing for the examinations at one time or another. In a very real sense Phan's supporters represented a link with the scholar-gentry resistance at the end of the previous century.

One prominent exception in Phan Boi Chau's list of potential supporters was the famous "Tiger or Yen The," Hoang Hoa Tham.[6] Born of mixed Sino-Vietnamese parentage in Thanh Hoa province, Hoang did not receive a Confucian education as a boy and, when orphaned at an early age, became a herder of buffalos. For a brief period in his early maturity he served in the Can Vuong, but when its power disintegrated he became a bandit along the railway from Vietnam to South China and was so troublesome that in 1894 the French granted him land in Bac Giang province on condition that he cease his activities. This agreement failed, but after he resumed his attacks in the area north of Hanoi, new negotiations succeeded in 1897, and for several years he led an apparently peaceful existence in Yen The province on land provided him by the French administration. Sometime in 1902, Phan, in an attempt to elicite Hoang Hoa Tham's support for his

4. *Nien Bieu*, p. 33.
5. Details on the life of Dang (also known as Ngu Hai) can be found in Marr, p. 101. Nguyen Thuong Hien was Phan's collaborator until his death in 1925. See Marr, p. 86.
6. Hoang was also known popularly as De Tham. Information on his life can be found in the biography *Hoang Tham: Pirate,* by Paul Chack (Paris, 1933). Also see Report no. 373, Governor-general to Minister of Colonies, Feb. 20, 1913 (Nouveau Fonds 592, Carton 49) held in the Archives Nationales de France, Section Outre-Mer in Paris. Hereafter this source will be referred to as AOM.

own cause, traveled to visit him at his residence at Phon Xuong.[7] Unfortunately, Hoang was ill, and Phan was able to see only one of his lieutenants, who did promise that Hoang's forces would rise in support if attacks by Phan's own group took place in the Center. Phan stayed about ten days, and then left for the South.

The Modernization Society

Phan Boi Chau's travels served to bring him into contact with a scattered band of patriots willing to join him in resistance to the French. By 1903 these patriots were ready to put the second part of his plan into action. In the spring of that year Phan met Nguyen Thanh, a former member of Can Vuong from Quang Nam province. Nguyen Thanh advised him that the rebels would need to enlist the support of a member of the royal family if they wished to obtain assistance from the noble families in Vietnam.[8] Nguyen first introduced Phan to Prince Ton That Toai of the royal family, but neither Nguyen nor Phan was impressed. They decided to locate someone in the direct line of Gia Long's eldest son Prince Canh in order to appeal to the rice-bowl South. The most likely candidate was Prince Cuong De, whose family had long been in disgrace at court for its flirtations with rebel units.[9] Upon being approached in March, the prince expressed a willingness to cooperate—in part because his father had been disgruntled by the failure of the French to offer him the throne after the flight of Ham Nghi in 1885.[10]

After having obtained the prince's promise of support and offi-

7. In *NTT,* Phan sets the date in June 1903; in *Nien Bieu* he states it was in the fall of 1902. This disagreement about chronology appears periodically in the two autobiographies. Tran Minh Thu takes *NTT* as more accurate, since it is closer to the events in time.

8. Nguyen Thanh (Tieu La) was the son of an official as well as a former member of the Can Vuong, and apparently had good connections at court. For information on his life, see Phan's own biography of him, *Truyen Tieu La* [The Story of Tieu La] in *Van Tho Phan Boi Chau Chon Loc* [Selections from the Writings of Phan Boi Chau] (Hanoi, 1967), pp. 414–420.

9. Cuong De discusses his own motives for joining the rebels in his autobiographical study, *Cuoc Doi Cach Mang Cuong De* [The Revolutionary Career of Cuong De] (Saigon, 1957), pp. 9–11. He was sometimes called Ky Ngoai Hau (Marquis of the External Principality).

10. AOM, Report no. 22, Governor-general to Ministry of Colonies, Sept. 1908, Dossier 598, Carton 50.

cially declared him the titular head of the group, Phan and Nguyen made a final trip to Cochin China in order to garner support. In early 1904 they then arranged a fateful meeting at Nguyen's house in Quang Nam province. Little information survives about the meeting because no written records were taken, in order to preserve secrecy, but it appears that there were about twenty participants, and the meeting was chaired by Cuong De. The basic motive for the conference was to formalize and expand the new anticolonial organization. It was agreed that there would be two facets to resistance activities—military and civilian. Some participants at the conference would attempt to obtain weapons in order to prepare partisan forces for an armed struggle against the French, while others would be entrusted with building schools and commercial associations. The new organization was called the Duy Tan Hoi (Modernization Society). It was the culmination of the process that had begun in 1900 with Phan's first simple plan to obtain support and evict the French.[11]

Returning to Hué in March 1904, Phan made an attempt to enlist the support of the bureaucracy by writing *Luu Cau Huyet Le Tan Thu* (Letter from the Ryukyus Written in Tears of Blood), in which he contended that independence could only be achieved through a transformation and revitalization of the national character.[12] The little book, Phan's first major work, was passed secretly to officials at the court, where it achieved a modest success and helped to bring his name to the attention of other prominent figures in Annam such as Tran Quy Cap and Phan Chu Trinh. It did not, however, have the desired effect on the officialdom. Many expressed their private sympathy, but few dared to offer their support. For Phan this was proof that the resistance movement could not count on the bureaucratic elite for assistance.

At this stage of his intellectual development, Phan's ideas were not distinguishable from those current in the anti-French move-

11. Eventually a written program was drawn up in South China, and 200 copies were sent to Vietnam. Suren Mkhitarian, *Rabochii Klass i Natsional'no-Osvoboditel'noe Dvizhenie vo Vietname* [The Working Class and the National Liberation Movement in Vietnam] (Moscow, 1967), p. 41.

12. This pamphlet is not extant, although a fragment may be located in *Van Su Dia* [The World of Literature], 33 (Oct. 1957). The contents are discussed in *Nien Bieu,* pp. 36–38, and in *NTT,* pp. 23–24.

ment as a whole. As the son of a scholar, he had read many of the Confucian classics as a youth, and it is evident from his early writings that he took very seriously the Confucian maxims of loyalty and filial piety.[13] In two short early works (no longer extant), he exhibited a fierce and uncomplicated patriotism, calling on the nation to rise in support of the rebels against the invaders.[14] There is little to indicate that in 1904 Phan and his colleagues had a profound understanding of the changes that were taking place in the world. Certainly the program of action drafted in 1900 completely ignored the complex problems that independence would bring. Yet it was at this time that he and his colleagues were just beginning to absorb knowledge from abroad, primarily through the writings of such reform-minded Chinese scholars as Liang Ch'i-ch'ao and K'ang Yu-wei. It was through these writings that what Phan called his "provincial mind" became gradually emancipated from the limitations of traditional thought. Also, from Darwin, he discovered "the struggle for survival in the world, the sad state of our country, and the decline of our race." From Western books he confirmed his view that the word *ai quoc* (love of country) was stronger than the Confucian *trung quan* (loyalty to the king).[15] In effect, he began to realize that to survive, Vietnam must change its ways. This process of emancipation took a remarkably short time, certainly less than had been required for most Confucianists in China, many of whom had wrestled with the problem of adjusting modern realities to their traditional assumptions for a decade or more.[16] Undoubtedly the relative rapidity and totality of Vietnam's defeat hastened this process. It is also probable that Phan and his compatriots found it easier to change since their intellectual mentors in China had already begun to make a similar transition.

In 1904, then, theory meant little to Phan Boi Chau and his colleagues. Preoccupied with the problem of finding sufficient sup-

13. Dang Thai Mai, *Van Tho Phan Boi Chau* [The Essays and Poems of Phan Boi Chau] (Hanoi, 1960), p. 30.

14. The titles are *Dinh Tay Thu Bac* [Defeat the Westerner and Restore the North] and *Song Tuat Luc* [A Tale of Two Years]. Both are described briefly in his autobiographies and in Dang Thai Mai, p. 62.

15. *Dang Thai Mai*, p. 33. The statement regarding Darwin is in *Nien Bieu*, p. 32.

16. Good examples are Liang Ch'i-ch'ao and Yen Fu.

port to evict the French, they gave little thought to abstract problems of the future, or to the "national heritage" that so gnawed at the consciences of their contemporaries in China. They were still monarchist, and their vision of the future state seemed to go little beyond the realization of independence. New ideas from the West had not yet greatly affected these men, who were prepared to be practical, but as yet had seen or heard very little of the world outside Vietnam. As Phan observed in one of his memoirs, a new era was dawning, but they were in a fog as to what it all meant. It was only when he went abroad that his ideas began to change.[17]

Japan, Model for All Asia

The most immediate problem facing the anticolonialists was to obtain financial support for their activities. They had gradually come to accept the necessity of searching for aid abroad. The natural tendency would be to turn to China, and Phan would have personally preferred to seek aid there, for reasons of history, geography, and race, but China had been forced to disavow its historic suzerainty over Vietnam in a treaty with France and was now concerned with defending her own territory against the West. With some reluctance, the Vietnamese turned to Japan, which since the beginning of the Meiji restoration in 1868 had been impressive in protecting its own interests against the West. The Meiji reformers had not only immeasurably strengthened Japanese economic and military capabilities, but had also inspired admiration elsewhere in Asia, where imitation of Western ways had proved so difficult. Such feelings were bolstered by Japan's victory in her war with tsarist Russia in 1904–1905.

At the same time, Japanese success also generated a certain sense of disquiet among some Vietnamese. After all, with its seizure of the Ryukyus and Taiwan, and its growing influence in Korea, Japan seemed to have developed some imperialist ambitions of its own. So although Japan appeared anxious to assist fellow Asians against the West, there was some suspicion that its reasons were not entirely altruistic. In the resistance movement, admiration eventually overcame distrust, and the Modernization

17. *NTT*, p. 26.

Society decided to send a delegation to Japan to ask for support.[18] When Phan indicated a reluctance to undertake such a delicate diplomatic mission without knowledge of Japan or its language, Nguyen Thanh suggested that Tang Bat Ho should go as his guide and interpreter. Tang, a former member of the Can Vuong who had spent many active years fighting and traveling in the Far East, was well acquainted with Japan. He had only recently returned to Vietnam and was in hiding in Hanoi.[19] Tang Bat Ho agreed to join Phan's forces and to accompany the latter on his trip to Japan.

After one more trip to his home province to say goodbye to family and friends, Phan, Tang, and Dang Tu Kinh, another disciple, left Haiphong in early 1905 for Japan, leaving Nguyen Thanh and Dang Thai Than in charge of the movement in Vietnam.[20] The group passed through Hong Kong, where Phan, posing as a Chinese merchant, had an opportunity to observe the effects of British colonial rule, and where he attempted to make the acquaintance of editors of progressive Chinese newspapers. He was unable to obtain an appointment with Hsü Ch'in, the editor of the constitutional monarchist newspaper *Shang Pao*, but he did manage to meet Feng Tzu-yu, editor of the *Chung-kuo Jih-pao* (Chinese Daily). Feng was sympathetic to the Vietnamese rebels, but warned Phan that the Vietnamese would have to wait at least thirty years until the Chinese revolutionaries could throw out the Manchus. He did suggest that the Vietnamese write a letter to the local governor-general of Kwangtung, Ts'en Ch'ün-hsuan. Phan did so. He wrote in a highly literary style, and reminded the Chinese official of the traditional tributary relationship of Vietnam to China. He promised that Vietnam would return to such an earlier relationship if help were obtained from China.[21] Phan re-

---

18. *Ibid.*, pp. 28–29; and *Nien Bieu*, p. 44, show Phan's attitude toward Japan.

19. For more detailed information on his life, see Buttinger, p. 78, and Phuong Huu, *Phong Trao Dai Dong Du* [The Exodus to the East Movement] (Saigon, 1950), pp. 59–63. He died in Hué before World War I of natural causes.

20. Dang was a former member of the Can Vuong who served Phan for years, without achieving any prominence in the movement. See *Nien Bieu*, *passim*.

21. *Nien Bieu*, p. 51. The text is located in *NCLS*, no. 90 (Sept. 1966).

ceived no reply, however. Members of the old feudal classes in China, he had learned, would give the Vietnamese rebels no assistance in their struggle for independence.

After a short delay while waiting for the end of Russo-Japanese hostilities, the Vietnamese contingent embarked from Shanghai on the final leg of their journey to Yokohama. Phan was aware that the Chinese constitutional monarchist Liang Ch'i-ch'ao, author of several modernist books and editor of the newspaper *Hsin-min Ts'ung-pao* (New People's Miscellany), was in Japan. He immediately wrote the Chinese reformer a letter asking for assistance in planning activities in Japan. Liang showed himself sympathetic to the Vietnamese cause and in several conversations discussed the problem of the liberation of Vietnam. When the Vietnamese told Liang that they hoped to obtain support from Japan, he was somewhat dubious. He said he thought that the Japanese would give military support to the Vietnamese only if Japan went to war with France. In addition, he warned Phan that in China's experience Japanese aid could be a two-edged sword—once the Japanese had an opportunity to intervene, they would never leave. He counseled Phan to think in terms of a three-point plan: (1) to develop internal strength, which could come only from the will and determination of the Vietnamese themselves; (2) to obtain weapons, not from Japan but from the South China provinces of Kwangtung and Kwangsi; and (3) to seek diplomatic aid, which the Japanese might be willing to supply.[22]

Although Liang was somewhat pessimistic about the possibility of obtaining assistance from Japan, he was willing to introduce Phan to some of his Japanese acquaintances, in particular to the Japanese politicians Okuma Shigenobu and Inukai Tsuyoshi. Phan was elated and wrote a letter of introduction to Okuma. In his letter he repeated the substance of his remarks to Ts'en Ch'ün-hsuan and argued that Japan had both moral and political obligations to intervene in Southeast Asia and to help with the liberation of the Vietnamese. He first appealed to the reader's altruistic sensibilities by pointing out that fellow Asians had been conquered by Europeans, and by asking rhetorically: is there no Asian power to protect weak Asian nations against outsiders? Phan was aware,

22. *Nien Bieu,* p. 55.

however, that security considerations would be more likely to stimulate Japanese action in Vietnam than moral ones. Always an enthusiastic amateur geopolitician, he attempted to convince Okuma that if France were not driven from Indochina, she might strike further north and take China's southern provinces. In turn, Russia would ally with France, and thus Japan's control over Taiwan and the Ryukyus would be endangered (Phan did not mention his opinion of the Japanese conquest of the latter, of course).[23]

Phan was able to obtain a personal meeting with Okuma, but his host responded to his arguments somewhat vaguely. It became apparent that, as Liang had predicted, the Japanese were reluctant to become involved. Okuma suggested that Cuong De come to Japan, and he held forth the possibility of future military assistance, but he stressed that Japan could take no immediate action in light of her recent war with Russia and the risk of future war with France. He did promise support for Vietnamese students wishing to come to Japan to study, and cautioned Phan that hasty action should be avoided until Japan was ready to give more active support. In effect, Okuma lent credence to Liang's own comment: God helps those who help themselves.[24]

Irritated with Japanese trepidation, Phan turned to Liang for comfort. The latter suggested that, for the moment, Okuma's offer be accepted and concerted efforts be made to bring young Vietnamese to Japan to study. In the meantime, he said, Phan could best serve the cause by writing stirring pamphlets condemning the French colonial regime in Indochina in order to persuade young Vietnamese with fire in their veins to come to Japan to prepare for revolt. As a first step, he agreed to publish Phan's newly written *Viet Nam Vong Quoc Su* (A History of the Downfall of Vietnam) in his own publication, *Hsin-min Ts'ung-pao*.[25]

Sparked by Liang's persuasive advice, Phan Boi Chau responded with an outburst of patriotic tracts designed to explain his ideas and to gain support for the anticolonialist cause within Vietnam. Many of his best-known works date from this period: *Viet Nam Vong Quoc Su, Hai Ngoai Huyet Thu* (Letters from Abroad

23. The text is located in *NCLS*, no. 90 (Sept. 1966).
24. *Nien Bieu*, p. 57.
25. *NTT*, p. 37.

Written in Blood), *Tan Viet Nam* (New Vietnam), *Ai Viet Dieu Dien* (A Lament for Vietnam and Yunnan), and *Viet Nam Quoc Su Khao* (An Outline History of Vietnam).[26]

Viet Nam Vong Quoc Su was probably written in 1905, shortly after Phan's arrival, and is thus thought to be the earliest of his major works. *Viet Nam Vong Quoc Su,* as its title suggests, was written essentially as a history of the conquest of Vietnam by the French, and as a projection of the possible future of the nation. The book demonstrates clearly the transitional nature of Phan's thought at this time. His analysis of the downfall of Vietnam in the nineteenth century is essentially Confucian. He attributes the downfall to a decline in civic virtue and moral fiber and finds the root cause of this decline in the corruption of the court and its isolation from the people.

Could Vietnam be saved, or would the yellow races all be swallowed up in a white sea, as Sun Yat-sen in China feared? In the concluding chapter of his book, Phan professes to be uncertain, but he voices the belief that if Vietnamese of all social classes were to join together in a sacred struggle, the invader could be driven from native soil.[27] If all Vietnamese, regardless of sex, of social status, or of vocation could unite as one to restore Vietnamese freedom, the future of the nation might be secured.

Phan's *Viet Nam Vong Quoc Su* was designed to be a rallying cry for the Vietnamese to rise in unison against their colonial oppressors. It was strictly patriotic in tone and gave few indications that he had advanced in his political thought beyond a fairly simple and uncomplicated Confucianism. Within a year, however, Phan followed up with two more works designed specifically to encourage the exodus of Vietnamese students to Japan to study.

The 11,000-character poem *Hai Ngoai Huyet Thu* was the first of these publications.[28] In this work there are still strong tradi-

---

26. *Hai Ngoai Huyet Thu, Tan Viet Nam,* and *Ai Viet Dieu Dien* have all been published in *NCLS* in quoc-ngu versions. *Viet Nam Vong Quoc Su* has been published in quoc-ngu and is also available in the original Chinese in *Chung-Fa Chan-cheng* [The Sino-French War] (Shanghai, 1957), vol. VII.

27. For a full list in English of the groups appealed to, see Marr, pp. 114–119.

28. The original, written in Chinese, is located in the *Yun-nan Tsa-chih*

tionalist overtones. Phan is again preoccupied with the reasons for the decline and fall of Vietnam. Once again the emperor and the court are taken to task for ignoring the welfare of the nation. But now the people themselves are also implicitly criticized for ignoring the affairs of the nation and for paying attention only to their own concerns. The main appeal is for national unity, the solidarity of all "bourgeoisie, officials, landlords, scholars, soldiers, hooligans, of all Vietnamese brothers and sisters" to rise against their common enemies.

The second work, written by Phan in 1906, was *Khuyen Quoc Dan Tu Tro Du Hoc Van* (Encouragement to Citizens to Contribute for Overseas Study). Phan attempted with this publication to spark the rage and determination of the Vietnamese people by comparing their weakness and ignorance with the unity and the strength of the Japanese during the Meiji period. He has strong praise for the Japanese warrior code (the Bushido) and the Japanese willingness to cooperate with each other, to study foreign customs and institutions in order to improve their own. By contrast, Vietnam has become a nation of slaves, he contends, and friends of Vietnam must think that it is about to disappear. He concludes by urging the Vietnamese to set up commercial associations to raise funds, and he appeals to rich families to provide financial aid for students coming to Japan to study.[29]

Phan also wrote an essay in late 1906 aimed especially at the 6,500 Vietnamese youth training for the civil service examinations. In *Hoa Le Cong Ngon* (An Appeal Bathed in Tears), Phan urges potential examination students to consider the real meaning of their obligation as leaders and models for the people. The traditional system, he explains, is now in the hands of the enemy, an enemy which has destroyed the national heritage and has left just the dregs of the emasculated civil service system to seduce the Vietnamese. How, then, Phan asks, can young Vietnamese who aspire to be virtuous leaders of men think in terms of following the time-honored path of a civil service career? He chastises those

[*Yunnan Journal*]. A later quoc-ngu version is in *Dang Thai Mai*, pp. 156–173.

29. The text is located in Phan Boi Chau, *Van Tho Phan Boi Chau Chon Loc*, pp. 44–49.

who would retreat from the crisis into their family obligations. The family and the nation are interrelated, Phan writes, and if one is lost, the other will inevitably be lost as well. His message is entirely traditional in tone, if not content. Solid old Confucian virtues are viewed as the means of cultivating one's own self and of guiding others until those virtues have spread to the population at large.[30]

Phan did not totally devote himself to propaganda, but also took periodic trips back to Vietnam in order to supervise the building up of his party and to encourage further contributions to provide opportunities for more students to travel to Japan, and to bring Prince Cuong De to Japan.

In Japan, he devoted his time to writing and to organizing his young resistance movement in exile.[31] Gradually, his efforts to build up a nucleus of Vietnamese students in Japan, what was to become famous in Vietnam as the Dong Du (Exodus to the East), began to take shape. In January 1906, he went to see the Japanese liberal politician Inukai Tsuyoshi. With Inukai was Fukushima Yasumasa, head of the Shimbu Military Academy, a private military school primarily for foreign students. Arrangements were made for three students to enter the academy and one to enter the Dobun Shoin (Common Culture School).[32] To provide training in Japanese for Phan's Vietnamese disciples, a special school was set up, the Binh Ngo Hien (The Eaves of 1906), and all new students automatically spent several months there for language study before going on to Japanese high schools.[33] As more students began to appear in Japan, a special organization, the Cong Hien Hoi (Public Offering Society), was founded in 1907 to control and direct their activities. Run by Cuong De and Phan Boi Chau, it became in effect the headquarters of a provisional government in exile to direct Modernization Society activities abroad.[34]

30. It is not certain that this work is by Phan Boi Chau. The text is located in *NCLS*, no. 56 (Nov. 1963), pp. 44–45.

31. Phan's activities in Japan have been chronicled in detail by David Marr, *Vietnamese Anticolonialism*. I have therefore restricted myself here to what is essential for the purpose of this book.

32. *NTT*, pp. 46–47.

33. *Nien Bieu*, p. 93. As more students arrived, they were sent to the Dobun Shoin which, as a party school, had no government connections.

34. Details are in *Nien Bieu*, pp. 97–98.

For a time, the activities of Phan's movement in Japan prospered, and by the summer of 1908 the number of Vietnamese students in Japan had increased to over 200, with half from Cochin China, 50 from Annam, and 40 from Tonkin. Success brought its problems, however, for with the numbers increasing, the organization began to have difficulties conciliating views of students from different regions. At one time personality conflicts became sufficiently serious to cause Phan to despair over his lack of personal ability to paper over the disputes.[35]

Constant exposure to foreign ideas and institutions—to the Japanese success story, to the effervescent revolutionary movement in China led by Sun Yat-sen, to the scintillating mind of such Chinese modernizers as Liang Ch'i-ch'ao—inevitably had its effect on the traditionalist mind of the now middle-aged patriot. By 1907, Phan was beginning to write more about his visions of the new Vietnam to come, and in so doing he showed the changes that were taking place in his ideas. He had previously thought primarily in terms of tactics rather than ultimate goals. Beyond independence he had demonstrated little inkling of the shape and form of a new postcolonial society. As for political institutions, his party had maintained the monarchy as the central focus, if more for symbolic value and to achieve support from traditionalist-minded Vietnamese than for its own intrinsic importance. By 1907, however, his writings begin to reflect the influence of the outside world.

In a pamphlet written in 1907, he described a vision of the future Vietnam as a *Tan Viet Nam* (New Vietnam), a modern, properous state built on the Western model, with representative assemblies, universal suffrage, fair taxes, and just laws. The king would be limited by a constitution, and ultimate sovereignty would rest in the lower house of parliament.[36] Industry and commerce would prosper, and social and economic equality would be guaranteed by universal education, social insurance, and private charity.

Phan's final major work written in 1908 in Japan was *Viet Nam Quoc Su Khao* (An Outline History of Vietnam). If *Tan Viet Nam* provided him with a forum to describe his desire for democracy and social and economic progress, *Viet Nam Quoc Su*

---

35. *Ibid.*, pp. 98–99.
36. The text is in *NCLS*, no. 78 (Aug. 1965), pp. 31–39.

Khao was designed to discuss in more specific terms his concept of nationhood and the role of man in society. Like *Viet Nam Vong Quoc Su,* it utilized history as a means to propagate a patriotic mentality, "a popular history to get the people to read about their past heroes and rise to save Vietnam," as he explained it.[37] Chapter 5 of the ten-chapter book provides the best description of Phan's evolving attitude toward political power and the relationship of man and society. Phan opens his discussion by quoting international law. There are, he states, three requirements for nationhood: people, territory, and a sovereign government. Without these factors, no human community can be considered a nation. And of these three, he adds, people are the most important, for nations must begin with a population. Phan concludes that the basis of a strong and independent nation is a free and educated citizenry. National wealth and power are virtually synonymous with a democratic system of government.

Like many Chinese progressives of the early twentieth century —and Liang Ch'i-ch'ao and Sun Yat-sen are only the most prominent examples—Phan apparently turned to democracy primarily as a solution to problems of national survival and independence. In *Viet Nam Quoc Su Khao,* he explains that history teaches that when the rights of the people are ignored, the power of the people is weak and the nation itself is powerless. In the democratic countries of the West, he writes, the power of the people results in a refined culture and a strong nation. In Vietnam, where the courts and the corrupt mandarins treat the people as "fish and meat," and trample on their rights and welfare, the result is inertia and stagnation, mutual distrust, and concern for self and family.

Phan's unhappiness with the nature of Vietnamese society and mores is highly reminiscent of the views of his mentor Liang Ch'i-ch'ao, who criticized public attitudes in China. Phan maintains in *Viet Nam Quoc Su Khao* that what Vietnam needs is a long-term goal, a concept of community benefit for which all will sacrifice their personal needs. In response to the question of whether "independence" means total freedom for each individual,

37. As far as I know, the full text is not available in this country, but Chapter 5 is printed in Phan Boi Chau, *Van Tho Phan Boi Chau Chon Loc,* pp. 120–138.

Phan states that total freedom would be total confusion. The meaning of independence (*doc lap*) in the West is that nations do not interfere in each other's affairs and are not dependent upon each other. Independence means that people in a nation join together to prevent outsiders from interfering in their lives. Thus independence comes from cooperation.

There is a deep irony in Phan's criticism of Vietnamese society, for cooperation and subordination to the community was a primary feature in Confucian theory and, to most Western observers, somewhat less prominent in the more individualistic West. Yet, in the context of the time, Phan's criticism takes on more validity. By the end of the nineteenth century, emphasis on community interests, so constant a factor in Confucian culture in China and Vietnam, had clearly degenerated in both countries to localism and what is often called "amoral familism." If community spirit had in the past served to ensure the survival of the Vietnamese nation, it had patently disappeared in modern days.[38] Instinctively, perhaps, Phan came to feel that a mere restatement of traditional values would not suffice to raise the patriotic sensibilities of the Vietnamese. More effective would be the demonstration that the secret of Western success lay in unity and cooperation. He did not disdain the basic values of the Confucian heritage, but he did not believe they could be revitalized for contemporary use.

Agitation in Vietnam, 1906–1911

While Phan Boi Chau and Prince Cuong De promoted the resistance movement in exile, other elements of the Modernization Society were building up the movement within Vietnam. One of the most important problems facing the party was that of obtaining money to finance its activities and, in particular, to train large numbers of students in Japan. To raise funds, commercial associations were formed and run by Vietnamese sympathetic to the cause. Traditionally, of course, the Vietnamese had not been especially active in developing commerce, and such trade as did exist was monopolized by enterprising Chinese who had immigrated from abroad. The scholar-gentry class was morally constrained

38. As David Marr has pointed out to me, this might be a reflection of the views of the scholar-elite rather than of the realities of Vietnam.

from engaging in commerce in traditional society. Therefore it was especially difficult for the scholar-patriots of the Modernization Society to initiate trading activities to further the anticolonial cause.

Attitudes were changing, however, and by the early years of the twentieth century, writings that blamed the stagnation of Vietnamese society on an inveterate contempt for commercial and manufacturing activities began to appear. In one of the most famous of these works, the anonymously written *Van Minh Tan Hoc Sach* (Civilization and New Learning), the author interprets Western power and prosperity in terms of advances in science, commerce, and manufacturing.[39]

The general idea to establish commercial firms as a means of developing Vietnamese commerce, of breaking the Chinese monopoly, and of raising funds for revolutionary activities, was, then, a consequence of the gradual change in attitude, manifest in publications such as *Van Minh Tan Hoc Sach*. It was Liang Ch'i-ch'ao, however, who, in a note written to Phan, recommended specific action. A number of Phan's colleagues in Vietnam took up the idea and began to form associations in various parts of the country. Most notable were the commercial firms formed in the South by the wealthy mandarin and naturalized French citizen Gilbert Chieu.[40] Chieu became a supporter of the resistance movement in 1906 or 1907, and soon took an active interest in the resistance movement. He promoted the dispatch of students to Japan, and, through the columns of two newspapers under his direction in Saigon—the Vietnamese–language *Luc Tinh Tan Van* (News from Six Provinces) and the French-language *Le Moniteur des Provinces*—provided a vehicle for revolutionary propaganda. He established hotels in My Tho and in Saigon as meeting places for rebels, and also built a soap factory in order to help finance the activities of the movement. Articles that criticized Chinese commercial control in Vietnam, that appealed for agricultural reforms and that elliptically attacked the French through parables began to appear in his publications. At least once, he urged his readers to disobey the orders of the governor-general. Eventually, French pressure

39. For a discussion of the book, see Marr, pp. 173–176.
40. His real name was Tran Chinh Chieu.

compelled him to draw in his head and restrict himself to commercial activities. In 1908, he was arrested. Although he was released a few months later for lack of evidence, all of his organizations had been uncovered and scattered. He became inactive in politics. After one more arrest and release, he died in 1913.[41]

French pressure was not the only problem for the newly formed commercial organizations. Most formed were small local handicraft producers, and financial difficulties were often severe. In part this was because few of the scholars-turned-shopowners were particularly good at business. Often they were incompetent. Many continued to wear their long gowns in the store and had their servants wave fans to keep them cool, practices which probably intimidated the local populace and kept the number of customers at a minimum. Many of the new shops closed after less than a year in operation.[42]

By late 1907, Phan's forces were ready to try their luck at an insurrection against the French. Phan visited Hoang Hoa Tham in 1907 in the latter's plantation in Bac Giang Province. Hoang agreed to make every effort to coordinate the activities of his own rebel forces with those of the Modernization Society and to recognize Cuong De as the legitimate ruler of Vietnam. It was further agreed that any uprisings by Phan's party in Annam would be followed by attacks on the French in the North by Hoang's own troops.[43] Soon after the visit, representatives of the two groups began meeting at a restaurant in Hanoi to make plans for a joint uprising which would center on a revolt by Vietnamese troops in French military garrisons in Hanoi. The plan was for low-level troops of the fourth regiment of colonial artillery and the ninth infantry regiment to poison the food of their French officers. They would then seize the local citadel and destroy rail and electrical lines. Meanwhile, units of Hoang's forces would attack on the left bank of the Red River and seize strategic points in the city. Hopefully, uprisings would then take place elsewhere in Vietnam and lead to a nationwide revolt.

Hopes for support elsewhere were based at least partly on con-

41. Phuong Huu, pp. 31–34.
42. Nguyen Hien Le, *Dong Kinh Nghia Thuc* [The Hanoi Free School] (Saigon, 1968), pp. 93–108.
43. *NTT*, p. 52.

ditions in Central Vietnam, where economic depression, high taxes, and mandarin exactions had created severe unrest. In March of 1908, peasants in Quang Nam province had marched to protest against forced labor, the monopolies on salt, opium, and liquor, and the confiscation of communal land by corrupt local officials and landlords. Within a month the riots had spread to Quang Ngai, Nghe An, Ha Tinh, and Thanh Hoa provinces. Although some prominent figures such as Phan Chu Trinh and Tran Quy Cap were involved, many of the demonstrations were spontaneous. In some places violence broke out, with villagers burning the houses of the wealthy, and beating or even killing tax collectors.[44]

The revolt by Phan Boi Chau's forces, several times postponed, was finally launched on June 27, 1908. On that date, the scheduled poisoning took place, but unfortunately for the rebels, the French had been forewarned and were able to blunt the attack and capture most of the rebel leaders. With the main attack thwarted, Hoang's troops did not attack, and the whole plan fizzled. In July, the French tried the instigators. Thirteen were executed, and thirty-one were given prison sentences. Phan, still in Japan, remained at large. Although Hoang Hoa Tham's forces had not attacked, the French were increasingly distrustful of his intentions, and in early 1909 launched a major attack on his headquarters. After four years of declining fortunes, Hoang Hoa Tham was finally killed and decapitated by bounty hunters.[45]

44. Georges Coulet, *Les Sociétés secrètes en terre d'Annam* (Paris, 1926), pp. 10–11.
45. *Ibid.*, p. 13. A description of Hoang's final days is given in Chack, p. 251.

Chapter 3

Phan Chu Trinh and
the Reformist Approach

Many of the scholar-patriots in Phan Boi Chau's movement had been conscious since the early years of their activity that a policy of violence alone would not achieve the goal of a united, independent Vietnam. Through the efforts of Phan Boi Chau and Nguyen Thanh, the fathers of the Modernization Society had agreed in their opening meetings that a combined strategy of armed struggle and educational efforts would be necessary to maximize the prospects of victory. Phan Boi Chau himself appeared to place a relatively high priority on educational and political activities, although his primary concern was to prepare for an armed uprising against the French.

There were, however, some in the scholar-patriot movement who, while agreeing with the general goal of national independence, were more antagonistic to the continued survival of the feudal monarchy than to the French, and who hoped to use the presence of the latter as a means to realize the necessary political and social reforms in Vietnam. Independence was the final goal, but the French were seen as an instrument of reform as much as a force to be resisted. The most representative figure of this view in the scholar-patriot generation was Phan Chu Trinh.

Phan Chu Trinh was born in 1872 in the village of Tay Loc in the province of Quang Nam.[1] He was the youngest of three children. His father, Phan Van Binh, was a low-level military officer

1. See Ton Quang Phiet, *Phan Boi Chau va Phan Chu Trinh* [Phan Boi Chau and Phan Chu Trinh] (Hanoi, 1956), pp. 70–74, for an account of his youth. Also see The Nguyen, *Phan Chu Trinh* (Saigon, 1956), pp. 9–10.

who studied for the civil service examinations but apparently never passed them. When the boy's mother died, his father decided to follow Phan Dinh Phung's resistance movement, but was eventually executed by the Can Vuong on suspicion of treason.[2]

Under his father's direction, the young Phan studied the military arts as a youth. His father believed that Confucian training was useless in the conditions prevailing in Vietnam. Following his father's death, however, Phan returned to classical studies in order to prepare for the examinations. After several years of studying under the direction of his older brother and with local scholars, he passed the first level examination (the *cu nhan*) in 1900 and then achieved the next level (the *pho bang*) the following year.[3] Assigned to minor duties in the administration at Hué, he soon grew bored and returned home to teach and await a better assignment. He was finally appointed to the Board of Rites in 1903. But Phan could not overcome his dissatisfaction with the bureaucracy. He was soon disgusted by the blatant corruption that prevailed in court circles, and in his spare time he began to read the reformist works of the Chinese modernizers. At about this time he met Phan Boi Chau for the first time.[4]

In 1905, Phan Chu Trinh lost patience and quit his job for a second time in order to travel and study. He went south with two fellow scholars, Tran Quy Cap and Huynh Thuc Khang. Stopping at Cam Ranh Bay they saw Russian warships sailing north to fight (and be destroyed) in the Russo-Japanese War. Later he went to Tonkin to visit Hoang Hoa Tham, but found the pirate leader disappointing. Finally he went to Hong Kong to meet Phan Boi Chau, and from there they went to Japan, where they observed the work being done by the Vietnamese movement in exile. Phan Chu Trinh expressed his approval of their educational activities, but he was less enthusiastic about the Modernization Society's acceptance of royal support and its adherence to the idea of a constitutional monarchy. Phan was willing to cooperate with France as long as

2. The Nguyen, p. 11.
3. *Ibid.*, p. 15.
4. The Nguyen and Ton Quang Phiet disagree on where they met. The latter maintains that they met in Nghe An province, while the former claims that their acquaintance began at the National Academy in Hué. The Nguyen, p. 16; Ton Quang Phiet, p. 74.

France opposed the Hué court and promised to transform Vietnam into its own image. Phan Boi Chau, on the other hand, did not trust the French. He advocated retention of the monarchy because he was convinced that the monarchical system was most appropriate to Vietnam at that stage of her evolution. In his view, the Vietnamese were culturally still well below the level of Europe, and to advocate immediate democracy for them was like "feeding a child a bone when his teeth are not firm and forcing him to chew it, whipping him to run when his legs are not yet solid." Whatever the theoretical virtues of democracy, he thought, the Vietnamese people were simply not ready for it, and a republic would only confuse them. The Vietnamese, he concluded, should set aside their ideological controversies and concentrate their efforts on winning independence. Then, he said, "ten years later if you bring up the idea again, I will be the first to stand by your side and applaud."[5]

The difference of opinion did not result in a complete rupture between the two men. They held several long conversations over a ten-day period, and argued goals and tactics. Phan disagreed with Phan Boi Chau concerning the role of institutions and in regard to Phan Boi Chau's espousal of violence. Phan emphatically opposed violence. "Violence is death," he often explained, and he was determined to obtain reforms in Vietnam without the necessity for bloodshed. In the end, however, the two "agreed to disagree" and to cooperate in their joint goal of independence.[6] Phan praised Phan Boi Chau and urged him to continue educating young Vietnamese in Japan, but he returned to Vietnam still determined to put his own reformist ideas into action. Although Phan Boi Chau did not reveal it in his discussions with Phan, his ideas were at that time in a state of flux, and within a few years he, too, would support the idea of republicanism. By the time he would do so, however, Phan Chu Trinh would be in exile in France.

In any event, the fissure between the two regarding tactics did not die, but rather initiated a schism in the Vietnamese resistance movement. Their disagreement prevented unity of action among

5. Dang Thai Mai, *Van Tho Phan Boi Chau* [The Essays and Poems of Phan Boi Chau] (Hanoi, 1960), pp. 156–157. The quote is from a letter to Phan Chu Trinh.
6. This dispute is discussed in *Nien Bieu*, p. 72.

the scholar-patriots and, in Phan Boi Chau's opinion, seriously diminished the chances that the Vietnamese resistance movement would succeed.[7]

Letter to Governor-general Beau

Upon his return to Vietnam, Phan lost little time in making public his views. In August of 1906, he wrote an open letter to Governor-general Paul Beau to express his feelings.[8] He explained first that his motive in writing was to bring to the attention of the governor-general the "extremely critical situation" in Vietnam. This critical situation, he hastened to say, was not the fault solely of the French. The French presence in Vietnam had brought many material blessings to the Vietnamese people. The problem lay elsewhere—in the behavior of the corrupt feudal bureaucracy which, under the benign protection of the colonial government, was rapaciously exploiting the Vietnamese. But because the protectorate tolerated this state of affairs, wrote Phan, it must share much of the blame. He explained that he had given up his career in order to travel and listen to public opinion. Now he was daring to present to the governmental authorities his interpretation of the mood of the Vietnamese people. In his view, mandarin corruption and the laziness and weakness of the imperial court in Hué had seriously alienated the population of Vietnam. This situation had existed for centuries, but since the French were now in charge they must share the blame. The French, having permitted the Vietnamese to perpetuate their own worst characteristics, had then compounded the problem by holding the Vietnamese in contempt, by loathing and despising them as an inferior race. Such conditions only lead to the creation of two nations apart, Phan argued.

What, then, should the government do? In Phan's view it should initiate comprehensive reforms in Vietnamese society—select able officials, reform the law codes, abolish the civil service examinations, expand the school system, and encourage industrial and

7. *Nien Bieu*, p. 86, has his comment.
8. A French version is located in *Bulletin de l'Ecole Française d'Extrême Orient* (March-June 1907), pp. 166–175. A quoc-ngu version is located in The Nguyen, pp. 81–100.

commercial education. Then Vietnam would be tranquil and content and its only fear would be the departure of the French.

There was nothing coy about Phan's appeal to the French. He saw the traditional bureaucracy as the major source of Vietnam's woes, but he courageously pointed out that the French now shared responsibility for the tragedy. In short, he felt that a continuation of the protectorate was preferable to a return to imperial control, and he was apparently confident that France would act to improve the situation if it became sufficiently aware of it. Quite likely, he saw himself as a Mencius, or as a K'ang Yu-wei—that is, one who would lead the government, through intelligent counsel, to implement proper reforms.

These were stiff words for the colonialists, and many French residents viewed Phan as simply another Confucian rebel anxious to evict the Europeans. Yet some in the government recognized that his attitude differed substantially from that of the Vietnamese exiles in Japan, and suggested that he be seduced with an offer of a position.[9] Governor-general Beau thought enough of Phan's ideas to have the letter published in France. Phan continued to speak for reform and became an ally of Phan Boi Chau in his struggle for a new Vietnam, without actually aligning himself to the resistance movement. A relationship between Phan and Phan Boi Chau's rebels was eventually achieved, with the formation of the famous Dong Kinh Nghia Thuc (Free School of Hanoi).[10] Patterned after the famous Keio Gijuku school of Fukuzawa Yukichi in Japan, the Dong Kinh Nghia Thuc was seen by advocates of reform and violence alike as a means of exposing hundreds of young Vietnamese to modern Western education, and of thus spreading literacy and modern ideas throughout Vietnamese society.

9. To Minh Trung, "Ban ve chu nghia cai luong Phan Chu Trinh" [A discussion of Phan Chu Trinh's reformism] *NCLS*, no. 67 (Oct. 1964), p. 36.

10. There is some disagreement over the meaning of the title. One scholar, Vu Doc Bang, rejects the idea that the words *Dong Kinh* stand for Hanoi, and contends that it is more likely that they refer to Tokyo. See Vu Doc Bang, "The Dong Kinh Free School Movement, 1907–1908," in Walter F. Vella, ed., *Aspects of Vietnamese History* (Honolulu, 1973), pp. 86–87. I feel that this is unlikely. For further discussion of the title, see David Marr, *Vietnamese Anticolonialism, 1885–1925* (Berkeley, 1971), p. 164.

The Dong Kinh Nghia Thuc

There is some disagreement among historians about whether the school was founded primarily as a consequence of the Modernization Society's strategy of starting an educational and propaganda organization in Vietnam to spread progressive ideas, or whether it resulted from the desire of reformists like Phan Chu Trinh to spur reform and avoid bloodshed.[11] There seems no doubt that Fukuzawa's school furnished the original model. Many Vietnamese in Japan, including Phan, had become acquainted with the Keio school and it appears that all agreed that the model could be usefully applied to Vietnam. Soon the idea spread to Vietnam itself and came to the attention of a number of progressive scholar-gentry who were acquainted, either personally or by reputation, with the leaders of the resistance movement—notably Luong Van Can, Hoang Tang Bi, Duong Ba Trac, and Nguyen Quyen.[12] Once founded, the school was supported by progressives of many types, some of whom were actively involved in the Modernization Society and who felt that the school would be useful as a propaganda device subordinate to the main goal of armed revolt. Others, like Phan Chu Trinh and founders Luong Van Can and Nguyen Quyen, preferred to follow the path of peaceful reform. They hoped that the school would create the conditions for social and political change and thus eliminate the need for political revolt. This conflict of interests did occasionally come to the fore. At one point director Luong Van Can proposed that the proponents of violence leave the school and go underground. They agreed, but the French closed down the school before the separation could take place.[13]

In sum, the question of the basic function of the school is not easy to resolve, for it was used as a tool by both groups. Most of the active leadership in the school appears to have been reformist,

11. Alternative explanations can be found in *Nien Bieu,* p. 59; in Nguyen Hien Le, *Dong Kinh Nghia Thuc* [The Hanoi Free School] (Saigon, 1968); and in Vu Doc Bang, pp. 36–37.

12. Luong Van Can became the director of the school, with Nguyen Quyen the principal. Luong, born of a poor family in Ha Dong province in 1854, had worked his way up to the *cu nhan* degree. Nguyen Quyen had been a district school superintendant. See Nguyen Hien Le, p. 45, and Vu Doc Bang, p. 37.

13. Nguyen Hien Le, p. 90.

however. Had the school continued to exist, this orientation may have predominated.[14] In the long run, the reformers, whatever their intentions, suffered along with the advocates of violent revolt, for the French were not inclined to draw any distinction and felt that the entire membership was simply a resistance front group.

During its brief life, the school was an active force in promoting reforms and Western ideas. Its stated goals, as indicated in the 1907 application to the French colonial authorities, were three: (1) to spread an interest in commerce, industry and the practical sciences; (2) to spread and popularize the use of quoc-ngu, the romanized form of the Vietnamese language, as the national means of written communications; and (3) to stimulate pride in Vietnamese history.

The Vietnamese waited a month for approval from the resident superior of Tonkin, who was apparently afraid either to approve or reject the application. Eventually someone suggested that the school open simply to teach quoc-ngu, since the government had not actually refused permission. Courses in language were therefore taught to seventy or eighty students of both sexes, mostly the children of founding members. The French were still not prepared to grant approval, however, and when a class was convened at a temple on a lake in Hanoi, two of the instructors were arrested while giving their lectures.[15]

One, Duong Ba Trac, was interrogated. He complained that the French had been in Vietnam for over twenty years and had not fulfilled their promise to civilize the people, so now the Vietnamese must do so on their own. In terms of injured innocence, he claimed that he was attempting only to encourage his students to develop industry in order to make the country more prosperous. How could that be dangerous? How could it not be in the governmental interest? The resident superior was apparently in a conciliatory mood. He said that he was withholding permission only until he obtained formal compliance from the governor-general. The two instructors were thereupon released, and one month later permission was granted to open the school in May, 1907.

Once opened for business, the school began to register students

14. Vu Doc Bang appears to agree. See pp. 73–74.
15. Nguyen Hien Le, pp. 120–121.

in eight grades on three levels, from elementary through higher secondary. Evidently, at least one thousand students were entered at one time or another.[16] Branches were eventually established elsewhere in Vietnam, mainly in Tonkin, and similar institutions appeared under separate management in the Center and the South. The school was financed by a variety of means. Most support, however, came in the form of gifts from sympathizers and contributions from parents and relatives. Within the school, several courses were taught, including geography, world history, mathematics, medicine, and the natural sciences. Particular emphasis was placed on practical subjects such as commerce and industry, apparently in the hope of spurring interest in commercial associations.

As for the traditional heritage, the school was somewhat ambivalent. Most of the instructors were relatively progressive in their views, and all seemed to share the general opinion that Vietnam had much to learn from the West. At the same time, there was a general consensus that the Confucian classics still had some value. Classes in the classics were taught, although the texts used were Chinese editions edited by such reformers as K'ang Yu-wei and Liang Ch'i-ch'ao.[17] Cracks were appearing in Confucian fundamentalism, for there was some desire among the instructors to modernize the civil service examination system.

This ambiguous attitude toward the past was not necessarily indicative of an emotional unwillingness to abandon the old system. It may have reflected simply a practical desire to utilize what was of value from the past. For example, surviving accounts of some of the talks given show the flexibility of thought at the school. On one occasion Phan Chu Trinh and a certain Phuong Son publicly disagreed about the role of religion in promoting social change. Phan maintained that Vietnam was weak because it lacked a religious spirit, a spirit of sacrifice. He cited the role of Buddhism in helping the Vietnamese to resist the Mongols in the thirteenth century. Here Phan was following Liang Ch'i-ch'ao, who had expressed the usefulness of Buddhism as a source of spiritual strength in building national unity. Phuong Son disagreed, pointing out that

16. Estimates vary from 400 to over 2,000.
17. Vu Doc Bang has details on course offerings. See pp. 37–38.

India, where Hinduism was strong, was nothing but a British colony. He then turned Phan's own example against him by asking how the Vietnamese had resisted the Ming in the fifteenth century when Buddhism was in decline in Vietnam.

At another time, Phan, who evidently had a weakness for vast historical generalizations, observed that Confucianism was the cause of the weakness of Vietnam, and asserted that Chinese studies should be abandoned. Once again Phuong Son rose to dispute the point. He agreed that the examination system had no part in a modern society, but retorted that Confucian concepts of loyalty and filiality had provided a moral foundation for the great heroes of Vietnam.[18] While such discussions were obviously highly theoretical, they did serve to stimulate thinking by young students and instructors alike about the future of Vietnamese society.

A more immediately practical aspect of the Free School's educational program was its treatment of the language problem. Since recorded history, the Vietnamese had lived with a complex language system. The native spoken language was used for everyday purposes. For official and literary written use, literary Chinese had been imported. All students training for the civil service examinations had to learn classical Chinese, including its thousands of complex written characters, in order to master the Confucian classics in the original. Finally, a synthetic written system called the *chu nom* (southern characters), was developed for spoken Vietnamese. It consisted of standard Chinese characters for those Vietnamese words that were derived from related words in Chinese, and of specially constructed Vietnamese characters for those words which had no Chinese equivalent.

In the seventeenth century, European Catholic missionaries had invented a phonetic system based on the roman alphabet—the quoc-ngu (national language)—primarily to facilitate the learning of Vietnamese by French missionaries. In the late nineteenth century, once French control was firmly established in Cochin China, quoc-ngu was deliberately popularized as a means of furthering literacy and also to promote French culture.[19] Within a

18. Nguyen Hien Le, pp. 79–82.
19. Details of the rise of *quoc-ngu* in the South can be found in Milton

generation, quoc-ngu became increasingly popular in the South, and many newspapers and journals began to appear in the medium. In Annam and Tonkin, however, traditionalist scholar-gentry, fearful that the advent of quoc-ngu would sound the death knell to Confucian classical education and, by extension, to the moral fabric of the nation itself, and fearful also that the development of the new form would render valueless their own long years of study in the secrets of literary Chinese, resisted the new writing system and refused to countenance its use.

With the Free School movement, however, the attitude of intellectuals in the Center and the North began to change as the advantages of quoc-ngu over its classical rival became apparent. In the first place quoc-ngu was much easier to learn than the Chinese written characters, which took the student years to master. Since the simple quoc-ngu phonetic system could be learned in a few weeks, it would be a means of simplifying the learning process for young Vietnamese. In the second place, it would be an easier tool for the introduction and translation of Western words, so necessary to the modernization of Vietnamese society. Finally, quoc-ngu could become the focus for a new Vietnamese (and not Sino-Vietnamese) identity. Thus, while the school taught in three languages, French, Chinese, and Vietnamese, quoc-ngu was used as the basis for all written texts at the elementary level.[20]

To further the promotion of the national written language, the school undertook to edit and publish books and pamphlets in quoc-ngu, and to spread them to the population at large. There were bureaus in the school for compiling and translating books and essays—particularly those with an emphasis on patriotism, self-strengthening, and modernization. The works of Chinese reformers, and the Chinese-language writings of Phan Boi Chau, were translated and distributed. In addition, a few original works, such as *Van Minh Tan Hoc Sach*—which itself advised its readers to study quoc-ngu and to develop a modern Vietnamese culture—were published. Another well-known work that was printed by the

Osborne, *The French Presence in Cochinchina and Cambodia* (Ithaca, 1969), *passim*.
20. Nguyen Hien Le, p. 44.

school was Nguyen Phan Lang's *Thiet Tien Ca* (Iron Money Ballad), a vigorous critique of French monetary policies. The critique was so effective that the Vietnamese boycott of French iron money forced the French to withdraw the money from circulation.[21]

All in all, the Free School's effect on Vietnamese society was felt in many areas, with progressives increasingly engaged in criticism of the old ways. Western clothes became fashionable and Western hair styles became increasingly common. Certainly Tonkin had not become as exposed to strong French influence as Cochin China, but under the stimulus of the Free School, a new awareness of the West was beginning to take place. If the members of the school were generally careful to avoid an overtly anti-French attitude, the Free School was, at least implicitly, critical of the French failure to spur reform.

What about the content of the Free School program? Can it be said, as some have, that the ideas promoted at the school went beyond those of Phan Boi Chau and his followers in Japan in terms of their reflection of Western influence? For more than one reason this question is difficult to answer. In the first place, the Free School scholars had no concerted program, but were simply a group of reform-minded individuals with a broad consensus on the need for change in Vietnamese society. The published works issued under the auspices of the school were not all the products of instructors at the school, and a full list of members of the school does not seem to be available. In effect, what we know about the school's attitudes toward questions of political and social significance is limited to a few recollections, and a handful of published works which reflected in only a general way the attitudes of the participants. Secondly, the participants in the school, unlike Phan Boi Chau who was able to write under no special constraint in exile, labored under the watchful and often hostile eye of the French administration, which no doubt imposed limitations on the content of the writings connected with the school.

Within these limitations some tentative conclusions are justified. In the first place, there is little substantial difference between the reformist goals of Phan Boi Chau and those of the leadership of the school. By 1907 and 1908, he had demonstrated a commit-

21. The text can be found in *ibid.*, pp. 163–166.

ment to modern ideas roughly equivalent to those expressed in such works as are available from the Free School. True, Phan still talked in terms of a constitutional monarchy, but there is no indication that the majority of Free School instructors were strongly republican. Phan and his movement differed from the Free Schoolers because of their strongly activist proclivities.

The Free School's promotion of cultural reform was not what caused the French to halt its activities. While they may have had objections to some of the aspects of the Free School program—particularly its potentially anti-French stance—they could not legitimately object to its cultural and educational aims, for official French policy was engaged in promoting similar goals. The French, however, were convinced that much of the Free School leadership was intimately tied up with the anti-French movement led by Phan Boi Chau, who remained in exile, and, further, that the alleged educational activities of the school were simply a front for its nefarious rebellious purposes. The governor-general's reports to the Minister of Colonies in Paris indicate an abiding conviction that the school's leadership was deeply involved in the resistance plots throughout Vietnam and also that it had direct ties with Hoang Hoa Tham, who was under increasing suspicion by the French.[22] The French, in short, were frightened by the prospects of a nationwide revolt, and reacted against the most visible symbol of Vietnamese nationalism. In December 1907, the French closed down the school. Although no immediate action was taken against its organizers (indeed, Nguyen Quyen and Duong Ba Trac were offered official posts), a number of participants in the school were later arrested.[23]

Phan Chu Trinh's career came to an abrupt halt in 1908, when he was arrested along with Tran Quy Cap and Huynh Thuc Khang for inciting violence in the tax riots in Annam during the spring. Tran, who was hated by the Hué court for his own detestation of the mandarin system, was executed, and Phan was condemned to death. The Ligue des Droits de l'Homme in Paris intervened, how-

22. Such conclusions emerge from the archival materials at the Ministère d'Outre-Mer in Paris. See the AOM reports from the Governor-general to the Ministry of Colonies, 1907–1910.
23. Nguyen Hien Le, p. 93. Nguyen Quyen and Duong Ba Trac were eventually imprisoned.

ever, and he was transferred to French control and sent to Con Lon island.[24] In French prison he received somewhat favored treatment, probably because of his influential friends in Paris. Eventually, in 1911, the French offered him a partial amnesty to show their preference of his approach as opposed to that of Phan Boi Chau.

Upon release, Phan was temporarily confined to the city of My Tho in the Mekong delta. He wanted either total freedom or a return to prison, however, and was permitted to go to France with Governor-general Klobukowski. He made contact with liberal and humanitarian elements in France and continued to voice his criticism of French policies in Indochina. In 1911, he published a petition in the *Cahier de la Ligue des Droits de l'Homme* in which he defended those who had been arrested for protesting taxes in 1908 and bitterly attacked the colonial government.[25] He also scorned French treatment of those Vietnamese who had cut their hair (the 1908 tax riots were called the revolt of the "cheveux coupés" by the French because many of the participants had cut their hair short to demonstrate their desire for reforms) and pointed out that Japan had compelled the Koreans to cut their hair for reasons of health. That, he said, is civilization. The French, on the other hand, hunt short-hairs down and call them rebels. He was also scandalized by the Hué government's execution of Tran Quy Cap and complained of a system which shot taxpayers, persecuted the scholar-gentry, and closed schools and shops founded with official permission. He warned the government that if it wanted to retain its prestige it would first have to acknowledge and correct its mistakes.[26] As a result of such statements, Phan lost the salary granted him by the French government and had to support himself as a photo retoucher.

24. The Nguyen, p. 16.
25. This article also appeared in series form in *Cloche fêlée* during the month of February 1926.
26. For a quoc-ngu version, see Truong Huu Ky, "Them mot so tai lieu ve cu Phan Chu Trinh" [some additional material on uncle Phan Chu Trinh], *NCLS*, no. 70 (Jan. 1965), p. 19.

Chapter 4

Lips and Teeth

By 1908, Phan Boi Chau's resistance movement had begun to make an impression on Vietnamese society, and all those forces opposed to French rule in Vietnam began to coalesce around him. Phan's group was surprisingly small, considering the reputation it had been able to build and the fear it had begun to inspire in the French. Some reports indicate that the total number of active members of the organization within Vietnam was not over one hundred.[1] Despite their diminutive size, they were playing a useful role in the formation of a movement for national independence. At a time when resistance to French rule had died out in many areas of Vietnamese society, the scholar-patriots were continuing the tradition of national resistance commenced by Phan Dinh Phung a generation earlier. They were building a bridge between the traditionalist goals of their predecessors and those of the modern men who would follow.

The immediate consequences of their early activity, however, had not been especially encouraging. Vietnamese society as a whole, from the rural population to the tiny but growing urban middle class, remained largely indifferent to the emotional blandishments of Phan Boi Chau and his colleagues.

The French were more observant. The colonial administration became conscious of the need to achieve a greater measure of cooperation with Vietnamese elites. It wanted to alleviate some of the more grievous injustices and to establish a regime of "mutual esteem and respect." By the early years of the twentieth century, French governors-general were expressing their desire to achieve

1. That figure would be at least doubled, of course, if the students in Japan were added to the total.

a policy of cooperation between the Vietnamese and the French administration in order to realize the mutually attractive goal of material prosperity and cultural advance. Although Governor-general Beau's tour of office was too short for many concrete accomplishments, his policy was continued by the flamboyant Albert Sarraut, who became the leading advocate of "association."

The initiation of a declared policy of association by the French did not mean that a change in French attitudes toward the resistance movement was imminent, however. Indeed, French administrators prided themselves on a policy of combining social reform with a rapid and brutal suppression of anticolonialist activities. For the most part, the early years of the Modernization Society were years of supposition, and after 1908, many of Phan's most trusted lieutenants in Vietnam—including Tang Bat Ho, Dang Thai Than, and Nguyen Thanh—either died or were executed by the French. Many others were thrown in prison. If the first few years of the anticolonial movement had brought considerable notoriety and a few converts to Phan Boi Chau's cause, it had also brought swift retaliation from the French and little in the way of concrete results. It was not a time of unbridled optimism for the revolutionaries.

Phan, during his years in Japan, had adhered to the general policy guidelines drawn up by the Modernization Society conference in 1904, and he shuttled back and forth from Japan to South China and Vietnam, composing pamphlets and exhorting his colleagues to increase their efforts. Through it all he had maintained his faith in the advantages of a Japanese connection. He continued to hope that ultimately his hosts would find it in their interests to give more substantial assistance to the Vietnamese resistance movement.

The course of international events shook Phan Boi Chau from his determined path. For a generation the leaders of Japan had been actively promoting the rapid transformation of that nation into a modern industrialized society. By the turn of the century, Japan had become economically prosperous and powerful, and was prepared to compete with its European rivals for influence in Asia. For a time the Japanese leadership toyed with the idea of becoming the leader of a resurgent Asia, and of becoming the avowed ally of the Asian colonialized peoples. No doubt many of

Phan's Japanese acquaintances sincerely hoped that Japanese foreign policy, once recovery from the war with Russia was complete, would eventually assume an anti-imperialist stance. But the government was about to adopt different tactics to transform Japan into a great power in Asia. Hegemony would be achieved not by a policy of hostility to the West, but by a process of accommodation. Given such premises, the past Japanese policy of supporting anti-colonialist movements was bound to lose its former validity. In France, meanwhile, there was a growing concern over Japan's sympathy and assistance for the Vietnamese resistance movement in exile. Among journalists and amateur strategists in France it had become the conventional wisdom to consider Japan a major threat to French domination in Indochina.[2]

In July of 1908, Japan and France reached an agreement that alleviated French concern and underlined Japan's new role as a responsible imperialist power. In return for financial concessions, Japan agreed to abandon its policy of tolerating Vietnamese anti-colonialists on her soil. Japan's decision to come to terms with France had lasting consequences for the Vietnamese resistance movement. Under Phan Boi Chau's leadership it now decisively turned to China as the nation most likely to be sympathetic to Vietnamese independence.

Phan had earlier made contact with Liang Ch'i-ch'ao's bitter rival Sun Yat-sen, after Sun had returned from the United States to set up his Revolutionary Alliance. Now, Phan decided to visit Sun at his residence. There, Sun criticized Phan's policy of supporting the monarchical system, since Sun had little liking for the constitutional monarchists in China. Sun did propose cooperation between his own group and the Vietnamese, but with the understanding that Phan's group would first help the Chinese revolutionaries expel the Manchus. Then, the Chinese would be happy to free Vietnam from French control. Phan Boi Chau, of course, wanted the Chinese to help liberate Vietnam first, and then use North Vietnam as a base area from which to attack the old dynasty on its weak southern flank. In Phan's own words, the conversation was "superficial," because neither really understood the

2. See, for example, Lt. Colonel Peroz, *France et Japon en Indochine* (Paris, 1906).

situation of the other. Although no decision was reached, the two maintained contact, and for a short period it was Sun's Revolutionary Alliance which kept the Vietnamese exiles financially afloat in Japan by giving jobs to Vietnamese students in need of funds.

Actually, Phan's hopes for assistance from China at this time rested less on aid from Sun's movement in exile than on support from Chinese in the southern provinces along the Vietnamese border—Yunnan, Kwangsi, and Kwangtung—where racial ties complemented historic and geographical proximity. Since 1906, Phan had been working as an editor for the *Yun-nan Tsa-chih* (Yunnan Journal), an organ of Yunnan revolutionaries in Japan. He occasionally wrote articles for the journal urging closer cooperation between Vietnam and the southern Chinese provinces. The best known of his articles on this subject is a brief essay, *Ai Viet Dieu Dien* (A Lament for Vietnam and Yunnan), written in 1906. In *Ai Viet Dieu Dien* Phan referred to the historic relations between Vietnam and South China and grieved over their recent humiliation at the hands of the West. He stressed the geographic, historical, and ethnic ties between the Vietnamese and the Yunnanese population, and alluded to the growing threat to the area posed by the construction of the French-built railway from North Vietnam to Kunming in Yunnan province. Quoting an old phrase familiar to Vietnamese as well as to Chinese, he pointed out that when the lips (Vietnam) are open, the teeth (China) are cold.[3] Yunnan and Vietnam, he concluded, should establish mutual cooperation in order to frustrate French plans to finish the railroad and extend their control over the "precious jewel" of Yunnan.

When news of the Japanese decision to evict the Vietnamese was made known, Phan clearly knew that he could not rely on Japan, and decided to look for help elsewhere. At first, having made contact with Japanese radicals who were attempting to create a multi-national organization of political emigrés in order to unite the anticolonialist elements in East and Southeast Asia against imperialism, he set up the Dong A Dong Menh Hoi (All-Asia Alliance). Composed of anticolonialists from India, the Philippines and Korea, as well as from Vietnam, China, and Japan, the new organization was aimed at world revolution by all oppressed peo-

3. The text is in *NCLS,* no. 56 (Nov. 1963), pp. 40–43.

ples.[4] It did not last long. Within five months it was hounded out of existence by Japanese authorities. Meanwhile, in an attempt to cement relations with the revolutionaries in South China, Phan established another organization, the Dien-Que-Viet Alliance (Yunnan-Kwangsi-Vietnam Alliance). The Dien-Que-Viet Alliance had no more success, however, than its pan-Asian predecessor, and was closed down within three months by the Japanese government in response to demands by the French and Chinese authorities.[5]

With the signature of the Franco-Japanese Treaty, the Vietnamese exile organization was forced to abandon its home in Japan. In late 1908, when the order came to leave, most of the students complied, although a few stayed to work. Cuong De and Phan Boi Chau were not ordered to depart until the next February.

They went to Hong Kong to make new plans and arrange passage for the evicted students. After a brief period in Hong Kong, where Cuong De decided to go to Europe to seek aid for Vietnam from sympathetic countries there, Phan arranged to take some of the students to Thailand. He had already visited Thailand the previous year and had made connections with officials in the foreign office in Bangkok. At that time he had asked one of his contacts in the royal family whether it would be possible for the Vietnamese to obtain land for an agricultural plantation. The king had promised to arrange it.[6] Because other affairs had intervened nothing had been done at the time, but now, with the Vietnamese activists lacking a headquarters, Phan renewed his effort to open a plantation in Thailand. By late September of 1910, permission was granted to give them land at Ban Tham, in a mountainous area four days travel from Bangkok. Tools were furnished by Thai well-wishers, and livestock was borrowed from neighbors. Soon Vietnamese students began to gather there. In early 1911, Phan himself went there to oversee operations and spent eight months, feeling "free, odd, happy." As an old literatus, he was somewhat awkward at farm labor, but he apparently thrived spiritually in

4. *Nien Bieu*, p. 119.
5. *Ibid.*, p. 120.
6. *Ibid.*, p. 125.

the bucolic atmosphere. He spent his leisure time writing poems and composing resistance songs for his disciples.[7]

The Restoration Society

For a decade, Phan Boi Chau had been at work in Vietnam and abroad for the nationalist cause. The results had been disappointingly meager. But prospects suddenly improved in late 1911 with the outbreak of the Chinese revolution. The apparent victory of the revolutionaries in the Yangtse Valley revived hopes for decisive change and cause a flurry of renewed activity in nationalist circles in Vietnam. Phan heard about the encouraging events while in Thailand. He was aware of their significance and made immediate arrangements to travel to China in order to renew his acquaintance with Chinese he had known in exile in Japan, and to seek their support for the liberation of Vietnam.[8]

Phan Boi Chau's immediate goal was to reorganize the Modernization Society into a more effective and streamlined organization to meet the changed exigencies of the time. The victory of Sun Yat-sen's revolutionary party in China seemed a good omen for the prospects of republicanism in Asia, and therefore the focal point of Phan's new plan was to establish a new ideological framework which would draw on the successes of the Revolutionary Alliance in China and also increase the latter's ideological sympathy for the Vietnamese resistance. In February 1912, he called a meeting of representatives from all three areas of Vietnam at the Canton residence of Liu Yung-fu, a Chinese whose Black Flag pirate band had fought against French forces in Tonkin in the 1870s and 1880s. The major issue of the day, obviously, concerned the monarchy versus republicanism. Whereas Phan had heretofore insisted on the retention of the monarchy, in the belief that only through the symbolism it provided could sufficient financial aid be obtained from within Vietnam to carry on resistance activities, now the situation had changed. In the first place, Vietnam's major hope of assistance lay with the new China. Sun Yat-

7. *NTT*, p. 63.
8. In his baggage was a new tract, *Lien A So Ngon* [Tract on the Unity of Asia] which discussed in superficial terms the unification of all Asia, and the need for Sino-Japanese cooperation. *Nien Bieu*, p. 138.

sen and his colleagues, for so long involved in bitter controversy with China's own constitutional monarchists, were unlikely to be sympathetic to a Vietnamese organization dedicated to maintaining the feudal monarchy at Hué. In the second place, Phan had himself been strongly influenced toward republicanism by the Chinese revolutionaries, and by his own reading of such Western classics as Montesquieu's *Esprit des Lois* and Rousseau's *Contrat Social*.[9] At the meeting, therefore, Phan strongly advocated abolition of the Modernization Society with its ultimate aim of constitutional monarchy and advocated the establishment of a new organization based on republicanism. While there was some grumbling among the more conservative delegates at the conference—mostly from Cochin China—the majority approved, and in consequence a new organization, based on the republican system of government, and called the Quang Phuc Hoi (Restoration Society), was founded.[10]

The organization of the new party was relatively simple, and was strongly influenced by Sun's own Revolutionary Alliance. Three administrative sections were created: (1) a commissariat, with Cuong De as chairman and Phan Boi Chau as vice-chairman and secretary general; (2) a consultative bureau, with representatives from all three areas of Vietnam, including Nguyen Thuong Hien from Tonkin, Phan from Annam, and Nguyen Than Hien from Cochin China; and (3) an executive council of ten members, divided into separate bureaus for military affairs, economic affairs, public relations, propaganda, and so forth.[11] The ultimate goal of the new organization was to overthrow the French and establish an independent Vietnamese republic.

Internal Revolt

Having taken preliminary action to bring the Vietnamese movement up to date, Phan left immediately for Nanking after the conference to renew his earlier contacts with Sun Yat-sen and his colleagues, and to remind Sun of his one-time promise to aid the

9. *Ibid.*, pp. 140–141.
10. *Ibid.*, p. 141.
11. Prominent members of the council included Hoang Trong Mau, Luong Lap Nam, Mai Lao Bang, and Phan Ba Ngoc. See *Nien Bieu*, p. 142.

Vietnamese once the victory of the Chinese revolution had been rendered secure. In Nanking, however, he found Sun preoccupied with negotiations over the form of the new government. Perhaps, too, Sun did not want to be reminded of his earlier commitments to Phan. In any event, Phan was fobbed off with Sun's lieutenant, Huang Hsing, who listened sympathetically to Phan's pleas for assistance, but who told him bluntly: "My country can hardly refuse the duty of helping Vietnam, but at this early moment we are simply unable to do so. What you should do is to select some students to enter our schools here, or some young men to join our army, and in this way to develop your talents. But this will take ten years. We'll help all we can, but we have no immediate plans to give you assistance."[12]

Huang Hsing's negative response was a sore disappointment to Phan, as his autobiography demonstrates. After over a decade of lonely and heart-rending struggle, involving the loss of some of his dearest comrades, such clichés about "developing your talent" and "gradual advance" were grinding on the ears, and ashes to the taste. For Phan Boi Chau, the time had come to make some crucial decisions. The need to rely on education and party building was forgotten. Now was the time for violent revolution, for glorious victory or equally glorious death—to wage the entire destiny of Vietnam on one throw of the dice.[13]

Thus set on armed revolt, Phan launched two related programs to obtain financial support. First, on the advice of a Chinese friend, revolutionary bank notes were issued, in amounts of five through one hundred piasters.[14] The notes were not backed by hard currency, but could only be redeemed if the Vietnamese revolution succeeded. If not, in his own words, it was as good a way as any to soak the rich. Second, he promoted the foundation of yet another Sino-Vietnamese organization for friendship and mutual support. Entitled Chan Hoa Hung A (Revive China, Restore Asia), it was set up at a meeting of over two hundred delegates from both nations in August 1912. A program and declaration were approved, including the usual appeal to China's sense of self-

12. *Ibid.*, p. 144.
13. *Ibid.*, p. 148.
14. *Ibid.*, pp. 148–149.

advantage and altruism, and new pleas for assistance in the liberation of India, Burma, and Korea, in addition to Vietnam. The leadership of the new group was divided among Chinese and Vietnamese, with Phan occupying the post of vice-chairman.[15]

After having taken about as much action as he could to call forth support from China, Phan now turned to the task of raising the decibel of discontent in Vietnam. For a time the revolutionaries limited themselves to attempted assassinations of prominent personalities in Vietnam, although in November 1912 an attempt was made on the life of Governor-general Sarraut. It failed. Other attacks were more successful—in April 1913 a district chief in Thai Binh province was assassinated, and the same month a bomb thrown by revolutionaries killed two Frenchmen at a hotel in Hanoi. Over two hundred suspects were seized. Seven were condemned to death by a hastily convened French criminal commission. Phan Boi Chau and Cuong De were sentenced to death in absentia.[16]

Such acts, of course, were only a substitute for major actions, but without aid from China, hopes for progress were considered fruitless. Phan attempted to get in touch with the governor of Honan province, T'an Yen-k'ai, but the situation in China had changed, and the revolutionaries were now on the defensive. In late spring 1913, the forces of President Yuan Shih-k'ai attacked the revolutionary sympathizer Ch'en Chiung-ming in Kwangtung and drove him out, replacing him with Yuan's own man Lung Chi-kuang. Yuan himself was not particularly hostile to the Vietnamese revolutionaries—indeed, his military subordinate, Tuan Ch'i-jui, had intimated to Cuong De that once the president had his hands free in a few years, he would be happy to assist the Vietnamese in obtaining their freedom.[17] Yuan's lieutenant in Kwangtung, however, did not share the president's benign attitude toward the Vietnamese, and when Governor-general Sarraut requested the arrest and extradition to Indochina of Phan and other members of his party as a result of the Hanoi bombing incident, Lung happily complied with the first part of the request. In January 1914,

---

15. Members included workers, merchants, and soldiers. *Ibid.*, p. 152.

16. Tran Huy Lieu, *Lich Su Thu Do Ha Noi* [A History of the City of Hanoi], (Hanoi, 1960), p. 129.

17. *Nien Bieu*, p. 159.

Phan was arrested and imprisoned in South China.[18] Cuong De had been arrested earlier in Hong Kong but was released on bail, at which time he fled to Europe.

While Phan was in prison, sporadic outbreaks of violence continued to occur throughout Vietnam, some under the direction of members of the party, others spontaneous. Lacking attractive alternatives, the revolutionaries surmised that conscription, taxes and the French monopolies had created incendiary conditions in Vietnam and hoped that a nationwide movement could be sparked by isolated attacks. In the meantime, a liberation army was being formed along the Sino-Vietnamese border. It would wait to invade at the appropriate moment. The French were privy to these plans, however, having planted an agent with Phan's entourage as early as 1913, and Sarraut was able to take precautions to reinforce the border posts.[19] At one time there was even the hope that Phan could be lured close enough to the Vietnamese border to be captured by French troops. For unexplained reasons the hope never materialized.

The revolutionaries planned to initiate, in June 1915, armed uprisings along the border areas in the mountain provinces of Tonkin. Apparently French harassment forced the attacks to break out six months early. These attacks, led by Hoang Trong Mao and Nguyen Than Hien were easily repulsed by the French, and the leaders were seized. Hoang was executed and Nguyen apparently died in prison.[20]

With the failure of these uprisings and with the arrest of the majority of the leaders, the back of the Restoration Society was broken. Other scattered uprisings occurred during the next few years but as a rule they were spontaneous and ill-coordinated. Several revolts broke out among the minority population in the mountain areas of Tonkin, but to no avail. In Cochin China, a revolt by a Buddhist religious sect, called the Thien Dia Hoi (Heaven and Earth Society), against the conscription of troops occurred in March of 1913. Even when the leader, Phan Phat Sanh, was cap-

18. *Ibid.*, p. 161; *NTT*, pp. 68–70.
19. AOM, Nouveau Fonds 605, Carton 51, report of Canton Consul Beauvais to Governor-general, Feb. 10, 1913.
20. David Marr, *Vietnamese Anticolonialism, 1885–1925* (Berkeley, 1971), p. 224.

tured, his followers continued to march on Saigon, and riots broke out in March and April.[21]

The most famous anti-French revolt of the war period, however, was the so-called Duy Tan uprising of May 1916 in Annam. Active resistance in the Center to the French protectorate had been at a low level since the crushing of the peasant tax riots in 1908, but anti-French sentiment still continued among some scholar-gentry followers of the Modernization Society and the defunct Can Vuong organization. In 1913, local resistance leaders sent two delegates to China to make contact with Phan's new Restoration Society. Upon their return the two delegates attempted to arrange for revolts in Annam to coincide with the planned 1914 attacks on the Chinese frontier. When the attacks in Tonkin failed, there was some discouragement in Annam, but desire for action against the French remained generally high. There were calls for immediate action, even though direct contact with the parent group in exile was difficult to maintain. The conspirators hoped to utilize the young Emperor Duy Tan—who had replaced his sick and erratic father, Thanh Thai, in 1907, and who had developed a sympathy with revolutionary aims. The original suggestion to focus the uprising around the figure of the emperor came from the conservative nationalist Tran Cao Van, who had been arrested in 1908 for his involvement in the tax riots of that year (he was released in 1913 after influential friends intervened on his behalf). At a meeting in February 1916 it was agreed to set an uprising for April in the Hué and Danang areas. Partisans in local areas would rise as the emperor secretly left the capital to lead the resistance forces. The rebels were hopeful that restless Vietnamese troops in Danang, scheduled to be sent to France to participate in the European war, would revolt and join them.[22] Unfortunately for the success of the movement, however, word of the plans leaked out. Some of the conspirators apparently talked too much. Even the monarch divulged the plot to members of his family, and news of the plan reached the ears of the French in the imperial capital.

21. Phuong Huu, *Phong Trao Dai Dong Du* [The Exodus to the East Movement] (Saigon, 1950), pp. 41–42.

22. Suren A. Mkhitarian, *Rabochii Klass i Natsional'no-Osvoboditel'noe Dvizhenie vo Vietname* [The Working Class and the National Liberation Movement in Vietnam] (Moscow, 1967), p. 107; Marr, p. 234.

The government immediately declared martial law throughout Annam and disarmed all Vietnamese soldiers in the area.

Incredibly, the conspirators themselves did not hear of the disclosure of their plot, and Duy Tan left the palace secretly in accordance with the plan and proceeded to Ngu Phong mountain, where he was seized within three days. Local partisan units, unaware of the events in the capital, rose in revolt and were easily subdued. The leaders of the uprising—Tran Cao Van, Thai Phien, and Thon That De—were all captured and beheaded. Duy Tan was deposed and sent to Reunion Island. His throne passed to Khai Dinh, the son of former emperor Dong Khanh.

Like so many of the events of this period, the ill-starred Duy Tan movement has inspired some controversy among historians of modern Vietnam. Was it, as some maintain, directly connected with Phan's movement in exile and aimed at the establishment of an independent democratic republic? Or, on the other hand, was it, as David Marr describes it, "a romantic aberration," a dying gasp of monarchist sentiment in Central Vietnam? Those who maintain the latter have pointed to the prominent position of Emperor Duy Tan in the movement and of the conservative Tran Cao Van in the planning and execution of the revolt.[23] A recent article published in Hanoi provides evidence, however, to dispute this view.[24] Some coordination with the Restoration Society in China did take place, and it appears that Duy Tan's participation was less active than had once been assumed. His participation in the uprising is no more an indication of the movement's ideological tendencies than was the participation of Cuong De in the Restoration Society.

Indeed, according to the recent articles cited above, there was considerable disagreement among the plotters over the future nature of the state. Some of the participants maintained that the population was not ready to accept democracy. They saw Duy Tan as the potential head of a future constitutional monarchy. Others felt that Duy Tan was useful only as a symbolic head of the move-

23. Marr, p. 233.
24. Le Trong Khanh and Dang Huy Van, "Cuoc khoi nghia cua Viet Nam Quang Phuc Hoi" [An uprising of the Vietnam Quang Phuc Hoi], *NCLS*, no. 22 (Jan. 1961), pp. 46–47.

ment during the military phase and looked forward to the ultimate establishment of a democratic republic.

This ambiguity was reflected in a draft declaration issued by the conspirators, which called for the emperor to participate in order to "reassure the population." The proposed new governmental structure, however, consisted of a president, a vice-president and seven ministers in a supreme organ called the Central Executive Yuan. Evidently there was no reference to the position of the monarch. Other articles called for the election of a legislative assembly, guarantees of freedom and democracy, and the abrogation of capitation taxes. Such provisions provide some indication that the Duy Tan uprising had sufficient progressive orientation to merit its inclusion in the general scope of the Restoration Society. Like the Free School of Hanoi, it probably contained ideological disagreement within its membership, but because it was short-lived and unsuccessful, the inner schisms never became a matter of obvious concern.

One final revolt, and perhaps the most substantial of the war years, took place in August 1917 in Thai Nguyen province northeast of Hanoi. Taking advantage of the resentment among local soldiers in the French colonial army, Luong Ngoc Quyen, son of Free School principal Luong Van Can and disciple of Phan Boi Chau since Japan days, made contact with a group of Vietnamese troops under Sergeant Trinh Van Can and made plans to seize the province and issue an appeal for nationwide support.[25] Although the first stage of the uprising was successful, and brief control over the city was achieved, divided views on strategy soon arose. Some members of the group, notably remnants of Hoang Hoa Tham's forces still active in the area, wanted to take the offensive in Phuc Yen, Bac Giang and Bac Can provinces in order to consolidate a base area throughout central North Vietnam. Luong, however, was more cautious and wanted to consolidate his strength in Thai Nguyen province while buying weapons and waiting for aid promised by the Restoration Society across the border. Luong's proposals eventually won out, but it soon became academic, for the French struck back quickly, seized the city and drove the revolu-

25. Mkhitarian, p. 108; Marr, p. 234.

tionaries into the mountains. By the beginning of the new year, the last of the rebels was captured. Luong had been killed earlier in the fighting, and Trinh committed suicide.

The Duy Tan and Thai Nguyen uprisings demonstrated that resistance to French rule in Vietnam was still alive, and that the imprisonment of Phan Boi Chau in South China did not totally cripple the Restoration Society. On the other hand, the nature of the revolts and their consequences showed that the nationalists were still far from attaining their goal. The uprisings themselves were markedly familiar. They were sporadic and ill coordinated, the leaders disagreed about tactics, and overall planning was virtually nonexistent. Participation of the local population was often left to chance. All in all, the revolts were amateurish in conception and execution. They are a good example of what happens when rebels decide to throw all of their resources into a last-ditch gamble for success. The age of the scholar-patriots was drawing to a close.

Chapter 5

Frustration and Defeat

In February 1917, Lung Chi-kuang was thrown out of power. At this point Phan Boi Chau had been in jail for three years. Lung had toyed with the idea of turning him over to the French but when they refused to permit him to use the Yunnan railway to move his troops he had decided against it. Now that Lung was gone, Phan was released from jail.[1] Although he may not have been aware that his days as the leader of an active revolutionary movement were over, the aging nationalist leader soon discovered the magnitude of his difficulties, for not only was his own organization disarmed, but foreign interest in the cause of Vietnam was at a low ebb. The revolutionaries had received a token gift of funds from Germany through the German consul in Thailand. Then the consul in Tientsin had made a tentative offer of weapons which would otherwise be confiscated because of the Chinese declaration of war on the Central Powers. But emissaries sent to negotiate were arrested and the plan failed. Elsewhere, Phan was equally unfortunate; Sun Yat-sen's forces in South China were preoccupied with their own problems. He went to Yunnan to seek aid from the local military leader T'ang Chi-yao, but T'ang avoided him. Finally, Phan settled down in China and, for lack of an alternative, decided to resume his writing. He became an assistant editor of the *Ping-shih Tsa-chih* (Military Affairs Journal), the official publication of the Chekiang government, and contributed articles under pseudonyms.

This failure to make progress toward independence helps to explain what has always been one of the most puzzling aspects of

1. *Nien Bieu,* p. 173.

Phan Boi Chau's long career. About a year after his release from prison he was approached by two of his revolutionary colleagues, Le Du and Phan Ba Ngoc, the latter a son of Phan Dinh Phung. Phan Ba Ngoc suggested that the Vietnamese nationalists should make conciliatory gestures to the new Governor-general Sarraut, a progressive who was returning after an earlier term in Indochina. Sarraut, they claimed, was planning a number of liberal policies concerning education, justice and political rights, and a receptive attitude by the Vietnamese revolutionaries would encourage the new governor-general to pursue such a moderate policy.[2] In his discouragement, Phan allowed himself to be convinced that the times called for flexible tactics, and responded by writing a brief tract, the *Phap-Viet De-Hue Chinh-kien Thu* (A Letter of Opinion on Franco-Vietnamese Harmony) in which he predicted a future war between Japan and the Western powers which would inevitably spill over into Indochina.[3] He contended that, whatever the brutalities of the present protectorate, French rule was preferable to Japanese (he pointed to the situation in Korea and Taiwan), and he advocated an increased effort on the part of both French and Vietnamese to establish amicable relations. The French should not consider the Vietnamese as "slaves and buffalos"; the Vietnamese should not look upon the French with hatred, but as teachers and able friends. They should join together against the Japanese. Without such cooperation, he predicted, the Japanese would have no difficulty in conquering Indochina, to the detriment of both Franch and Vietnam.

Phan's response was carried to Sarraut, who then offered to send a representative to China to discuss the possibility of cooperation. In May 1919, a French delegate arrived at West Lake near Hangchow to talk with Phan and present the French proposals. Sarraut offered Phan a high post at court, on condition that he return to Vietnam and publicly renounce his career as a rebel. By this time, however, Phan was having second thoughts, and refused the French conditions, insisting that he had been duped.[4]

2. *Ibid.,* p. 186.
3. *Phap-Viet De-Hue Chinh-Kien Thu,* trans. Nguyen Khac Hanh (Hanoi, n. d.), p. 10.
4. *Nien Bieu,* p. 188.

Not surprisingly, there has been considerable controversy over the meaning and implications of the entire incident. Pro-French sources have often cited the letter to show that Phan had been converted to a policy of cooperation with France. Nationalists are inclined to concede that it was a regrettable incident, "naive and clumsy," in an otherwise impeccable career as a patriot, but point out that he returned to an anti-French stance in later writings.[5] They further assert that Phan had been seduced by Le Du and Phan Ba Ngoc, both of whom had sold out to the French. It is probable that the latter explanation is the more correct one. Phan did go through a period of discouragement after his release, and for a time he began to advocate peaceful reform in the cultural sphere in place of violent struggle, and the letter to Sarraut may well have represented his views at that time. On the other hand, what he had in mind was certainly not a simple amnesty for himself, and the terms presented by the French were insulting. In addition, he later claimed that the quoc-ngu translation of the original Chinese version misinterpreted his real views.[6] In any event, when he realized that Sarraut had no real intention of modifying French policy, but was merely trying to neutralize the old patriot's influence, he repudiated his gesture of conciliation and returned to his earlier posture.

Whatever the final truth of the incident, Phan Boi Chau played a passive role in the nationalist movement in the postwar period, limiting his participation to that of propagandist and elder statesman. He continued to contribute articles to revolutionary Chinese journals, and a number of his major works date from this period. Unfortunately, much of the material on Phan's activities at this time is only now being gathered and gradually published in Hanoi. Many of his works dating from the postwar era are not yet widely

5. For a pro-French position, see the introduction by Nguyen Khac Hanh, p. 10. For a nationalist reaction, see Tran Huy Lieu, "Phan Boi Chau, tieu bieu cho nhung cuoc van dong yeu nuoc o Viet Nam dau the ky XX" [Phan Boi Chau, the model for all patriotic movements in Vietnam in the early 20th century], *NCLS*, no. 105 (Dec. 1967), p. 6.

6. Chuong Thau, "Phan Boi Chau qua mot so sach bao mien nam hien nay" [Phan Boi Chau through a number of articles and books published in contemporary South Vietnam], *NCLS*, no. 67 (Oct. 1964), p. 14. The Chinese original is not currently available.

available to scholars, and researchers are forced to rely on scattered references and excerpts in North Vietnamese sources.[7]

The best known of his works written during this period are *Trung Quang Tam Su* (also known as *Hao Tran Dat Su*), *Du Cuu Nien Lai So Tri Chi Chu Nghia* (My Contentions for the Last Nine Years), *Y Hon Don* (Medical Prescription for Curing the Soul), and *Thien Ho De Ho* (O Heaven, O God).[8] *Trung Quang Tam Su* (History of Trung Quang) was a short history about a peasant tax revolt in fifteenth century Nghe An against the Ming conquerors, but by implication was a call for national resistance against the French. *Du Cuu Nien Lai* and *Y Hon Don* were both written at a time when Phan suffered from depression and they seem to reflect the same tendency away from violent revolution as *Phap-Viet De-Hue Chinh-kien Thu*. The first, dating from 1920, was evidently written in support of the idea of a "cultural revolution."[9] *Y Hon Don* discussed favorably the passive resistance doctrines of Mahatma Gandhi which at that time were popular in many parts of Asia.

With *Thien Ho De Ho*, however, it is clear that Phan had revived his spirits and his confidence in the prospects for Vietamese liberation. Probably the last of the aforementioned works to be composed (in 1923), it is a harsh diatribe against the policies of cultural genocide which the French government was allegedly following in Vietnam. In the author's opinion, the policies followed by the French in the fields of religion, education, and politics were designed to erase the Vietnamese people's awareness of themselves as a nation. He placed particular blame on the role of Christianity and called on Christians to behave according to the real message of Jesus—according to brotherhood and equality.[10]

7. Chuong Thau, "Anh huong cua Phan Boi Chau doi voi mot so to chuc cach mang Trung Quoc" [Phan Boi Chau's influence on Chinese revolutionary organizations], *NCLS*, no. 56 (Nov. 1963), pp. 36–37.

8. Of these, only the text of *Trung Quang* is available to me. See *Van Tho Phan Boi Chau Chon Loc* [Selections from the Writings of Phan Boi Chau] (Hanoi, 1967), pp. 211–247.

9. Chuong Thau, "Tinh hinh nghien cuu Phan Boi Chau tu truoc den nay" [The situation regarding research on Phan Boi Chau from past to present], *NCLS*, no. 104 (Nov. 1967), p. 12.

10. *Nien Bieu*, p. 194. Nguyen Thuong Huyen in an article published in 1960 contended that Phan wrote it in praise of Christianity. Fragmentary evidence available to me indicates, however, that it is more likely a reflec-

Do Phan Boi Chau's postwar writings indicate any significant changes in his ideas? For the most part, they appear to reflect ideas current in China at that time and give little indication of any real intellectual growth. Most provocative of the new ideas to affect his own thought was Marxism. Until 1920 he had given no indication of even a passing acquaintance with socialism. He had maintained contact with members of the Chinese Socialist party in Kwangtung province, but in none of his writings was there expressed any interest in the doctrine. In 1920, however, he read a book in Japanese on Soviet Russia. Curious, he managed to obtain an introduction to two Russians in Peking, one an aide to Russian ambassador Karakhan, and discussed communism with them.[11] From all indications, he received a generally favorable impression of the Russian experiment, and expressed an interest in sending Vietnamese students to Moscow to study. Nothing came of it, however.

Most of the evidence regarding growing socialist influence on his thought during this period, however, is based on a work which he wrote in late 1924, *Truyen Pham Hong Thai* (The Story of Pham Hong Thai). Pham Hong Thai was born in 1893 in the province of Nghe An. He was the son of a former Can Vuong scholar-patriot who had later become an educational officer in a Franco-Vietnamese school in Hanoi. The young Pham himself was educated in the Franco-Vietnamese educational system and, after becoming radical in his ideas, quit school to work in industry as a manual laborer. In 1923, he and revolutionaries Le Hong Phong and Ho Tung Mau joined with other radicals and went to Canton, where they formed the radical nationalist group, the *Tam Tam Xa* (Association of Like Minds).[12] At some point, Pham and his colleagues had determined to assassinate Governor-general

---

tion of the anti-Christian views common in China at the time. For a criticism of Nguyen's view, see Chuong Thau, "Phan Boi Chau qua," pp. 15–16.

11. *Nien Bieu*, p. 189.

12. Tran Huy Lieu et al., *Tai Lieu Tham Khao Lich Su Cach Mang Can Dai Viet Nam* [Historical Research Materials Concerning the Modern Revolution in Vietnam], 12 vols. (Hanoi, 1958), IV, 123–124. Hereafter this material will be cited as *TLTK*. The Tam Tam Xa group originally belonged to Phan Boi Chau's Restoration Society, but broke away when they felt Phan's party was ineffective.

Martial Merlin during the latter's ceremonial tour of East Asia. Failing to achieve their goal in Japan because of tight security precautions, they were finally able to make a bombing attempt on June 19, 1924, while Merlin was attending a state banquet at the Hotel Victoria in the French concessional area of Canton. Although their attempt on the official's life was unsuccessful, the explosion mortally wounded five other French citizens attending the dinner, and Pham died by drowning while trying to escape.[13]

Phan Boi Chau had not participated in the planning of the assassination attempt, and indeed had no knowledge that it was about to take place. But he, like many other Vietnamese nationalists, saw the event as a symbolic blow against French imperialism in Asia. In a declaration written on June 23, four days after the attempt, he expressed the view that the Vietnamese patriot had committed the act, not as a personal insult to the governor-general, but as a retaliation against the inhumane and savage acts perpetrated by French imperialism in Indochina. In his declaration he referred to Pham as "we," apparently in the assumption that the assassin had been a member of his own nearly defunct organization. The French, he asserted, had been practicing great power imperialism on others since the days of Napoleon, and the Vietnamese were only the most recent victim of their behavior. Our rights have been ignored, we have been subjected to brutal treatment, he stated. Is it worse, he cried, to kill than to oppress? Phan followed his gratuitous explanation with a series of demands that the French abandon their dictatorship, grant political amnesty, permit political activity and initiate constitutional government. In the long run, he said, the Vietnamese must have self-determination and independence under a constitutional republic.[14]

13. Huong Pho, "Gop phan danh gia tu tuong cua Phan Boi Chau" [A contribution to an analysis of the thought of Phan Boi Chau], *NCLS*, no. 94 (Sept. 1967), p. 24.

14. The declaration is in *Van Tho Phan Boi Chau Chon Loc*, pp. 258–262. Statutes which appear to be of Phan's organization are located in AOM, Service de Liaison avec les Originaires de Territoires de la France d'Outre-Mer, formerly known as Service de Contrôle et d'Assistance en France des Indigènes des Colonies Françaises, Series III, Carton 3, Case 2, Dossier 1. The tone of the statutes and program generally resembles that of Sun Yat-sen's writings in China. The French in this report mistakenly believed that the program and statutes related to the Paris-based Parti An-

Later in the year, after having written a funeral oration for the young martyr, he wrote *Truyen Pham Hong Thai,* which purported to be a history of the life and motivation of the young nationalist, and which was published in Canton in 1925.[15] In the author's treatment, the history of Pham Hong Thai becomes a vehicle for the expression of his own ideas, his own regrets, and his own changes of attitude. As Phan portrays him, the young Pham had once been convinced that only a peaceful revolution would suffice, a "cultural revolution" that would achieve the gradual liberation of the Vietnamese people. Ultimately, however, he came in contact with Ho Chi Minh, a Vietnamese communist who had recently returned to Asia from Moscow. In a long conversation with Pham Hong Thai, the communist revolutionary (according to the author) not only convinced him of the need for violence but also of the necessity for a social revolution which would "burn down the palace of imperialism."[16] According to Ho the peasant and worker masses were strongly oppressed, but they were too apathetic to revolt by themselves. What was required was that Vietnamese intellectuals arouse the Vietnamese masses to rise against their exploiters.

Sparked by the comments of Ho Chi Minh, Pham Hong Thai, according to the author, decided to commit a single brilliant act that would frighten the enemy and electrify the Vietnamese masses. Thus came the inspiration for his assassination attempt on the life of Martial Merlin.

Textual analysis indicates that there are a number of inaccuracies in Phan's account, suggesting that he was probably taking liberties with historical truth in order to express his own views.[17]

---

namite de l'Indépendance, to be discussed in part II of this work. This archival source, called SLOTFOM for short, contains reports and documents of the French Sûreté Générale in Indochina between the two world wars. While the reliability of the information contained in these files cannot be accepted without question, the reports and documents in SLOTFOM were for internal use and, for the most part, appear to be accurate. I am greatly indebted to Milton Osborne for pointing out the existence of this to me. Hereafter this source will be cited in this study as SLOTFOM.

15. Phan Boi Chau, *Truyen Pham Hong Thai* [The Story of Pham Hong Thai] (Hanoi, 1967).

16. *Ibid.,* p. 126.

17. It is unlikely that Pham Hong Thai ever met Ho Chi Minh. Phan Boi Chau did, of course, and it is possible that he was simply repeating Ho Chi

Still, if *Truyen Pham Hong Thai* does not appear to be a reliable account of the life of the young assassin, it tends to confirm the supposition that Phan Boi Chau still believed in the need for violence against the French, and that his brief conversations with the revolutionary Ho Chi Minh in China had considerable effect on his own thought.

It is conceivable, then, that the influence of Ho Chi Minh on Phan Boi Chau and his revolutionary organization would have been more extensive had the circumstances been different. After Ho returned to Canton from Moscow in late 1924, he suggested modifications in Phan's Restoration Society (probably in imitation of the recent reorganization of Sun's Kuomintang along Leninist lines). Phan apparently gave at least tentative consent, for he went to Hangchow to talk the matter over with colleagues, and intimated that a new party, the Viet Nam Quoc Dan Dang (Vietnamese Nationalist Party), would replace the old party. Apparently this proposed reorganization never took place.[18]

In June 1925, Phan left Hangchow to return to Canton with his private secretary Nguyen Thuong Huyen. They traveled by rail to Shanghai where they would transfer to another train going to Canton. Phan was arrested by French authorities at the train station in Shanghai, however, and was returned to Hanoi to stand trial for treason. On November 23, he was brought before the Criminal Commission where the prosecutor demanded the death sentence. Despite massive demonstrations by the Vietnamese protesting the government's treatment of the old patriot, he was given a sentence of life imprisonment at hard labor. A few weeks later, on December 24, he was pardoned by the new governor-general, Alexander Varenne, and his sentence was commuted to house imprisonment in Hué.

The circumstances surrounding the arrest of Phan Boi Chau have become one of the more controversial aspects of his long and active life. Phan concluded in his autobiography that he had been betrayed by his secretary and disciple, Nguyen Thuong Huyen,

---

Minh's comments to himself. Whatever the truth of the matter, the author's portrayal of Pham Hong Thai seems to mirror changes that had taken place in his own ideas. The most extensive account of Pham's life is To Nguyet Dinh, *Pham Hong Thai* (Saigon, 1957).

18. Chuong Thau, "Anh huong," p. 22.

who had claimed to be the grandson of Phan's long-time colleague Nguyen Thuong Hien.[19] This charge has been supported by communist historians in Hanoi. But Nguyen vehemently denied the charge and in an article in the journal *Cai Tao* claimed that the culprit was another of Phan's colleagues, Lam Duc Thu, who later became a member of Ho Chi Minh's Revolutionary Youth League.[20] This version has gained wide currency in South Vietnam and in the West, where several students of the period have concluded that it was Ho Chi Minh who was responsible for the betrayal of Phan Boi Chau to the French, for the dual purpose of creating a martyr for the revolutionary cause and of receiving the reward money.[21] Lam's guilt is underlined by Cuong De's autobiography, in which the author states that Lam Duc Thu bragged about his act in later years. Communist historians in the Democratic Republic of Vietnam vigorously deny these assertions and point out that Ho Chi Minh had considerable respect for Phan Boi Chau and had no reason to turn him over to his enemies.[22]

   Given the lack of irrefutable evidence indicating the real source for Phan's betrayal, a categorical conclusion does not seem justified. On the one hand, Lam's later reputation for high living in Hong Kong adds some substance to the charges against him. On the other hand, the arguments in favor of Ho Chi Minh's involvement seem to be far-fetched. There is no indication that Lam took Ho into his confidence. Lam appears to have been an independent operator who, whatever his ties with the Revolutionary Youth League, had his own activities on the side. Ho would have had every reason to attempt to utilize Phan Boi Chau as a patriotic symbol around which to build a Leninist united front against imperialism. Phan could not possibly have been a danger to him—indeed, the old revolutionary was apparently just preparing to reorganize his own party along lines desired by Ho himself. As the potential figurehead leader of a broad Leninist national movement

   19. *Nien Bieu,* pp. 202–203.
   20. Chuong Thau, "Phan Boi Chau qua," p. 17.
   21. For example, see Joseph Buttinger, *Viet-Nam: A Dragon Embattled* (New York, 1967), I, 80.
   22. Cuong De, *Cuoc Doi Cach Mang Cuong De* [The Revolutionary Career of Cuong De] (Saigon, 1957), p. 120, has his version. Chuong Thau, "Phan Boi Chau qua," has a communist point of view.

under communist domination, he was an ideal figure from the communist point of view. Ageing and somewhat infirm in his ideas, attracted to socialism without being firmly committed to a Marxist world view, he would in all probability have posed little obstacle to communist control of the movement. But as a patriot of long standing, charismatic and widely revered throughout Vietnam, he would attract wide support from forces unwilling to commit themselves to a movement openly dedicated to a social revolutionary goal. If Ho indeed plotted for his capture in return for a few handfuls of silver, it was one of the few truly shortsighted decisions of his long career.

The Return of Phan Chu Trinh

Not long after Phan Boi Chau's arrest in Shanghai, the other grand old man of Vietnamese nationalism was about to make his own final appearance in Saigon. Phan Chu Trinh had lapsed into a silence after his prewar criticisms of French policies in Indochina that was broken only in 1922 when he wrote an open letter to Emperor Khai Dinh.

In 1925, ageing and ill, Phan Chu Trinh returned to the political arena. As always, he was equally critical of both French and Vietnamese. In a speech in Paris in February 1925 he contended that France could not achieve her mission in Vietnam unless she relied upon Vietnamese support. Yet in a letter written to a student friend at approximately the same time he criticized the Vietnamese anticolonialist movement in exile for its policy of empty *revanchisme*. Of what use to the Vietnamese people, he asked, are a few brave men throwing their lives away like knight-errants?[23]

In May of 1925, he convened a conference of eight hundred Vietnamese and progressive Frenchman in Paris to draw up a list of desiderata to present to the president of the republic and other high dignitaries. Founding their demands on Phan's well-known belief that violence was not the road to progress, and that only frank and sincere collaboration between France and Vietnam would effectively achieve the realization of the common goal, the

---

23. For these comments, see Tran Van Giau, *Giai Cap Cong Nhan Viet Nam* [The Working Class of Vietnam] (Hanoi, 1961), p. 276. Hereafter *Giai Cap.*

conference participants echoed Phan's original public letter to Governor-general Beau in calling for social and political reforms and the establishment of a constitutional government.[24]

In June, Phan Chu Trinh was permitted to return to Vietnam for the first time in nearly fifteen years. On his arrival in Saigon he was given a patriot's welcome. He quickly demonstrated that his view of his own role had not changed since his 1906 letter to Governor-general Beau. Eschewing active political work, he indicated that he still preferred to play the part of the philosopher-patriot, viewing Vietnam's struggle for justice from above the tumult and the clamor. In a pair of major speeches that he gave in Saigon in late 1925 he addressed himself to two crucial questions: the synthesis of East and West in Vietnam, and the form that a future government for the Vietnamese people might take.[25] In "Quan tri chu nghia va dan tri chu nghia" (Monarchy and Democracy), he criticized not only the Vietnamese monarchy but the institutions of monarchy itself, and praised Western democracy as more appropriate for a modern nation. His second, and more sophisticated address, "Dao duc va luan ly Dong Tay" (Morality and Ethics of East and West), made a serious attempt to approach the problem of the assimilation of Western values into Vietnamese civilization.

Phan was spurred to write about cultural exchange by a desire to refute statements by contemporaries who contended that Vietnamese culture should be preserved in order that the nation could survive in the twentieth century. He conceded that all nationalities should have their own distinct history and culture, but this did not justify a retention of all traditional values and institutions. On the contrary, the problem was not that Vietnam had lost its old morality but that it had not yet attained a new one. The traditionalists, of course, retorted that Vietnam should return to the old Confucian virtues. In Phan's view, however, such virtues had long since disappeared from society. The Confucian scholar had become an anachronism, Confucian ethics just a form of slave mentality. This was not to say that Confucius was totally irrelevant to the

24. The text of the document is in Georges Garros, *Forceries humaines* (Paris, 1926), pp. 179–182.
25. The texts are in *NCLS*, no. 67 (Oct. 1964); and *NCLS*, no. 66 (Sept. 1964).

needs of contemporary Vietnam. Phan asserted that the real essence of Vietnamese morality was not the autocracy and humiliating enslavement of state Confucianism, but the higher morality of Confucian-Mencian humanism—the teaching that ruler and people are of equal importance, and that the ordering of society must start with self-cultivation. It followed that for Vietnam to follow the West would not mean that it was being untrue to itself. Western morality, he contended, is not only compatible with Confucian morality, it is superior because Europe already had struggled through its own period of autocracy to a higher level of civilization. To bring in Western culture was thus equivalent to restoring and enriching the original meaning of Confucianism in Vietnam. Even China, he asserted, is moving toward the West and toward republicanism.

Reading Phan Chu Trinh's two essays is like reading a composite of the writings of the Chinese reformists during the first decade of the twentieth century. The author is brightly optimistic about the nature of Western civilization and its applicability to an Asian culture, and naively certain that democracy and national wealth and power go hand in hand. On the surface, Phan's ideas are reminiscent of K'ang Yu-wei's in that Phan is eager to demonstrate the continued utility of Confucian values in a modern society. But this resemblance is artificial, for Phan is clearly less concerned about the survival of traditional values than is K'ang. The comparison of Confucian-Mencian philosophical ideas with Western ones in Phan's essay is more for the purpose of persuading traditional thinkers to accept the justification for reform than for the purpose of preserving these values per se. Having become a convert to Westernization, Phan seldom showed concern for the Vietnamese past.

Phan had returned to Vietnam a sick man. In March of 1926, he died.[26] His death was an occasion for national mourning, thousands turning out for his funeral in Saigon. Resistance figures like Phan Boi Chau and Huynh Thuc Khang wrote elegies. The Francophile Bui Quang Chieu spoke at his funeral, pledging willing-

26. His death is often cited as occurring on the twenty-fourth, but he may have died a day or two earlier. See William H. Frederick, "Alexander Varenne and Politics in Indochina," in Walter Vella, ed., *Aspects of Vietnamese History* (Honolulu, 1973), p. 158.

ness to give his own life for Phan's ideal of Franco-Vietnamese harmony. The emotion surrounding the funeral demonstrated Phan's enduring popularity in Vietnam, and this historical image has continued to this day. He is customarily ranked immediately after Phan Boi Chau in the pantheon of modern Vietnamese heroes, and his lifelong resistance to oppression is praised by all factions in Vietnam.[27]

How can he be placed in the perspective of his age? In his refusal to countenance the use of force, he was always clearly distinct from the scholar-patriots who surrounded Phan Boi Chau, and he was closer to what might be called the "national-reformist" group that typified the majority at the Hanoi Free School.[28] His rejection of the use of force was by no means an indication of lack of courage, or of lack of determination in struggling against oppression. But although he was willing to criticize the French on many occasions, he always refused to consider them as the main enemy of the Vietnamese people, or to consider violence as the instrument of national liberation. While willing to take the French to task for their failure to end the oppression of the court, and for their condescension to the Vietnamese, he retained to the end the hope that they would live up to their promise to reform Vietnamese society and never directly demanded that they leave. A letter he wrote not long before his death to a French acquaintance, Jules Roux, expresses his views: "I am wretched, have left my village, my wife, and my children for nine years. I have endured a hundred humiliations, a hundred miseries. It is my wish that the peoples of France and Vietnam will sincerely cooperate. And if my death can serve to benefit your country and mine, I can die happy."[29]

27. He is sometimes criticized by Vietnamese Communist historians. The current view of his career in Hanoi is that he was a sincere but misguided patriot, who failed to distinguish the main enemy of the Vietnamese people —the real enemy was not the old feudal regime, which was a mere scarecrow, but the French imperial regime which upheld it. If Phan Boi Chau was misguided in some respects, he at least understood the nature of his real enemy. For a discussion of Hanoi's attitude, see my article "Hanoi Scrutinizes the Past: The Marxist Evaluation of Phan Boi Chau and Phan Chu Trinh," in *Southeast Asia*, 1, no. 3 (summer 1971), 242–254.

28. This term is not used in its Marxist sense, which refers to such quasi-collaborationist groups as Bui Quang Chieu's Constitutionalist Party. As used here, national reformism refers to clearly nationalist groups and figures whose basic tactic is reformism rather than insurrection.

29. The Nguyen, *Phan Chu Trinh* (Saigon, 1956), p. 50.

As for his ideas, they are certainly more pro-Western and more anti-feudal than those of most of his contemporaries. Yet there is a marked lack of sophistication in his theories, and considerable naiveté about the nature of the West.[30] The complexities of synthesizing East and West seemed to escape him, and the events in Europe after the war had little effect on his ideas. One radical said, after attempting to talk to Phan just before his death about Bolshevism and class struggle, that Phan Chu Trinh was still living in the world of the eighteenth-century *philosophes*.[31] For him, the West was still the world of Natural Man, Reason, and the Enlightenment, not of violence, irrationality, and class struggle. For this reason, the serviceability of his thought to his contemporaries was somewhat limited, and it was his patriotic spirit more than his ideas that was mourned in 1926.

Old Man in Hué

For fifteen years after his arrest, Phan Boi Chau lived on in Hué. He was by no means immediately forgotten, and remained for many the living symbol of Vietnam's desire for self-determination. Representatives of many parties, overt and covert, came to him for advice and support, including Nguyen Thai Hoc's Viet Nam Quoc Dan Dang (VNQDD) and Ho Chi Minh's own Revolutionary Youth League.[32] Visitors found in the old patriot a variety of emotions and ideas. Most observers felt that he retained the indomitable spirit of independence and courage that had motivated his life for so many years. Of the parties which emerged in Vietnam in the 1920s, he apparently felt the strongest spiritual affinity for the ardently nationalist VNQDD. At the same time many noticed a perceptible softening of his attitude toward politics, at least in his public statements. French visitors to his home—such well-known critics of French colonial policy as Louis Roubaud and

30. Marr contends that "he succeeded in raising many of the significant questions" about long-term Westernization and modernization in Vietnam. See p. 275. This is true, but the superficiality of his understanding of the West is often striking.

31. Tran Huy Lieu, "Nho lai ong gia Ben Ngu" [In memory of Phan Boi Chau], *NCLS*, no. 47 (Feb. 1963), 41–44.

32. Chuong Thau, "Nha yeu nuoc va nha van Phan Boi Chau" [Phan Boi Chau: Patriot and Literary Figure], *NCLS*, no. 136 (April 1971), p. 42. These parties will be discussed later in this work.

Andrée Viollis—found him critical of France but also of his own people as well. Roubaud, in his well-known book, *Vietnam: La Tragédie indochinoise,* quotes Phan Boi Chau as saying:

The grave malaise which you have noticed is explained by the fact that the Annamite people are an infant; they do not know how to walk but they have reached and even surpassed the age where a baby takes its first steps. Their mother would have taken them by the hand and helped them to run a few steps and educated their little legs. But the Annamite people have no mother; they are orphans. Its tutor, France, feels that a child is easier to control when he is unable to run. France does not want its pupil to learn to walk. So, the baby tires, cries, kicks, and throws tantrums.[33]

Phan found the cause of this immaturity in the nature of the French educational system, which had destroyed traditional values and thus created a generation of uprooted people on their own soil. Moreover, the French restricted the elementary rights of citizens in Vietnam and denied the people any meaningful role in the political life of their own country. It was no wonder, he said, that the Vietnamese were willing to turn to anyone who offered them a helping hand. Referring to the rising support for communism in Vietnam, he said that the Vietnamese people, like he himself, did not understand what it was, but added that it was not surprising that such ideas appealed to the starved soul of Vietnam, which received no intellectual stimulation from the suffocating French regime.

In a similar conversation with the French reporter Andrée Viollis in 1931, Phan repeated these criticisms of French policy, which, in his view, destroyed Confucianism and left nothing in its place. In a familiar complaint, he said that the French treated the Vietnamese with contempt and did not practice in Asia what they preached in Paris.[34] On the other hand, he was equally critical of the Vietnamese. Since he had returned to Vietnam, he confided, he had come to realize that the Vietnamese, a "soft and pacific people," were not ready for independence; if the French had really offered collaboration, he added, the Vietnamese would have readily

33. Louis Roubaud, *Vietnam: La Tragédie indochinoise* (Paris, 1931), pp. 232–241. The term "Annamite" was commonly used by the French to refer to all Vietnamese during the period of French colonial control.

34. Andrée Viollis, *Indochine S.O.S.* (Paris, 1935), p. 96.

forgotten even the word independence. In conclusion, Phan said to his listener: "Tell the French people that the old revolutionary Phan Boi Chau sincerely desires loyal collaboration with France. But hurry—otherwise it will be too late."

Such impressions of mellowing are strengthened by the comments of Vietnamese nationalists who visited him, and by his writings at the time. He still retained a certain curiosity about socialism, and even attempted to write a book about it. But, like many Chinese of the time, he found its roots in Chinese culture at the time of Confucius two millennia before. One historian later attached to the communist movement, Tran Huy Lieu, observed that Phan's socialism was of the utopian variety, filled with a simple love for humanity. He advised him to write his autobiography instead. As Tran observed, Phan was just a nationalist "no more and no less," who, to the astonishment of his listener, "didn't even see the wickedness of Bui Quang Chieu."[35]

If to some observers, French and Vietnamese, Phan Boi Chau appeared to have mellowed in exile, the French colonial administration had reason to believe that his behavior was simply a ruse. Through informants, the resident superior of Annam kept track of his activities, which were sufficiently disquieting to cause anxiety. By 1930, when the situation in the area had deteriorated to the point of open revolt, some officials were convinced that the old patriot was actively involved in anti-French activities and wanted to get rid of him. Informants reported that he sympathized with the communists and "only blamed the communist movement for its actual methods adopted."[36] In Phan's view, the harsh policies followed in the villages of Annam only alienated potential supporters of the nationalist movement and drove them into the arms of the French. Forwarding this information to the governor-general's office in Hanoi, the local security chief commented that Phan Boi Chau apparently felt that the discontent in the central coastal provinces was fomented by members of his own exile or-

35. Tran Huy Lieu, "Nho lai ong gia Ben Ngu" [In memory of Phan Boi Chau], p. 34. Bui Quang Chieu will be discussed in a later chapter.

36. AOM Carton 327, Dossier 2643, confidential note number 2546 from the Chef de Service de Police et Securité at Hué to the Directeur de la Sûreté Nationale. When Phan was asked if the Russians would aid the Vietnamese he said that if Vietnam achieved its own independence the Russians would then help them with weapons and financial aid.

ganization, and that they had only adopted communist methods for tactical reasons. Phan himself allegedly preferred a policy of terror and persuasion against Vietnamese collaborators to compel them to abandon their support of the French regime. Pushed into a social and financial crisis, he felt, the French would be desperate. Then, the Vietnamese would be able to impose their own conditions.

Among the French, opinions were divided on how to handle the problem. Resident superior Le Fol of Annam felt that Phan's presence was dangerous and advised his deportation. Acting Governor-general René Robin was of the same mind and in December of 1930 wrote to Paris proposing that he permanently be removed from Vietnam. This proposal was received with caution by the Minister of Colonies, however, and when Governor-general Pasquier returned to his post in early 1931 he voiced his objections to Robin's proposal, asserting that this would only make Phan Boi Chau a martyr.[37] In the end, no action was taken and Phan remained unmolested in Hué.

At this point it is difficult to know what was going on in Phan's mind. Probably his calculated gestures to the French were meant to deceive them and permit him greater freedom to give support to the activities of the nationalists throughout Vietnam. Yet from his writings in Hué it does appear that in some respects his ideas were changing. During his final years, he was relatively active as a writer, and he turned out a number of books and pamphlets for the edification of his fellow-countrymen. Now, however, he combined a tenacious love of country with the dispassionate wisdom of a moral philosopher. Most of his writings were designed to educate the Vietnamese people in how to be better citizens, and showed a manifest Confucian influence. In *Cao Dang Quoc Dan* (A People of Quality), written in 1927, he set forth those qualities which the Vietnamese people would find it necessary to possess in order to build a strong and independent state—courage, mutual love, independence of character, sincerity, rationality, righteousness, frugality, and an end to superstition. The old master Confucius would

37. AOM Carton 327, Dossier 2643, report of resident superior Le Fol to the governor-general, April 29, 1930; letter of René Robin to Minister of Colonies, Dec. 31, 1930; letter of Pierre Pasquier to Le Fol, May 27, 1931.

have been pleased. In a perhaps ironic stab at his own failures he added that they would need an ideology, and a program to follow.[38]

In *Khong Hoc Dang* (The Light of Confucius), written two years later, he continued these moral musings in the form of a book on Confucian social ethics. The sayings of the Confucian classics were set forth to provide examples of the need to develop humanism (*nhan dao*) in Vietnam. In Phan's works, the path to truth and knowledge consisted of combining the best of the old with the best of the new. Knowledge, he said, is like building a house; old studies (and here he clearly meant the Confucian philosophical classics) are the foundation, and new studies (and here he meant Western science) are the superstructure. Both were needed, the one to modernize society, the other to provide a sense of identity for the people.[39]

A third major work on the moral question was Phan's *Nam Quoc Dan Tu Tri* (What Our Male Citizens Should Know), in which he discussed the concept of individual freedom and the role of man in society. He was again full of praise for the old virtues—mutual love, sincerity, service to community, self-control, and filial piety—but his main theme was the need for a strong nation, and for that nation to be built on responsible citizens. The foundation of the nation he found in the family, and his concern for the family system was strong throughout the book. Phan clearly was not using *Nam Quoc Dan Tu Tri* merely to voice a desire to return Vietnam to familism, but to build up the consciousness of nationhood. For the nation, in his view, is simply a large family, and it needs support and love as much as the family itself. This all tied in with the concept of freedom, for although modern independent states must be built on a free citizenry, beyond this freedom lay the transcendent obligation of individuals to subordinate their interests to the broader needs of the society, for only through unity and the cooperation of all elements in the community could the state protect its citizens.[40] Citizenship means not only privi-

38. Phan Boi Chau, *Cao Dang Quoc Dan* (Hué, 1957), p. 43.
39. Phan Boi Chau, *Khong Hoc Dang* (Hué, 1957), foreword.
40. Located in Luu Tran Thien, *Phan Boi Chau, Tieu Su va Van Tho* [Phan Boi Chau, a Short History and Selected Writings], (Ngay-Mai, 1940), pp. 113–127.

leges, but responsibility. Freedom, he said, is not license, which is "the freedom of thieves."

Unquestionably Phan Boi Chau's writings during his final years demonstrate an emotional step back toward a Confucian vision of society. He had not abandoned his dream of an independent parliamentary republic. (In his conversation with Louis Roubaud in 1930 he had stressed that if the Vietnamese had their choice they would build a democratic republic with legislative assemblies responsible to the people, and initiate social reforms and universal education.) But he had belatedly discovered some universal truths in the old traditions, and it was to those that he gave his time in his final years on earth. The New Vietnam of 1908 had become filled out with a moral ethic highly reminiscent of the precolonial period. Concern for the physical independence of Vietnam gave way to concern for its spiritual vitality. Culturalism was belatedly replacing nationalism.

On October 29, 1940, Phan Boi Chau died peacefully in his house in Hué. Two days later, his testament to the Vietnamese people was printed in Huynh Thuc Khang's newspaper *Tieng Dan* (Voice of the People). The old man apologized for his massive failure, and expressed his gratitude to the Vietnamese people who did not criticize him but sympathized with him in his grief.

Epitaph for a Simple Patriot

It need hardly be said that the arrest and trial of Phan Boi Chau in 1925 simply underlined the symbolic truth that the age of the scholar-patriots had come to a close. In fact, Phan's Restoration Society never recovered from his arrest in South China and the abortive uprisings in the years 1913 to 1916. Although Phan and a few of his supporters attempted to revitalize the movement after World War I, conditions had changed and a new generation was ready to turn to new leadership.

The failure of Phan Boi Chau to bring the labors of the scholar-patriots to a successful conclusion has not seriously tarnished his reputation as a hero of the Vietnamese resistance. In the nearly half a century that has elapsed since his arrest, he has been generally revered as the leading nationalist figure of his generation, the symbol of Vietnamese patriotism and resistance to French colonial control. He has come to stand for many of the qualities so necessary to the Vietnamese in their struggle against oppression and outside control. It is significant that even communist historians today give Phan high marks as the greatest Vietnamese patriot for the first quarter of the present century. While conceding that in many respects Phan's ideas and tactics were old-fashioned, they point to the essential validity of his basic assumption that the matter of highest priority for the Vietnamese people was to overthrow the colonial regime, and to cease being slaves in their own country. Whatever his limitations as an ideologist—and most communist students of his life concede that he did not move significantly toward socialism even at the end of his life—the view from Hanoi today is that Phan performed a vital role in arousing the national consciousness of the Vietnamese people, a consciousness that was itself of major assistance to the Vietminh movement in the postwar period.[41] Like Sun Yat-sen in China, Phan is viewed by contemporary commmunist historiography as moving his society a significant step toward the final victory of the socialist revolution.

Whatever his merits as an inspirational leader for the Vietnamese resistance movement, however, it is equally evident that there were serious flaws in Phan Boi Chau's understanding of the social forces at work in Vietnam, and in his ability to formulate an effective strategy to counter his adversary. These weaknesses were sufficient to hamper his life-long attempt to build up a force to overthrow the French. He had little comprehension of how to go about organizing and building a highly disciplined revolutionary movement. Although he was constantly preoccupied with the desire to build a strong and united party, and spent a great deal of time traveling throughout the country attempting to carry out his plans, he did not seem to understand the means of creating a truly professional organization. His party was more an extension of his own personality than a well-organized movement in its own right, and it often reflected the vicissitudes of his own character. Phan himself was aware of this weakness. In the introduction to his autobiography he wrote, regarding his view of affairs and people: "[I] only paid attention to the big things, and for small things I

41. For the views of a Marxist on Phan's socialism, see Chuong Thau, "Anh huong," pp. 12–26, and Huong Pho, "Gop phan," pp. 24–28.

judge only the outline; therefore many times I will fail at a big thing for a small reason; I am careless, not cautious."[42]

This lack of discipline not only affected his own actions but those of his party as well. Lacking the patience to build a well-disciplined organization, he was constantly let into incautious, and, as the communists might phase it, "adventuristic" actions that perhaps served to vent his frustrations but in the longer term only resulted in setting back the prospects for final victory. At one point in his autobiography he observes that there are times when it is better to throw it all on one chance—to gamble and die a glorious death—than to die in inactivity and slavery.[43] Devoid of the patience that the times required, he squandered the strength of his movement on ill-considered and worse-prepared attacks which only resulted in increasing French oppression and the death of some of his closest comrades. It would be totally unfair to place the entire blame for such results on him alone, for his impatience was undoubtedly shared by most if not all of his colleagues, and he may have felt that daring attacks on the government were necessary to keep up the spirits of his disciples. Lacking the sense of certainty that the materialist dialectic provides the Marxist, the scholar-patriots under Phan Boi Chau could not rely on historic inevitability. Only by keeping before the public eye could they hope to attract volunteers and contributions. In the long run, of course, the result was that the potential strength of the movement was often squandered for the superficial value of the image of success. Reality was sacrificed for appearance.

A related weakness in Phan's approach was his failure to utilize the potential force of the peasantry in the war of liberation. This may seem paradoxical, for it can also be said that in his realization of the importance of mass support he had progressed a significant step beyond his traditional predecessors. Phan was strongly conscious of the need for a truly national effort to unite all elements of society—from the mandarins to the lowly servants in the wealthy villas of the French colonialists. His propaganda efforts were directly at all sections of society, and to most of the major vocational and religious groups. In this respect, he was cer-

42. *Nien Bieu*, pp. 22–23.
43. *Nien Bieu*, p. 148.

tainly one of the first to see the struggle for independence as a truly *national* one, and as time went by he became increasingly conscious of the possible role of the peasantry as a basic resource for the liberation of the nation. This appears strongly in his historical work *Trung Quang Tam Su* when by implication be called on the peasantry to join in the struggle as they did in the "people's war" of the fifteenth century. Later he became even more aware of the specific uses of the masses as a consequence of his reading in Marxism.

But, as was so often the case with Phan Boi Chau, there was a failure in execution. For despite his constant calls for unity, for "ten thousand nameless heroes" to coalesce in the sacred cause, he seemed unaware how to enlist the support of the mass of the population, and his appeal for sacrifice and virtue was more effective with the scholar-gentry elite, steeped in Confucian concepts of loyalty, duty, and sincerity, than with the millions of peasants. Apparently unconscious of the need to use a different psychological approach and different slogans with the peasants, to focus on their predominant concern with high taxes, the corvée, and the monopolies, he failed to put forth a program which would be clearly beneficial to the farmer. Certainly he talked of the evils of French economic measures, and sympathized with the poverty and ignorance of the Vietnamese peasant masses; but, apparently in the belief that the scholar-gentry itself could rally the masses to the cause, he concentrated his efforts on recruiting the elites, and spent little effort in promoting support at the village level. In consequence, there was inevitably little lower-class participation in the movement, and Phan's gallants were more in the image of the knight-errants of old, slashing like Vietnamese Don Quixotes at colonial windmills, and spending more time glorying in their dashing image of sacrifice and revolutionary heroism than in the tough, day-to-day work of educating the populace and winning support at the village level.

But if the scholar-patriots were unable to find the key to unlock the secret door to modernity and independence, it was due to the spirit of the age as much as to their own weakness. Few Vietnamese were willing to follow their example in resisting the French; of those that did, fewer still understood the complexity of the task that faced them. Whatever their frailties, the scholar-patriots possessed a preeminent moral stature that placed them high in the respect of their contemporaries. This was not a negligible quality in the history of the Vietnamese nationalist movement.

More to the point, perhaps, the age of Phan Boi Chau marked the emergence of modern nationalism in Vietnam. If Phan Boi Chau only imperfectly understood the nature of the world he lived in, he had managed to grasp some important truths which served to move the Vietnamese resistance movement a significant step toward its final goal—a Vietnam strong and prosperous, its citizenry united and stubbornly determined to protect its identity as Vietnamese. If he must be seen in history as a transitional figure, too traditionalist, too inflexible, too unimaginative, to play the role of an effective leader in the modern world, at the same time he must be seen as clearly more than this. The nationalist movement in Vietnam was bound to undergo a period of trial and error, a period of growing national awareness but of insufficient understanding of the implications of modern forces and challenges, a period when the symbol of resistance would be raised and unfurled, but success not yet achieved. In this sense, Phan Boi Chau and his colleagues played their part well. They left behind them a spirit of indomitability, a consciousness of the greater duty of the Vietnamese people to unite behind the great idea of national independence, and this image is sufficiently vital even today for the communists of North Vietnam to call upon the old scholar-patriot as a model for young Vietnamese to emulate. If Ho Chi Minh is the paragon of all revolutionary virtues, Phan Boi Chau was his flawed but still revered predecessor. As Ho Chi Minh himself said: "[Phan] sacrificed his family and his fortune to flee from the invaders of his country, to a life far from his native soil, tracked down and lured into countless traps, condemned to death *in absentia,* dragged into prison and pillorized, with the specter of the guillotine day and night over his head . . . [Phan Boi Chau] the hero, the apostle, the martyr of independence, venerated by 20 million slaves."[44]

44. Chuong Thau, "Nha yeu nuoc," p. 35.

PART II

URBAN NATIONALISTS

Chapter 6

Francophiles

Some years before the age of the scholar-patriots came to a final symbolic end with the arrest and trial of Phan Boi Chau, signs of a new era in Vietnamese nationalism had already begun to appear. For during World War I, the industrial and commercial development of Indochina began to accelerate rapidly. The war had created new opportunities for local commerce as French imports and investments in Southeast Asia dropped considerably owing to French preoccupation with the war effort. As a result, the number of Vietnamese-owned commercial establishments began to increase, and Vietnamese became active in such areas as rice milling, printing, textiles and weaving, and the processing of *nuoc mam* (fermented fish sauce). This commercial growth in the cities coincided with the appearance of a native landed aristocracy, mainly in the Trans-Bassac area of the Mekong delta, when the French government sold land to speculators at cheap prices.[1]

Side by side with the emergence of this new and generally prosperous urban leisured class arose other products of the increasing urbanization of colonial society—workers, students, petty merchants, and clerks. Living on the fringe of the modern sector of the economy, this new petit bourgeoisie was, like its more prosperous counterpart, beginning to reflect the influence of Western culture.

By the end of the war, these new urban classes began to flex their political muscles and to exert a greater degree of influence in Vietnamese society. Small informal political parties and factions

1. Pierre Brocheux, "Les Grands Dien Chu de la Cochin Chine Occidentale pendant la periode coloniale" in Jean Chesneaux, ed., *Tradition et révolution au Vietnam* (Paris, 1971), p. 150.

began to form, particularly in the urban areas of Cochin China, where a greater degree of open political activity was permitted. By the middle of the next decade, the rise of these new classes, combined with the declining fortunes of the scholar-patriots, resulted in the gradual appearance of a new form of nationalism in colonial Vietnam. For with new social classes came new attitudes and new political goals, which in turn led to a new type of nationalism—more sophisticated and more conscious of nationality as a concept. With these developments, the second stage in the growth of modern nationalism appears.

In many colonial societies in Asia, the emergence of urban nationalism presaged the formation of united resistance movements, led by a Westernized elite but gradually attaining considerable support among the mass of the population.[2] In Vietnam, however, the rise of urban nationalism did not result in unity among resistance groups, for the goals and tactics of the urban nationalists were highly diverse, running the gamut from quasi-collaborationism to violent anticolonialism. It might be broadly stated that the increasing urbanization of Vietnamese colonial society spawned two divergent forms of response to French rule: (1) a moderate reformism rooted primarily among the wealthy and often French-educated urban bourgeoisie, and (2) a potentially more radical urban nationalism based on an amalgam of working class elements and the petit bourgeois intelligentsia.

The wealthy urban bourgeoisie often received benefits from the French presence and were generally Francophile in political orientation. On the other hand they had begun to feel more frustrated over their lack of influence and status in colonial society. For a time they became a potentially influential force in the nationalist movement. Their political aims were decidedly limited in scope, however. They were ambivalent on the question of independence and were unalterably opposed to violent resistance in any form. The political orientation of various factions within the bourgeoisie ranged from reformist nationalism to pure collaborationism; and once the French government showed a willingness to accede to

2. Some examples are the Sarekat Islam in the Dutch East Indies, the Congress Party in British India, and the Anti-Fascist People's Freedom League (A.F.P.F.L.) in Burma.

their minimum demands for reform, they faded from the political scene almost entirely.[3]

The amalgam of working class elements and petit bourgeois intelligentsia was strongly anti-French and therefore often distrustful of the quasi-collaborationist Francophiles. It was more inclined to condone the use of violence in the struggle for national liberation. Although nationalists in this category shared an anti-French orientation, they could not unite on tactics and ideology. Some vacillated between reformism and revolution; others joined radical parties dedicated to the violent overthrow of colonial authority; ultimately a significant proportion of this segment of urban nationalism drifted into the communist movement. Petit bourgeois nationalism in Vietnam thus displayed many faces, from national reformism, to non-Marxist radicalism, and to Marxism-Leninism.

One of the salient characteristics of urban nationalism was its exposure to Western culture. This posed a problem for nationalists, for the brilliance of Western civilization had an undeniable allure to many educated Vietnamese, and not a few nationalists conceded that the French presence could be used as an instrument for achieving reforms in Vietnamese society. A relatively progressive French policy would be likely to defuse some of the sources of anger in Vietnamese nationalism and might even bring a few over to a policy of cooperation with the French administration. Whether the government would have the vision to adopt such a policy, of course, was another question.

It is not necessary here to discuss in detail the intricate debates that took place over the nature of France's civilizing mission. Suf-

3. The urban upper middle class is discussed in a recent article entitled "The Faithful Few: The Politics of Collaboration in Cochinchina in the 1920s" by Milton Osborne, in Walter F. Vella, ed., *Aspects of Vietnamese History* (Honolulu, 1973). Some feel that this group does not qualify for the nationalist label. There is some validity in this contention. On balance, however, I feel it is advisable to include them in this study. For a time they were a marginal force in the nationalist movement, and the nature of Vietnamese nationalism is incomprehensible without discussing their role in modern Vietnam. Also, as Milton Osborne points out, many of them did have a sincere conviction that collaboration was the best strategy for Vietnam. There is perhaps no adequate label for this group. *Collaborateur* can be misleading, for some did oppose the French on certain issues. Yet another label, Francophile, tends to have cultural more than political connotations. For convenience, I will use the latter term in this study.

fice it to say that colonial policy vacillated between assimilation and association, between the attempt to transform Vietnamese society and a desire to leave it alone. These precise distinctions lost clarity, of course, when put into practice. Nevertheless, there were concrete differences between French policies in different areas of Indochina, and these differences had discernible effects on the growth of the nationalist movement.

Before the turn of the century some French officials appeared to be attuned to Vietnamese sensitivities, as when Governor Paul Bert promised that Vietnamese institutions and traditions would be scrupulously respected by the new rulers.[4] Such comments were hardly applicable in Cochin China, however, where a policy of assimilation was already under way. French and quoc-ngu were being officially promoted to facilitate the introduction of Western ideas and governmental policies, Roman Catholicism was being proselytized, and the administrative structure was almost entirely in French hands. With the old political system discarded and a new one, dominated by officials sent from France, put in its place, only one reasonably effective conduit for Vietnamese feeling remained —the Colonial Council, established in 1880, which had some Vietnamese membership.[5]

Even in the North, Bert's promises were not kept by his successors. Under the Protectorate established by treaty in 1884, imperial authority in Tonkin was to be represented by an imperial viceroy (the *kinh luoc*) who was theoretically to have extensive powers to maintain court authority in the area. By 1897, however, a centralizing trend had developed in the office of the governor-general, the office of the viceroy was abolished, and direct administration of Tonkin was imposed, with the French resident superior in Hanoi taking over the duties of the *kinh luoc*. This action was symptomatic of the orientation of French policy in the North at the end of the century, as increasing centralization took place. Only in the Center did the emperor retain a modicum of his past authority, and even there he had become in effect a puppet of the French, on the throne at the whim of the local resi-

4. For his opening speech, see Guy Lebel, *Deux aspects de l'évolution du Protectorat Français en Annam et Tonkin* (Paris, 1932), pp. 23–24.

5. Milton Osborne, *The French Presence in Cochinchina and Cambodia* (Ithaca, 1969), p. 50.

dent superior, with French advisers at all upper levels of the bureaucracy. In Annam, as in Tonkin, local customs were at least temporarily untouched at the village level, but a progressive destruction of village authority, village education, and the communal system was taking place nonetheless.

In reality, then, the policies put into effect by the French colonial officials by the end of the nineteenth century were highly varied—and certainly not systematic—but they seemed to be predicated more on assimilationist than on associationist assumptions. Whatever the philosophical assumptions of French colonial officials in Paris, governmental policy in Vietnam was simply authoritarian, and took little account of opportunities to achieve cooperation with willing Vietnamese. This was particularly true during and after the centralizing regime of Governor-general Paul Doumer (1897–1902), whose byword was efficiency and who assumed that the French government must take an active interest in social change. Later governors-general, even when evoking the spirit of association in their dealings with native officials, found themselves following assimilationist assumptions. By 1906, Governor-general Paul Beau, who described association as "cette parole généreuse," was convinced that the duty of France was to take charge not only of the material development of Vietnam, but also of the reform of its customs and institutions. In his hands, the French administration would talk about association while presiding over a comprehensive reform of many aspects of Vietnamese society: "Indochina cannot rest isolated from this great movement which carries all the people of Asia toward progress, and it would be unwise to seek to prevent its evolution under the pretext of security or of respect for tradition."[6] Beau's immediate successors, Klobukowski and Sarraut, while speaking of collaboration, would implement measures of social and political change—if not for the ultimate benefit of all Vietnamese, then certainly to facilitate the exploitation of natural resources in Indochina.

The major instrument of modernization in Vietnam, of course, was the educational system. The government gave at least sporadic attention to developing a modern system which would inculcate Western ideas into the population at large. The extent of this edu-

6. Lebel, p. 49.

cational effort should not be exaggerated, for most attention was concentrated in spreading French education among the elites in the big cities and provincial capitals. In Cochin China this effort was particularly extensive, and for those fortunate youngsters exposed to this modern system little remained of the traditional except an occasional course on morality in the public schools.[7] In the Center and the North, however, the traditional system was permitted to continue at the village level, and until the World War I students continued to study for the traditional civil service examinations. Franco-Vietnamese education was limited to a few secondary schools in the big cities like Hanoi and Hué.[8]

One important aspect of the problem was reform of the written language. The traditional form of written communication—based on Chinese characters—was considered a major obstacle to modernization. To hasten its demise the government began moving simultaneously in two other directions—toward increasing the number of French-language courses to accommodate those Vietnamese who needed to know French, and toward the establishment of schools at the village level to expand the use of quoc-ngu among the mass of the population. Because each program offered advantages as well as disadvantages, the government took a schizophrenic approach to the problem and appeared to push both at the same time. In a general way, however, the government promoted French primarily in the urban schools and at the upper levels of the educational system, and quoc-ngu in the villages and at the primary level.

By 1906 the government had begun to systematize its efforts. It created a public educational system based on three levels, the highest level being the new University of Hanoi which was composed of colleges of literature, law, and natural science.[9] Primary education was based on the vernacular, and textbooks in quoc-ngu were provided, while Chinese and French were added at the higher

7. Henri Gourdon, "l'Education des indigènes dans l'Indochine Française", in *Asie Française*, March 1931, p. 163. This journal will be cited hereafter as *AF*.
8. There were a few reforms in the civil service system. See Gourdon, p. 163.
9. Details can be found in Tran Huy Lieu, *Lich Su Thu Do Ha Noi* [A History of the City of Hanoi] (Hanoi, 1960).

levels. The number of courses in modern subjects such as mathematics, geography, and science was increased. At the same time, the civil service examinations added questions on modern subjects.[10] It should be kept in mind, however, that this system was limited to a relatively small proportion of the population, for even after World War I only about 10 per cent of the total student-age population of Vietnam were attending the Franco-Vietnamese schools.

Governor-general Beau made the first serious attempts to create a form of representative government in line with his publicly stated desire to gain the cooperation of the Vietnamese in France's mission in Southeast Asia. Provincial councils and advisory chambers at the regional level, with fiscal and administrative powers, were established in Annam and Tonkin.

By the early years of the twentieth century, then, many of the old traditions of Vietnam had begun to break down, either as a result of official policy or sheer desuetude. At the apex of the political pyramid, the hallowed authority of the emperor was dangerously and perhaps fatally compromised by the French habit of making decisions without bothering to consult the court officials.[11] Within the social system, the Confucian moral and intellectual foundation was being undermined, sometimes deliberately, by French policy which discouraged classical education and the Chinese written language which propagated it. As French and quoc-ngu began to replace Chinese characters, Confucianism became the inevitable casualty. A new generation of Vietnamese elites, channeled through the Franco-Vietnamese educational system, was being formed. At the village level, many peasant families continued to live as they had for ages—following traditional ceremonies of marriage, death, and the harvest cycle—but other aspects of village life were beginning to break down. The communal system was eroded by the confiscation of the villages' common land by speculators. The traditional village leadership was undermined by French administrative policy. In a number of respects, the

10. Gourdon, p. 163.
11. The most prominent example is the discarding of Emperor Thanh Thai by the French resident superior Levecque. The latter chose Duy Tan as the emperor's successor despite the wishes of the Imperial Council for another candidate.

traditional way of life was beginning to erode and a new elite increasingly influenced by French culture was beginning to emerge.

The New Journalists

In 1911, the French government, spurred by criticisms in parliament of its repressive policies, appointed Radical Party deputy Albert Sarraut as the new governor-general of Indochina. Sarraut, a strong personality and an eloquent orator, was an outspoken advocate of association, and on his arrival in Indochina in 1911 he painted in glowing terms a future of fruitful Franco-Vietnamese friendship and cooperation. He was capable of dealing firmly with rebels, but he was also sympathetic to the need for a more open French attitude toward cooperation with the indigenous population under its control. Joseph Buttinger, in his massive history of modern Vietnam, points out that Sarraut, in spite of his grandiloquent promises, accomplished little in concrete terms.[12] On the record, it is true that his administrations (1911–1914 and 1917–1918) were not marked by significantly more legislation than any other during the period. Nevertheless, Sarraut was undoubtedly highly effective, at least on the short term. In government, style is often as important as substance, and Sarraut, by seeming to understand the aspirations of young Vietnam and by promising a brighter future (whether or not he himself took his statements seriously), made it respectable for Vietnamese elites to promote cultural reform rather than wage political revolution. Had he and later governors-general been willing to take advantage of this tolerance on the part of the indigenous elite, the first steps toward Franco-Vietnamese collaboration might have been possible. For by his wooing of the moderates, Sarraut had begun to create the necessary psychological conditions for a regime marked by cooperation. The real problems lay in the future, in the mid-1920s, when moderates began to see the gap between Sarraut's statements and the realities of colonial policy.

In any event, the policy of conciliation initiated by French officials such as Sarraut coincided with the rise of moderate Francophile elements among the urban wealthy bourgeoisie, particu-

12. Joseph Buttinger, *Viet-Nam: A Dragon Embattled* (New York, 1967), I, 87–91.

larly in the big cities of Saigon and Hanoi. This new generation of moderate reformists preferred to avoid direct political action, choosing instead to express its interest in the comparatively uncontroversial areas of cultural reform and journalism. Indeed, the true home of moderate reformism in the interwar period became the world of journalism, and it was primarily through the pages of the journals, some in French and some in quoc-ngu, that the moderates would express their message of reform rather than revolt.

The most immediate contribution of the new journals was the promotion of quoc-ngu as a medium for the voicing of the aspirations of the new Vietnam. The first publications in quoc-ngu had appeared in Cochin China, where the French had attempted to propagate the new written form as a means of ending the domination of the Chinese written language over Vietnamese language and culture. The first publication to be issued in quoc-ngu was the famous *Gia Dinh Bao* (The Journal of Gia Dinh), which appeared with official French encouragement in 1865.[13] It was, of course, pro-French in its political orientation, and its main Vietnamese contributors were two prominent Vietnamese catholics, Petrus Ky and Paulus Cua. For its time it became a major vehicle for the transmission of French culture as well as the new written language to the literate population of Cochin China.

Publications in quoc-ngu were slower to appear in the Center and North. Indeed, French regulations made it more difficult, for Governor-general Doumer had decreed in 1898 that no journal or newspaper in quoc-ngu or Chinese could be published in protectorate areas without the advance permission of the government, and permission was not granted to a publication not headed by a French citizen.[14] In effect, any Vietnamese wishing to publish a journal, no matter how pro-French, had to locate a French citizen willing to take on the managerial responsibility. The first breakthrough was made by a young Vietnamese named Nguyen Van Vinh, often considered the founder of modern Vietnamese journalism and a major figure in the growth of modern Vietnamese literature. Born in 1882 in Ha Dong province of a commoner family, Nguyen early developed an interest in the West. He entered

13. For details, see Osborne, pp. 91–95.
14. Tran Huy Lieu, p. 133.

the translation school in Hanoi, from whence he graduated in 1896. He became a clerk in Lao Cay, and was later transferred to Haiphong, Bac Ninh, and then to Hanoi.[15] In 1906, he was sent to France to attend an exposition in Marseilles. While there his enthusiasm for French culture intensified. He also became acquainted with the possibilities of using journalism as a means of promoting the cultural renaissance of the Vietnamese people. In early 1907, he returned to Vietnam to put his plans into action, and soon made contact with a Frenchman named Schneider, who was publisher of the newspaper *Dai Nam Dong Van,* the first Chinese-language paper in Hanoi.[16] With Nguyen Van Vinh's collaboration, Schneider changed the name of the publication to *Dang Co Tung Bao* (Old Lantern Miscellany), which was issued half in Chinese and half in quoc-ngu. The first issue appeared in March 1907 with Nguyen Van Vinh as editor. Although its aims were to promote Western culture and the use of quoc-ngu in the North, it was not successful for the simple reason that few people in the area were yet able to read quoc-ngu.[17] The publication ceased to exist after just a few issues.

At about the same time, with the aid of another Frenchman, Dufour, Nguyen set up a publishing house and translation bureau for works in quoc-ngu and put out such popular favorites as *Kim Van Kieu* and the Chinese epic *Romance of the Three Kingdoms.*[18] With the failure of *Dang Co Tung Bao,* Nguyen briefly put out the French-language paper *Notre Journal* in 1908 and 1909, and then went with Schneider to Saigon to publish another quoc-ngu newspaper, the *Luc Tinh Tan Van.*[19] In 1913, now convinced that conditions in the North were more favorable for the establishment of a quoc-ngu press in that area, he returned to Tonkin (again with Schneider in tow) and founded the first all-

15. *Pham Quynh Va Nguyen Van Vinh* [Pham Quynh and Nguyen Van Vinh] (Saigon, 1958), p. 25.

16. Tran Huy Lieu, p. 134. The newspaper was started in 1893. Also see Tran Huy Lieu, "Lich su bao chi Viet Nam" [A history of journalism in Vietnam], *NCLS,* no. 1 (March 1959), p. 11.

17. Pham The Ngu, *Lich Su Van Hoc Viet Nam* [A History of Vietnamese Literature] (Saigon, 1961), pp. 96–97.

18. *Ibid.,* 97.

19. This bears the same name as the newspaper of Gilbert Chieu. I have not been able to determine if it is the same publication under new ownership.

quoc-ngu journal in North Vietnam, the *Dong Duong Tap Chi* (Indochinese Review). Like its predecessors, the *Dong Duong Tap Chi* was aimed at spreading French culture and quoc-ngu. It presented in its columns essays on morality, translations of such French works as *Gil Blas,* women's columns, and a course in Vietnamese for French speakers. Writers such as Tran Trong Kim offered comments on pedagogy, and in early issues the young Pham Quynh occasionally published articles on Eastern-Western cultural problems. The overall tone of the magazine was strongly pro-Western and antitraditional, with occasional articles criticizing Chinese thought as "a hedge providing a barrier to progress."[20]

In 1915, the magazine changed somewhat. By that time Nguyen Van Vinh and Schneider had put out the *Trung Bac Tan Van* (Central Tonkin News), a Hanoi newspaper in quoc-ngu devoted to politics. With the publication of the new daily, the *Dong Duong Tap Chi* became less political and turned into a primarily cultural organ, with a literary column by Phan Ke Binh, studies of classical literature, and translations of Chinese short stories. In 1919, it underwent a final change. Abandoning its interest in learning to Pham Quynh's *Nam Phong* it became just a pedagogical journal for Tran Trong Kim's work.

Through the work of Nguyen Van Vinh, quoc-ngu and French culture began to penetrate slowly into the still strongly Confucian North Vietnamese society. Although *Dong Duong Tap Chi* had only a short existence as a major force for cultural change, it opened the door for successors such as *Nam Phong,* and served as a mouthpiece for Nguyen Van Vinh's progressive thought.

Nguyen saw himself not only as a promoter of modern literature, but as a voice for political and social progress in Vietnam. Outspokenly pro-French, he openly praised Western culture and Western political institutions in the pages of his journal. In a series of articles in *Dong Duong Tap Chi* he attempted to teach his readers about the functions of government in the West. He was particularly interested in problems connected with the reorganization of village administration, apparently because the question had been placed before the Consultative Assembly of Annam, of which he had become a member.

20. Pham The Ngu, p. 97.

Paralleling his admiration of Western culture was a dislike of traditional society. Like Phan Chu Trinh he felt hostility toward the past, and this emotional reaction extended to traditional mores as well as the feudal structure. In a series of articles, he exposed to merciless ridicule all the bad old customs of the pre-colonial days that the Vietnamese should get rid of—the corruption of village notables, irresponsible religious habits which prevented the Vietnamese from having any enthusiasm to undertake a major challenge, shallow learning that created a class of gentry "who eat the rice and wear the clothes of society," without performing any useful purpose, and such assorted other traditional evils as gambling, fuzzy and clumsy talk, and mystical beliefs.[21] He had words of advice for women, too; in a column devoted to women's affairs, he talked of some weakness of Vietnamese women—of primitive childbearing habits, careless nursing, the chewing of betel nut, female fickleness and lust. Buddists also were the subject of some scathing criticism: in an article in *Notre journal* he criticized Buddhism for its "disorderly thought, superstition, and waste."

In his admiration for the West and dislike of the past, Nguyen Van Vinh resembled the foremost spokesman for a reformist approach during the early twentieth century, Phan Chu Trinh. Yet there are marked dissimilarities between them. Where Phan could probably agree with Nguyen Van Vinh's statement that "although the colonial government has not taken us to the apex, still, compared with the past it has been 100 times better in giving us a breath of freedom and a taste of democracy," he was much more conscious of the failures of French rule and more willing to take them to task for mistakes.[22] Where Phan had the courage to complain of French authoritarianism, condescension, arrogance and hypocrisy, Nguyen Van Vinh would only rarely refer to such problems, while concentrating his anger on "reckless individuals" who preached rebellion against the French. Only such irreconcilables were oppressed in Vietnam, he said, while anyone who was astute and publicly submissive enjoyed a considerable measure of freedom. He opposed Phan Boi Chau's Exodus to the East movement, claiming it would only lead to the restoration of feudalism,

21. *Ibid.*
22. The quotation is from *Ibid.*, p. 112.

and described Phan Boi Chau, who had the admiration of Phan Chu Trinh, as "a small man, inflated with a sense of self-importance, who escapes abroad to incite people to cause trouble and sow disaster."[23] In key areas, then, Nguyen Van Vinh differed in attitude from Phan Chu Trinh, and it is small wonder that the latter received considerably more respect from the activist elements within the Vietnamese nationalist movement.

Nguyen Van Vinh's period of ascendancy in Vietnam was fairly brief. After 1920 he turned to translation, and until 1930, when he briefly returned to prominence in a new controversy, his star dimmed. For a short period of time he was a figure of some importance in Vietnamese culture. But he was a lightweight in the eyes of other resistance leaders, who ridiculed his fear of offending the French, and who considered him a collaborator. The French, too, showed little fear of him; where they made a few moves to placate Phan Chu Trinh, they appeared to view Nguyen Van Vinh as a "friendly" who could be safely ignored. As for his ideas, they were not particularly distinctive within the progressive community. From the materials available it seems that he reflected the antitraditional and promodernist views that were characteristic of many graduates of the Franco-Vietnamese school system. Apparently he made no attempt to evaluate the deeper problems of synthesis and absorption of foreign and native values. Contemporaries generally considered him one of the most obviously pro-Western of the Vietnamese moderates, with his Western suits and his Western motorbike, and his lavish praise of everything French.

Perhaps, though, his greatest contribution was as a promoter of quoc-ngu. It was he, more than anyone else, who carried the torch for the new written form which had been originally lit by the scholars of the Free School of Hanoi. The French encouragement of quoc-ngu had not proceeded as far in the North as it had in Cochin China, and it was Nguyen's promotion of the new form in *Dong Duong Tap Chi* that provided a major impetus for its increasing popularity. He had seen the need for quoc-ngu as the instrument by which Western culture could be brought into Vietnam, seeing it as a "life and death issue for us Vietnamese."[24]

23. *Ibid.*, pp. 114–120.
24. *Ibid.*, p. 117.

Quoc-ngu would be the key to escaping the prison of Chinese culture and of feudal society in general. It opened the way to progress and modernization.

Pham Quynh and Nam Phong

Nguyen Van Vinh was soon to be followed by another and more important figure in the history of modern Vietnam. Pham Quynh was born in the year 1892 in the village of Luong Ngoc in Hai Duong province.[25] Son of a poor but hardworking scholarly family, he was orphaned at an early age and raised by a paternal grandmother. At twelve he attended the Protectorate School (Trung hoc bao ho), successor of the original interpreter school set up in Hanoi by the French in 1886. Graduated from higher primary school in 1908, he went on to the famous Ecole Française d'Extrême Orient. Pham's education at the Ecole, where he received his initiation into classical culture and Vietnamese, made an indelible impression on him and made him a unique figure within the ranks of Vietnamese nationalism. After a decade at the Ecole Française d'Extrême Orient, Pham Quynh became in 1913 an occasional contributor to Nguyen Van Vinh's journal *Dong Duong Tap Chi*. His articles hinted at the political and philosophical orientation of his later writings.[26]

It was during World War I that he got the major break that eventually would make him one of the most prominent literary figures in colonial Vietnam. The French were concerned about German propaganda in China during the war that was being spread by means of a German-owned newspaper in Tsingtao; this problem was the particular responsibility of Louis Marty, chief of the governor-general's political bureau and later director of the French Sûreté Générale, who had been put in charge of an office to counter German propaganda efforts in East and Southeast Asia.[27] Pham Quynh came to the favorable attention of Marty, and at the latter's request Pham and Nguyen Ba Trac agreed to

25. He often used the pen names Thuong Chi and Hong Nhan. See *ibid.*, p. 125.

26. *Ibid.*

27. Marty's background is given in *ibid.*, p. 128. He started working in the office of the resident superior of Tonkin in 1907, and became an assistant to the Political Bureau chief in 1914. Later he became director of National Security.

found a Chinese-language paper, *Au Chau Chien Su* (The European War), which presented the French view of the conflict. It was published in one thousand copies and sent to be read in China.

By 1917, Marty began to see the potential value of a pro-French quoc-ngu journal in Vietnam, and asked the two Vietnamese to use their facilities to put out a propaganda organ for sale in Vietnam. The two agreed and thus was born *Nam Phong* (Wind from the South), the second major quoc-ngu journal in North Vietnam. Thus, with French sponsorship, the journal *Nam Phong* was founded in July 1917. It was destined to be one of the longest-lasting journals in modern Vietnamese press history. encompassing two hundred ten issues, over a total of seventeen years until its demise in December 1934. Beginning as a monthly half in Chinese and half in Vietnamese, it soon expanded to include a French section.

The aims of the journal—and the lifelong goals of the editor—were to blend Western science with Eastern philosophical values and to achieve the synthesis of East and West in Vietnam.[28] A second but hardly less important goal of the new journal was to enrich Vietnamese language and literature as a living monument to the people, and for this purpose the magazine would not only do its utmost to promote the creation of original works in quoc-ngu, but also to provide translations in quoc-ngu of the great works in foreign literature, as well as to publish quoc-ngu versions of the Vietnamese classics.[29]

In terms of contents, *Nam Phong* was divided into eight sections. There were essays on contemporary affairs, literature, philosophy, science, and international events, as well as a literary corner, short stories, and a section of miscellany. The Chinese section, headed for a while by Nguyen Ba Trac, was devoted to literary essays and poems. In the journal were found translations of *Le Cid* and de Maupassant, and discussions of famous French philosophers such as Rousseau, Bergson, and Descartes. Of a higher general literary quality than *Dong Duong Tap Chi*, *Nam Phong* was also more broadly cultural, and helped to create a more fluent

28. *Ibid.*, p. 29.
29. Nguyen Duy Dien, *Luan De ve Nam Phong Tap Chi* [Essays on Nam Phong magazine] (Saigon, 1960), p. 13.

and robust national language. Where before *Nam Phong*'s appearance there were just a few stories in quoc-ngu, written by Petrus Ky and Paulus Cua, through *Nam Phong*'s promotion the number of new and translated works grew rapidly.

Over the years, Pham Quynh was assisted by a number of well-known scholars, many from old Confucian families, and the magazine rapidly became a focus for the expression of philosophical values and the literary classics of the past, as well as for the promotion of French culture. Most prominent were Nguyen Ba Hoc, teacher and writer, and a specialist on education and ethics; Nguyen Trong Thuat, an admirer of Confucianism and Buddhism and, in *Nam Phong,* a popularizer of traditional culture; Nguyen Huu Tien, a prolific writer on Eastern culture and philosophy, and translator of ancient and modern Chinese works; and Duong Ba Trac, a degree-holder who had become a convert to modern learning and an active participant in the Hanoi Free School, later imprisoned on Con Lon island after the 1908 tax riots.[30]

Under the forceful editorship of Pham Quynh, *Nam Phong* became a popular and influential journal, expressing the political and cultural views of the relatively conservative, but sometimes cautiously modernist scholar-gentry of North Vietnam. For a time it was blatantly pro-French, but after 1923 it became somewhat more oppositionist in tone, although it never lost the derisive sobriquet conferred upon it by more progressive elements—"the *Dong Kinh Nghia Thuc* of the colons."[31]

At all times, until 1932 when Pham Quynh turned over the editorship to Nguyen Trong Thuat, the journal was primarily the vehicle for the expression of Pham Quynh's philosophical, political, and cultural ideas. A catholic thinker, a prolific writer, cultured and at ease in Western as in Eastern culture, Pham Quynh became a distinctive figure in Vietnam. His writings encompassed a remarkably broad scope—translations of French philosophers like Barrès, Maurras, Le Bon; philosophical studies of eighteenth-century *philosophes* such as Voltaire, Rousseau, and Montesquieu, and of moderns such as Bergson and Comte; literary criticism of French, Chinese, and Vietnamese works like *La Poésie*

30. Pham The Ngu, p. 129.
31. Nguyen Van Trung, *Chu Nghia Thuc Dan Phap o Viet Nam* [French Colonial Ideology in Vietnam] (Saigon, 1963), p. 202.

annamite and *L'Idéal du sage dans la philosophie confucéene;*
studies of Vietnamese folk literature and *ca dao;* and works on
Buddhism, countless essays on philosophical, moral, and political
topics, many eventually printed in two well-known volumes entitled *Essais franco-annamites* and *Nouveaux essais franco-
annamites.*[32]

Much of Pham Quynh's written work was superficial—more in-
terpretive than creative. Yet in one respect he was an unusual
and significant figure in the history of modern Vietnam. One of
the major characteristics of the anticolonialist movement in the
early years of the twentieth century was its failure to devote much
attention to the problem of adapting modern Western values and
institutions to a society still strongly traditional in tone. As was
observed in the last chapter, the major intellectual figures of the
scholar-patriot era, Phan Boi Chau and Phan Chu Trinh, had
given relatively little thought to the problem of synthesizing East
and West in Vietnam. Phan Boi Chau showed no interest in the
problem until his arrest in 1925. He seemed to feel that Vietnam
could assimilate Western culture indiscriminately without confusing the Vietnamese sense of destiny in the modern world. Independence was the panacea for all problems. Phan Boi Chau's ne-
glect of the problem was symptomatic of the lack of concern within
the scholar-patriot movement as a whole. Only Phan Chu Trinh,
with his habit of intellectualizing, gave much attention to the
problem, and, until 1925 when he returned to Vietnam for the
last time, he limited his attention to discussions at the Hanoi Free
School.

It is curious that Vietnamese intellectuals did not feel a greater
need to discuss the question, for their counterparts in China—
from K'ang Yu-wei and Liang Ch'i-ch'ao to Sun Yat-sen—were
often preoccupied with the problem of finding a new philosophy
of life and a new political system to replace the traditional one.
But in Vietnam, it was only with Pham Quynh that the problem
was raised in a serious manner, and that an attempt was made to
weave together the threads of a fairly coherent political and social

32. A list of his writings can be found in Pham The Ngu, pp. 134–135,
and in Nguyen Duy Dien, pp. 20–21.

philosophy that would resolve the cultural problems accompanying Vietnam's exposure to the Western world.

In the modern history of Vietnam he stands clearly as a figure of conservatism. Certainly he was not the most reactionary of Vietnamese, but he was the most prominent, the most vociferous, and possibly the most intellectually gifted of those who warned against the consequences of a policy of wholehearted Westernization in Vietnam. What frightened Pham Quynh above all was the possibility of Vietnam losing its own distinct characteristics. Vietnam's loss of independence was unfortunate, he conceded, but looked at from the long-term viewpoint, the conquest of Vietnam by the French was "just a small drama in the larger drama of the East-West conflict." The major concern for Vietnam was less political than it was cultural, for it is many times more dangerous to lose the soul of the nation (*quoc hon*) than merely to lose independence. And the foremost danger to Vietnamese society was that the cultural essence of the Vietnamese nation would be submerged in a sea of Western ideas and technology. Independence can be lost and the national soul retained, but without a soul there can be no nation at all to revive. Conservation is thus as important as progress.

Pham Quynh was by no means totally opposed to Western culture. Like Phan Chu Trinh and Nguyen Van Vinh, he was critical of some of the more deadening aspects of traditional Confucian civilization in Vietnam—ignorant superstitions, formalism and ritualism, subservience, bowing and scraping, "taking the four books and the five classics as sacred books synthesizing all knowledge in the world for mankind." Such a narrow and limited view of the world could only lead to the decline of the Vietnamese nation.[33]

For this reason, Pham Quynh welcomed the intervention of France in the nineteenth century. The coming of France, he felt, was a "breath of fresh air" which brought its humane influence to Vietnam. The first Vietnamese did not see it that way, of course,

33. In a famous speech given in Paris in 1922, "L'Evolution intellectuelle et morale des Annamites depuis l'établissement du Protectorat Français," Pham had criticized traditional culture in Vietnam as "a pale image of China." See Pham Quynh, *Nouveaux essais franco-annamites* (Hué, 1937).

and resisted French culture. Even to learn French or quoc-ngu was considered a humiliation by the lettré class. But gradually the Vietnamese have learned to accept the French presence in their country as inevitable. And now the beneficent influence of France has brought a vision of a better society to Vietnam— reformed law codes, an improved educational system, and the gradual creation of a representative system of government.

The crux of Pham Quynh's thought was thus how best to preserve what was of value in traditional Vietnamese culture while at the same time absorbing what was useful from the outside world. And the answer, provided in a series of articles in *Nam Phong*, lay in a mixture of conservatism and progress, in a careful selection of values from East and West to achieve a harmonization (*trung dung*) of contrasting cultures. Only thus could society both retain its roots and keep up with environmental changes.[34] To prove his point, Pham Quynh cited the example of the Western nations building a modern civilization based on science and technology, while still maintaining their cultural roots in the values and philosophical ideals of Greek and Roman antiquity. In a similar fashion, he contended, modern Vietnam should retain its ties with its own Confucian past.[35]

The value of the tie with France, as he explained in the opening issue of *Nam Phong* in 1917, was that France was bearing the heavy responsibility of bringing Western culture to Vietnam while, unlike other imperialist powers, never attempting to replace the Vietnamese national heritage (*quoc tuy*) with French values and institutions.[36]

Theorizing about the synthesis of East and West was a common pastime in early twentieth-century Asia, of course, and more practical thinkers would have been justified in asking Pham Quynh just what he meant by the "national heritage," and precisely what aspects of Western civilization could be usefully applied in Viet-

34. Pham's ideas on the synthesis of East and West are given in "Bao thu va Tien bo" [Conservatism and Progress], *Nam Phong*, no. 156 (Nov. 1930).

35. Pham The Ngu, p. 232.

36. Hoang Hanh, "Su thong nhat ve tinh chat phan dong cua Pham Quynh trong linh vuc chinh tri va van hoc" [The unity in the reactionary nature of Pham Quynh's thought in the political and literary spheres], *Van Su Dia*, no. 48 (Jan. 1949), p. 63.

nam. Pham Quynh was not blind to the possible charge of remaining at the theoretical level in his analysis, and scattered throughout his writings are indications of what he had in mind, but he apparently never attempted a major systematic analysis of Eastern and Western civilization in order to determine in what manner the synthesis could be applied. In occasional articles he referred to the elements in the "national heritage" that should be maintained: the Confucian concepts of the Way (the *Dao*) and of self-cultivation (*tu than xu the*), filial piety and the concept of loyalty and subordination of the individual to the community.[37]

From such indications it is evident that Pham Quynh's vision of the future of Vietnamese society was strikingly different from the view of most of his nationalist-minded contemporaries. Indeed, Pham Quynh's view of the ideal Vietnamese society in many respects seemed not markedly different in spirit from the traditional Confucian world of his forefathers, a hierarchial world in which members of the governed class obeyed their betters, an organic world in which the individual was subordinate to social units like the family to preserve order with society. Freedom, equality, and individual liberty he scorned as the delusions of the post-Rousseau modern world. To say that the individual has indelible rights, he contended, is wrong. The individual has rights only within the sphere of the family and the nation. People cannot live for the self alone, but for the family and the community.[38]

The key to maintaining the order of society was religion and the monarchy. Buddhism, which Nguyen Van Vinh had scorned with its monks and temples and useless relics of the past, Pham Quynh saw as providing important spiritual strength, The monarchy was necessary to provide the solemnity and majesty necessary to maintain social stability, and to provide the people with a mediator to represent their needs before the Almighty.[39]

37. A brief indication of Pham's ideas on the national heritage can be found in his article, "Dao 'hieu' va dao 'trung' trong luan ly cua Khong giao" [The concepts of "filialty" and "loyalty" in the ethical philosophy of Confucius], in Chu Dang Son and Tran Viet Son, *Luan De ve Nhom Nam Phong Tap Chi* [Essays on the Group at Nam Phong Journal] (Saigon, 1960), p. 133.

38. Pham Quynh, *Thuong Chi Van Tap* [The Essays of Thuong Chi] (Saigon, 1962), IV, 301.

39. Hong Hanh, p. 68, citing *Nam Phong*, no. 9 (1917), p. 211.

A cursory view of Pham Quynh's views on society, on politics, and on ethics, might leave the impression that he had constructed his universe almost totally without recourse to Western thought. Strictly speaking, however, Pham Quynh was strongly influenced in his views by some of the harsher critics of Western bourgeois civilization in Republican France—Maurice Barrès, Paul Bourget, Gustav Le Bon, and, in particular, Charles Maurras. He often quoted with relish Maurras' criticisms of Western liberalism, and agreed with Maurras' organic view of human nature and society.[40] Following Maurras, Pham Quynh saw liberty, equality, and fraternity as a sham. Pham Quynh, like Maurras, had thus declared war on the libertarian tendencies of modern Western thought, and its glorification of human potentialities. The primordial problem for societies is to preserve themselves from the disintegrating effects of human greed and irrationality. And this order could only be safeguarded by means of authority, of hierarchy, of discipline, and by the hereditary monarchy. Human society would be built on ancient institutions—religion, the family, the monarchy—and the function of the individual would be to serve and protect these institutions, even at the expense of his own freedom and individuality, for without them society would disintegrate, and chaos would result.

It need hardly be said that Pham Quynh's views on the surface seem very reminiscent of Confucian doctrine. At the same time it would be misleading to view Pham Quynh's thought simply as an attempt to synthesize Confucianism with Western democracy. In his view of human nature, Pham Quynh departed significantly from the Confucian view (or at least from the strongly humanistic Confucian-Mencian tradition), for he had considerably less confidence in the nature and educability of man than Confucius and his more humanistic successors. It is apparent that his attraction for Maurras is due primarily to the latter's own harsh criticism of the bourgeois democratic world of the French Third Republic. As such, Pham Quynh was making a frontal attack on the liberal democratic orientations of most of his nationalist contemporaries.

Pham Quynh's strongly traditional world view raises the ques-

---

40. Pham Quynh's views on Maurras can be found in his *Charles Maurras, penseur politique* (Hué, 1942).

at he felt Vietnam had to learn from the scientific and
:" West. And indeed Pham was not clear in explaining
ly he meant when he said Vietnam had to learn about
n the West. In one article in *Nam Phong* he talked
eed for Vietnam to assimilate the scientific research
methods of the West, in order to evaluate Vietnam's own past and
to determine what of the traditional period should be revitalized
for the twentieth century.[41] And when he talked in general terms
about the nature of the synthesis to be achieved between East and
West in Vietnam he referred to the need to match Eastern emphasis on "virtue" with the Western emphasis on "materialism."[42] Yet
he certainly did not have in mind the importation into Vietnam of
Western materialism and liberal democracy, those elements which,
in the view of Charles Maurras, had created such a decadant society in the West. Indeed, it is not clear whether Pham Quynh
really did want Western science, for he was much more bothered
by social disorder than by poverty, dictatorship, or disease. In his
view, Vietnamese society was "passably incoherent and disorganized" and gave the impression of "a crazed crowd which is
looking for a way and does not know exactly what it is doing or
where it is going."[43] Under these circumstances, he felt that a
French protectorate was inevitable and indeed desirable, and to
be patriotic it was first necessary to be pro-French, for the "peuples
mineurs" like the Vietnamese were inevitably going to enter the
orbit of one great power or another, and France obviously was
preferable to any alternative. This opinion had been uttered in
France in 1922, and though a decade later he was pressing the
French government to grant greater autonomy to the Vietnamese
monarchy, there is no indication that he ever desired to throw off
French overlordship entirely—since France, in his mind, was the
only protection for Vietnamese against the demographic threat of
China and the military threat of Japan.

But Pham Quynh's importance cannot be assessed without con-

41. Pham Quynh, "Ban ve quoc hoc" [Talks on national studies], *Nam Phong*, no. 163 (June 1931), pp. 515–522.
42. Pham Quynh, "Ban phiem ve van hoa dong tay" [Further discussion on East-West culture] *Nam Phong*, no. 84 (June 1924), pp. 447–455.
43. Pham Quynh, "Vers une doctrine nationale", *Nouveaux Essais*, p. 457.

sideration of his influence in literature. For, like Nguyen Van Vinh, perhaps his most lasting importance in Vietnamese history lies in his encouragement of the development of a national literature and a national language. It was his contention that the most valuable contribution a Vietnamese could make was in the area of culture, not of politics. Critics have maintained that in so doing he was simply acting as a catspaw for the French by siphoning off resentment and frustration into the relatively innocuous realm of culture. This is probably a true estimate of the French attitude. On the other hand, Pham Quynh's feeling about the need to attack on the cultural plane is not necessarily irrational, given his view of the nature of society. Like many of the Confucianists in China he saw the vital role of the intellectual elite in changing society, and it was his specific view that writers were the most important people in society, for wherever writers go, the people will surely follow.[44]

So, in establishing *Nam Phong,* Pham Quynh saw the journal as the focus for activity directed at saving Vietnamese culture and preserving Vietnamese identity through the creation of a national language and a national literature. Quoc-ngu was beginning to develop in Tonkin as a result of the Free School and Nguyen Van Vinh's promotional work. At the time of the establishment of *Nam Phong* in 1917, however, there was still much to be done, for the language was still restricted in serviceability and had a limited vocabulary in many professional areas. It would be the destiny of Pham Quynh and his journal to carry a major burden in remedying this deficiency.

In undertaking this activity Pham Quynh had to struggle against opposition in cultural circles in Vietnam. In the past, the main hostility to quoc-ngu had come from traditional elements anxious to protect the Confucian heritage. Now, however, the attack came from other quarters. Some graduates of the Franco-Vietnamese school system simply wanted to abandon Vietnamese altogether and adopt French as a more cosmopolitan and useful language to bring Vietnam into the modern world. Indeed, some Vietnamese spoke French better than their own native language. Pham Quynh vigorously opposed the abandonment of Vietnamese and the adop-

44. Hong Hanh, p. 69.

tion of French. In an article written in *Nam Phong* in 1918, "Chu Phap co dung lam quoc van duoc khong" (Can French be used as our national language), he first denied that Vietnamese was lacking the qualities of a national language and then added that all Vietnamese do not need to communicate with the outside world or the government, and thus have no need for French. Finally, he defended quoc-ngu, because "to maintain the national language is to maintain the *quoc hon,* the metaphysical spirit of the nation, to nourish a hope for tomorrow."[45]

In his view, this literary and language revolution would take place primarily through the enrichment of Vietnamese culture by means of assimilation of cultural influence from China and France. French influence would come through the translation of French classics into Vietnamese, and the adaptation of selected words and phrases into quoc-ngu forms. A similar process would serve to bring words and compounds from literary Chinese into the Vietnamese language. It was through the efforts of Pham Quynh and others on the staff of *Nam Phong* that quoc-ngu began to develop a large Chinese vocabulary, particularly at the level of philosophy and politics.

It is not easy to place Pham Quynh in the perspective of his age. His ideas often appear more sophisticated than the naive musings of Phan Boi Chau and Phan Chu Trinh, or the hasty Westernization on Nguyen Van Vinh. He certainly was more aware of the problems of psychological identity which the Vietnamese people would endure as they entered a new age. Yet at the same time Pham's ideas were hardly more practical. This is ironic because above all he prided himself on his realism, and he must have felt that his support for France was based at least in part on a realistic assessment of the nature of world society. His theories, however, have a rustic, scholarly, medieval quality (the king in his castle and the peasant, warm and content, in his cottage). As such, Pham Quynh completely ignored the social realities of his time. Too attracted to a vision of peace and order, he failed to see the trend of the age, the rising confidence in Man, the irreconcilability of the concept of hierarchy with the new spirit of freedom. These trends were clearly evident in Vietnam. Even if Pham Quynh were to be

45. Pham The Ngu, p. 176.

right in his assessment of the nature of man and human society, he picked a bad time to say it.

Yet he is still a significant figure in the history of modern nationalism in Vietnam. Although a friend of France, he did focus attention on the need for Vietnamese to search within themselves and their own traditions for particular answers to their problems, a service neglected by other, more progressive figures. By promoting quoc-ngu as a national language, he provided the Vietnamese with a tool and a symbol of their own identity in the modern world. If he was guilty of seriously misreading the temper of the age, he still had an awareness of one aspect of the challenge faced by modern Vietnam, an aspect little considered by others in the movement. Curiously, Pham Quynh's legacy was taken up by a kindred figure a generation later—the mandarin President Ngo Dinh Diem—who was similarly conscious of the awesome cultural gap between Vietnam and the West. Like Pham Quynh, Diem felt that Vietnamese society required a solid ideological foundation based in part on traditional concepts of obedience, virtue, and community. But both, whatever their self-images as modernists and realists, were running against the spirit of the times; their call to tradition, and distrust of human nature, was simply ludicrous to many of their contemporaries. By the time they had raised the issue, it was already too late.

Albert Sarraut and the Association Policy

In order to accept the validity of the approach of the Francophile elements in the nationalist movement it was before all else necessary to accept one basic premise—that the French would actually carry through on their implicit promise of fulfilling a "mission civilisatrice" in Indochina. Up to World War I, French performance had been sporadic, rich in promises but poor in results. But when Albert Sarraut, that outspoken advocate of Franco-Vietnamese association and friendship who had earlier served a term as governor-general from 1911 to 1914, was reappointed for a second tour in January 1917 it looked to some as if there were indeed a chance for a new Golden Age, or, as Pham Quynh put it, a "Meiji period" in Vietnam. Indeed, if there ever was a Golden Age in Indochina, it probably took place under the reign of Albert Sarraut. For it was Sarraut's special ability to be able to soothe the resentment and frustration of moderate nationalists with promises of reform and change. Nothing could be done with the most outspoken opponents of French rule—although Sarraut had made an effort to lure Phan Boi Chau into surrender—but there were a substantial number of Vietnamese who, although they were anxious for reform and an increased role for Vietnamese in society, were willing to settle, at least temporarily, for less than total independence. And, unquestionably, Sarraut was the man with the personal style and the oratorical eloquence to win the reluctant or wholehearted support of such moderate nationalists.

What were the demands of the more cautious reformists at this period in history? A look at the moderate and pro-French newspaper *Tribune indigène,* founded in 1917, gives an idea of the interests of Saigon intellectuals and the middle-class elite. First of all, the moderates wanted greater representation in the Colonial Council—preferably parity with the French—and more positions for Vietnamese in the Cochin Chinese administrative hierarchy. Second, there was growing criticism of the domination of the economy of the South by Chinese and the *chettys,* the Indian money-lenders. Although there may have been some resentment of French commercial interests, it was at this point still unspoken. Finally, the middle class wanted more educational opportunities, particularly for their own children at the highest levels, but more generally for all Vietnamese. The number of schools was insufficient, and provision for higher education had been inadequate since the University of Hanoi was closed in 1908.

During the next decades, French administrations would have to find solutions to these problems sufficient to defuse moderate discontent in Vietnam, while at the same time avoiding policies that would arouse the fears and opposition of the French colonialists in Indochina; they would have to grant additional rights and privileges to the Vietnamese population without endangering the political and economic domination of the area by the French. For Sarraut, apparently, the solution was to mollify Vietnamese nationalists by promises of a better world to come, while keeping actual changes minimal enough to avoid unduly irritating the local French population. Indeed, Sarraut's promises were broad in their scope. "I want to give you," he said to a Vietnamese audience before leaving France for Indochina in 1917, "the instrument of liberation which will gradually lead you toward those superior spheres to which you aspire."[46] He had for long been an advocate of cooperation between French and Vietnamese, and in his speeches in Vietnam he often seemed to promise that the end of the Great War was opening a new era in which Vietnamese would play a larger role in their own affairs, "new times" which called for "flexible policies" on the part of the government. In actual performance, the regime of Sarraut was less impressive, and only a few structural changes took place under his direction. But up until the time of his departure he continued to stress the changes that would inevitably take place. The Vietnamese, he promised, would receive "a perceptible extension of their political rights," including greater representation in existing assemblies, and an enlargement of suffrage.

Vietnamese moderates were only too happy to respond to Sarraut's lyrical promises. Until the end of his term of office, *Tribune indigène* continued to praise his efforts and his magnanimity.[47] In the North, the primary indication of collaboration was the new association, the Khai Tri Tien Duc (Association pour la Formation Intellectuelle et Morale des Annamites, or AFIMA), formed at the behest of Sarraut and Louis Marty by Vietnamese Francophiles like Pham Quynh, Nguyen Van Vinh, and Hoang Trong Phu, son of the former viceroy Hoang Cao Khai. The aim of AFIMA was to promote East-West collaboration, to develop French influence in Vietnam, and to arrange for the translation of Western classics into quoc-ngu. Pham Quynh became the general secretary, and *Nam Phong* its press organ.[48] Vietnamese patriots often tended to see AFIMA as a pure propaganda tool of the French, while some French colonialists looked at it with suspicion as a new Hanoi Free School. The former were closer to the mark; the members consisted primarily of bureaucrats, notables, village chiefs, merchants, and wealthy landlords, and most joined probably to protect their status. As Sarraut himself admitted, it was the only organization of its kind open to Vietnamese. By the mid-1920s it numbered about 2,000 members.[49]

46. Georges Garros, *Forceries Humaines* (Paris, 1926), p. 51.
47. For example, see the issues of Nov. 5 and 26, 1918.
48. Nguyen Van Trung, p. 153.
49. *Ibid.*

This state of collaboration between the French and the Vietnamese moderates was not destined to become a constant fixture on the political scene, however, as the fruitless trip of Emperor Khai Dinh to Paris in 1922 demonstrated. Khai Dinh, son of Dong Khanh, who had succeeded Duy Tan in 1916, was on friendly terms with Pham Quynh and took seriously the latter's advocacy of a revitalization of the old 1884 treaty of protectorate between the Vietnamese monarchy and France. In 1922, Khai Dinh went to Paris with the specific intention of achieving French agreement on Pham Quynh's proposals, but Paris was not amenable and he returned empty handed. Khai Dinh's failure had repercussions in Indochina where it was another straw in the wind that Pham Quynh's optimism over French intentions was misplaced. Under the governor-generalship of Maurice Long in the early 1920s the government began to initiate some reforms which increased Vietnamese representation in consultative chambers. The number of Vietnamese in the Colonial Council in Saigon increased from six to ten, and more Vietnamese were put into the Cochin Chinese administration.[50] But such reforms smacked of tokenism when compared to the still-remaining degree of French authority in Vietnam, and even Pham Quynh, on his return from France in 1923, became increasingly independent in his statements; in 1925 he broke off relations with AFIMA, presumably to demonstrate his dissatisfaction with French policies. Even among its friends, the French government was having difficulties in satisfying the hopes aroused by Sarraut.

In one area, Sarraut had moved to make specific reforms. When he took office in 1917, the reorganization of Vietnamese education which had begun at the beginning of the century was only partially completed. Most importantly, it reached only a small proportion of the populace—only three thousand of the more than twenty-three thousand communes in Vietnam had a village school—and thus the vast percentage of school-age children were deprived of any educational opportunity at all.[51] Sarraut's contribu-

50. At the same time, the number of French members was increased from twelve to fourteen.
51. Figures on education are located in *AF*, July 1925, p. 228, and in

tion to the education of Vietnamese was his comprehensive reform entitled the "Code de l'Instruction Publique," which carried on the developments begun by Governor-general Beau but made some major changes in substance. Under the new system, two separate types of school were created, French and Franco-Vietnamese. The French schools followed the system in metropolitan France and were designed primarily for children of French parents, while the Franco-Vietnamese schools were for Vietnamese. Both would culminate in a common university program in the newly-reopened University of Hanoi. There was no immediate provision for increasing the number of schools or the number of students being educated, but one major change called for education at the basic level in both types of schools in French. In effect, the great apostle of "association" had become convinced that all Vietnamese who were educated should have a basic grounding in the French language.[52] For the moment, because there were insufficient instructors able to teach the language, the regulation was not enforced in some villages. Tradition still had a minor place in the educational system with a few courses offering Chinese and traditional morality, but the emphasis was strongly on modernization. In 1918 the last civil service examinations were given in Central Vietnam.

Sarraut's new educational program created considerable stir among Vietnamese middle class elites. Many approved of the new emphasis on French as the only locally used language which was cosmopolitan and appropriate to the needs of a modern people.[53] The new regulations predictably brought forth an outcry from Pham Quynh, however, who criticized the new system as "assimilationist." Pham complained that many French and some French-educated Vietnamese thought of quoc-ngu as just a "patois" and retorted:

Nguyen Anh, "Vai net ve giao duc o Viet Nam tu khi Phap xam luoc den cuoi chien tranh the gioi lan thu nhat" [Some figures on education in Vietnam from the time of the French conquest until the First World War], NCLS, no. 98 (May 1967), p. 46.

52. These educational statutes are reproduced in Tribune indigène, May-June, 1918.

53. For example, see the article on education in Tribune indigène, May 13, 1918.

A language which is spoken by 18 million people, which over the centuries has successfully resisted Chinese conquest, which, although having borrowed extensively from Chinese characters from which it is indeed in part derived, like French from Latin, has been able to conserve its own individuality, and which, although not having produced a particularly rich literature . . . has nevertheless its originality, its charm, and its beauty, well, that language is not a formless patois. It deserves to live.[54]

Pham Quynh had no success with Sarraut or his successor Maurice Long, but found a more appreciative audience in the new Governor-general Martial Merlin, who succeeded to office in 1923. Merlin, who had already considerable colonial experience in Africa, has been accused by Joseph Buttinger of being a "professed enemy of higher education for the natives."[55] That is true enough, although Merlin's attitude was probably determined more by problems of unemployment of skilled Vietnamese than by an innate dislike of education for natives. In any event, Merlin expressed himself in favor of increasing educational opportunities, but at the basic level, and for useful purposes. Education at the secondary and college level he might classify with many French colonial residents as creating "not one coolie less but one rebel more." To deal with this problem, he reduced the number of Vietnamese high school students and created a local baccalaureate, so that graduates of the Franco-Vietnamese system could not proceed with their education in French universities, but had to attend the University of Hanoi.

Such policies, by themselves, did not meet with Pham Quynh's requirements, and when the latter reproached Merlin for continuing the emphasis on the French language, the governor-general responded in September 1924 with a directive that dropped the emphasis on French and specified that for the first three years of instruction in Franco-Vietnamese schools, instruction would be in quoc-ngu.[56] This in itself created some problems, for with the use

54. *AF*, March 1923, p. 225. Some French agreed with this assessment, as in 1917 when the new resident superior in Annam fired all Vietnamese professors of Chinese characters. AOM Carton 332, Dossier 2684, report of Resident Superior Le Fol of June 6–10, 1931, p. 11.

55. Buttinger, I, 103.

56. Nguyen Anh, "Vai net ve giao duc o Viet Nam tu sau dai chien the gioi lan thu nhat den truoc cach mang thang tam" [Some figures on educa-

of Vietnamese at the elementary level, those students who went on to the higher level found it difficult to cope with French, so a special course had to be set up to prepare students for French language instruction.

---

tion in Vietnam after the First World War to the August Revolution] *NCLS*, no. 102 (Sept. 1967), p. 32.

Chapter 7

Crisis in Cochin China

While Pham Quynh was busy promoting cultural and educational reform in the North, similar forces were at work chipping away at the edifice of colonial authority in the South. The character of this movement rising after World War I in Saigon differed in some respects from that led by Pham Quynh in Hanoi and was symbolic of the changing nature of society in Cochin China. For in Saigon, accelerating commercial activity was creating a wealthy indigenous bourgeoisie that was simultaneously modernist and pro-French in its basic orientation.[1]

By nature, this new Cochin Chinese elite was caught in the familiar dilemma. Proud and status-oriented, it instinctively wanted a larger political and economic role in society. Yet by vocation and education its members were tied to a continued French presence and inclined toward moderation and compromise, wanting reforms and increased influence but without the risks of incurring irreconcilable hostility from the French government.

In the early 1920s, however, this new Cochin Chinese elite was politically aware and conscious of a need to utilize its potential influence to modify French policy to its own advantage. In a number of respects, this rising middle class was dissatisfied with conditions in Vietnam. In the first place, Vietnamese still had limited political rights within their own country. The primary forum in Cochin China for the new urban middle class was the Colonial Council, a regional elected body established in 1880 to consider

1. See Ralph B. Smith, "Bui Quang Chieu and the Constitutionalist Party in French Cochin China," *Modern Asian Studies,* 3, part 2 (April 1969), 130–150. Some came from a lower class background, but many others were from affluent families. Most were successful professionally.

problems of a social and economic nature, and pass the budget. But this council was dominated by French interests, and even after the reforms of 1922 there were only ten Vietnamese in a council of twenty-four members, elected by a constituency of twenty-two thousand.[2] Similar restrictions existed in the Chambers of Commerce and Agriculture. There was dissatisfaction, too, over the repressive political climate. Some press freedom existed, and a number of French- and Vietnamese-language papers had been established, but the quoc-ngu press in particular was closely monitored by the government, and the rights of association and the right to travel were subject to severe limitations.[3] In the economic sphere the most galling problem for the Vietnamese was the virtual domination of the commercial sector of the economy by the French and the overseas Chinese, particularly in the areas of banking and foreign trade. There were other, more serious problems, of course, for the poor in the cities and the rural areas— oppressive taxation; the monopolies on alcohol, salt, and opium; the long working hours and poor conditions. These problems were aired in the moderate press, although with somewhat less vehemence than issues of direct concern to the middle class.

By the early 1920s, the nucleus of a new movement based on these interests had begun to coalesce around the Constitutional Party and its leading figure, the French-educated journalist Bui Quang Chieu (1873–1945). Son of a Confucian village official in Ben Tre province in the Mekong Delta, Bui Quang Chieu received his education in France, graduating from the National Institute of Agronomy as an agricultural engineer in 1897. After several years in the Indochinese government service after his return to Asia, he became interested in politics and joined with Nguyen Phu Khai in establishing the French-language newspaper in Saigon, *Tribune indigène*. With the appearance of this publication was born the Constitutionalist Party, a new political organization representing moderate nationalist views.[4] More an interest group of like-minded men—civil servants, teachers, merchants, and landlords—than a political party, the Constitutionalists did not attempt

2. *TLTK*, IV, 12–13. See also Ralph B. Smith, "Some Vietnamese Elites in Cochin China, 1943," *Modern Asian Studies*, 6, part 4 (Oct. 1972), 480.
3. Georges Garros, *Forceries humaines* (Paris, 1926), p. 52.
4. Smith, "Bui Quang," p. 132.

to develop a concrete ideology or a mass following. Rather, they agreed on the necessity of some specific changes in governmental policy, and cooperated in order to achieve these reforms with a minimum of political effort. In the first issue, the editors of the *Tribune indigène* showed their moderate and pro-French orientation. After expressing their concern about the common danger to both French and Vietnamese posed by German militarism, the editors stated:

[the journal] openly expresses all the pride of the Annamite peoples in being associated in the common endeavor. To condense the expression of our love, to exalt the moral factors which are needed to reinforce our young patriotism, to rally the hesitant to the French cause, in a word, to glorify the moral beauty of our adopted country, that is the work which we undertake with regard to our compatriots. We will then attempt to promote the diffusion of French ideas among the educated elements of the Annamite population.[5]

But the new party did have some specific complaints, and in their press organ and through the speeches of Constitutionalist Diep Van Cuong in the Colonial Council they began to air them before the government. The first cause that seemed to stimulate a sense of emotional concern was that of reducing Chinese monopoly control over the Cochin Chinese economy. As an early article in the *Tribune indigène* complained, the overseas Chinese monopolized virtually all of the major commerce in the Saigon area, and many members of the Vietnamese bourgeoisie after the war began to blame the Chinese for the economic problems in the colony. The *Tribune indigène* took an active role in the effort to break down the Chinese monopoly. A series of articles was printed in the newspaper reviling the Chinese as "Rois de négoce" (merchant kings), and a fake letter was printed indicating that the Chinese felt contempt of the Vietnamese.[6] Influential Vietnamese such as the journalist Nguyen Phan Long called on the Vietnamese to enter commerce in self-defense, and leaflets were distributed calling on Vietnamese to boycott Chinese goods. An article of July 8, 1918, in the *Tribune indigène* was typical: "The Chinese hold us by their solidarity. That is a terrible weapon, but we have one as well. The thing is to know how to utilize our own weapon. Let

5. *Tribune indigène*, Aug. 20, 1917.
6. *Tribune indigène*, April 11, 1918.

us then be polite, and return an eye for an eye. To the Chinese Association, let us oppose the Annamite Mutual Benefit Association, and we will then see who of us will have the last word." It is interesting to note that at this stage it did not occur to the Vietnamese to question the French role in the process, and an article in Nguyen Phan Long's *Echo annamite,* a newspaper with political views similar to the *Tribune indigène,* called on the French "mother" to help her Vietnamese offspring against the overseas Chinese.[7]

By the early 1920s, the Constitutionalists became bolder and more willing to castigate French economic domination over the economy—notably in 1923 when some members of the party attempted to block an attempt by the French consortium "Homberg" to obtain a twenty-year monopoly on rice exports from the port of Saigon. Until then, rice exports had been controlled informally by Chinese merchants, and French interests, allied with a few Vietnamese landlords like Le Quang Trinh, Le Phat An, and Nguyen Huu Hao, tried to obtain a legal monopoly of their own on the pretext of breaking down Chinese domination. Other Vietnamese elements led by Bui Quang Chieu and the *Tribune indigène* were hostile, saying that a free market was needed, while the proposal before the Colonial Council simply exchanged one monopoly for another. Although the presence of influential French *colonialists* like Outrey and de la Chevrotière managed to push the bill through the Colonial Council, other French liberals took the issue to Paris and ultimately the government prevented the resolution from being put into effect.[8] One effect of the controversy was to drive a wedge between various elements in the moderate Vietnamese camp, with the group around Le Quang Trinh leaving the Constitutionalist Party and forming its own newspaper, *Le Progrès annamite.* Then, a similar crisis erupted over the manufacture of *nuoc mam.* For years, the popular fish sauce was manufactured primarily by the Vietnamese, except for a brief and unsuccessful attempt by Chinese interests to produce an ersatz sauce at cheaper prices. Then in 1920, a French company attempted to obtain a monopoly for the manufacture of *nuoc mam* and was able to persuade the govern-

7. The letter appeared in August 1920.
8. *TLTK,* IV, 88–89.

ment to issue a declaration that the fish sauce produced by Vietnamese firms did not meet with health standards, but Vietnamese commercial interests organized protests in the early 1920s, and the plan to establish a French monopoly was abandoned.[9]

The Constitutionalists were also active in pressing the French for political reforms. Nguyen Phan Long's journal *Echo annamite* observed in 1921 that the Vietnamese had roads and schools and economic prosperity (presumably the author was unaware of conditions for the mass of the population), but "to make us happy, one basic thing is still lacking, and that is political power."[10] By 1923, the Constitutionalists were not only demanding more Vietnamese participation in the organs of government, but also a constitution and Canadian-style dominion status. In some French colonial circles, Bui Quang Chieu began to be considered as a dangerous radical, and his proposals were ridiculed as visionary. They saw Bui Quang Chieu and his ilk as Bolsheviks, or as affected bullies, guilty of duplicity and bad faith, "the prototypes of our culture, deprived of traditional beliefs and uprooted from their ancestral soil—totally ignorant of Confucian morality, which they despise because they don't understand it."[11]

By the early 1920s, the Constitutionalists had marked out a relatively progressive position within the narrow spectrum of open political expression. They were not revolutionaries, to be sure, and while distrusted by the French right, they aroused equal dislike on the Vietnamese left. But they stood for change and were demonstrating an increased tendency to oppose French interests on issues basic to them. Under the leadership of Bui Quang Chieu and Nguyen Phan Long, the party began to gain support, mainly among middle-class Vietnamese but also in the worker community because of Constitutionalist proposals to abolish forced recruitment. In particular, the party became influential in the Colonial Council, where Bui Quang Chieu, Nguyen Phan Long, and Le Quang Liem waged a constant struggle for administrative reform.

The Constitutionalists were only one of several political factions which became active in the frenetic years of the mid-1920s

9. *Ibid.*, pp. 90–92.
10. *Giai Cap*, p. 274.
11. Paul Monet, *Français et Annamites: Entre deux feux* (Paris, 1928), p. 40.

in Cochin China. Other, more radical groups began to organize in the interests of promoting changes in French policy. None was well organized, and few had any concrete ideology. The most prominent, perhaps, was less a political party than a clique around a single political personality—the so-called *Thanh Nien Cao Vong* (The Hopes of Youth) of Nguyen An Ninh. Born in 1900 in Gia Dinh province near Saigon, Nguyen An Ninh came from a scholar-gentry family, his father having been local representative for the Hanoi Free School and later a member of the *Dong Du* movement. Young Nguyen received his education in the Franco-Vietnamese school system, including the famous Chasseloup-Laubat school in Saigon. In 1918 he left the Ecole de Droit in Hanoi and went to Paris, where he took his law degree in 1920. While in France he developed a strong admiration for the ideals of French civilization, translating Rousseau's *Contrat social* into quoc-ngu and studying the Confucian-Mencian classics and Buddhism in French.[12] At the same time he became increasingly concerned about the failure of the French to put their ideals into practice in Indochina, and when he returned to Vietnam after a couple of years working in France, he founded a French-language newspaper, *Cloche fêlée* (Cracked Bell), and began to give talks on contemporary problems that were attended by hundreds of young devotees.[13]

Under Nguyen An Ninh's leadership, *Cloche fêlée* had no specific political point of view—it was just directed at youth concerns, and at the need for Vietnam's young intellectuals to take responsibility for the fate of their nation. In its columns, *Cloche fêlée* occasionally criticized the French. They criticized the "louts" Paris sent out as administrators, the French enslavement of the Vietnamese people in their own land, the lack of political equality, and the muzzling of the press. The newspaper rapidly became popular in the Saigon area, among workers and peasants as well as among intellectuals. Copies were passed around until they were dog-eared, and those who could not read French had friends read

12. The major source for his life—but a disorganized one—is Phuong Lan, *Nha Cach Mang Nguyen An Ninh* [The Revolutionary Nguyen An Ninh] (Saigon, 1971).

13. Phuong Lan gives two reasons for the name: first, that he felt himself untalented, and, second, that Vietnam was itself lacking in culture. See *ibid.*, pp. 146–147.

it to them out loud. At the same time it aroused the concern of the government, and when Nguyen was unable to find anyone willing to sell it for him, he distributed it himself.[14]

Beyond his editorship of *Cloche fêlée,* Nguyen An Ninh was a significant figure in the Vietnamese nationalist movement. He had long been an admirer of French civilization, and, like Phan Chu Trinh, he was convinced that Vietnamese society must borrow from the West—particularly in the area of science and democracy —in order to survive. In the early years, he apparently had placed confidence in French reformism, and blamed the plight of Vietnam on its own citizens. The Vietnamese people, he felt, had a slave mentality and were unprepared to achieve their own liberation. Revolt therefore was irrelevant, for what Vietnam needed was a spiritual rebirth. In imitation of the work of Rabindranath Tagore in India, he felt that the proper course for Vietnam was to build up the spiritual and intellectual talents of the people, in order to create a "moral force" capable of leading the people to achieve their own salvation. Further, Nguyen felt that it was the intellectuals who would have to put this program into effect, and he therefore developed the idea of arranging for talks by famous Vietnamese at the Salle d'Enseignement Mutuelle in Saigon. Phan Chu Trinh spoke there in 1925 after returning from France; the progressive lawyer Phan Van Truong spoke about conditions of the Vietnamese exiles in Europe, and Nguyen himself gave talks.

One of the best indications of Nguyen's attitude is found in a famous speech which he made at the Salle in October 1923.[15] The speech, above all, was an appeal to the heart and the spirit of young Vietnam. The editor of *Cloche fêlée* contended that the problems of Vietnam were as much spiritual as political, and that the solution to these problems could only come about through the "creative force" of the Vietnamese, a revitalization of the national spirit. In this sense, Nguyen An Ninh shared Pham Quynh's strong sense of concern for the national culture of the Vietnamese people, and felt that a people could not achieve true independence without possessing an intellectual culture of their own. Nguyen differed from the editor of *Nam Phong,* however, in his evaluation of the

14. *Ibid.,* pp. 145–147.
15. The text is in *Cloche fêlée,* Jan. 7 and 14, 1924.

traditional culture of Vietnam and its utility in the modern age. While professing himself an admirer of Confucius and his philosophy of society, he emphatically denied that it possessed the whole truth a society required in order to build a culturally rich and advanced civilization. The problem with Confucianism in Vietnam was that it had stifled the creativity of the Vietnamese people, and even other intellectual giants like Lao Tzu were smothered in its suffocating embrace. Confucian culture was an advantage to China, where it was indigenous and helped to avoid the disintegration of native culture during a period of foreign conquest. In Vietnam, however, Confucianism was "an article of exportation" and ended up by becoming a massive handicap to the development of a native Vietnamese culture.

In consequence, the great tragedy of modern Vietnam was that it almost totally lacked a national culture on which to build for the future. Traditional society left little solid heritage, and what did exist, in Nguyen's eyes, was decadent and totally inappropriate to the modern world. He did not conclude from this, however, that the lack of native culture released modern-day Vietnamese from concern about the spiritual and cultural base of a new Vietnamese society. On the contrary, Vietnam today more than ever needed a "common ideal" on which to construct its own future, and he had vigorous criticism for those Vietnamese nationalists who saw the problem of Independence in only political terms. "They speak of politics," he said, "as if it were there, and there alone, from which will come the realization of our promises, as if the vital problem of our races were a political one and not a social one."

The solution could only come though action, and through borrowing from the West. Nguyen heaped scorn on those who only dream of independence and national rebirth. We must learn to count on ourselves alone, he said, and what we must fight against is not simply the colonial government but our own inertia. The value of France is that it is in French culture that Vietnam must find the source for her own renaissance, and it is the duty of the French government to assist Vietnam in the process, for protectorate means tutelage, and tutelage does not mean "éternelle minorité." But, as for the present, the famous "French miracle in Asia" had only resulted in lowering Vietnam's cultural level another notch, and precipitating the Vietnamese people into complete servitude.

In his conclusion, Nguyen An Ninh lapsed into reverie. We must leave this environment, he said, and reach a summit, where "in solitude, we would be able to feel all of our force and possess our soul, and with a look around us full of life and love, comprehend the world and our harmony with it. And then we will leave that summit . . . which for a time was for us a land of exile, and return to society, where we can utilize the maximum of our creative force."

Nguyen An Ninh's exhortation was somewhat vague, and certainly lacked in specifics. Yet his words possessed a certain force and sensitivity, and there was no denying their effect on his audience. If much of what he said was not understood by his listeners —and Nguyen An Ninh himself confessed that they responded more to his criticisms of the status quo than to his appeal for spiritual revival—there was a general recognition that his was a call to action. And in 1923, such a voice had not been heard on a public platform for several years.

If in late 1923 Nguyen An Ninh had avoided direct criticism of France, and had concentrated on the moral responsibilities of the Vietnamese themselves, by mid-1925 he was ready to place more blame on the colonial protector. In an article written in April of that year, and published in *Cloche fêlée,* he had strong words of warning for the government.

When a race is trapped to the point of having a choice only of death or of slavery, to face death is the more courageous. Violence should be condemned where it is not necessary. But there are cases where it must be resorted to because it is the last resource.

If the masses brave death rather than accept injustice, and if the colonialists do not want to renounce their policies of oppression and unscrupulous exploitation, it is the duty of the most courageous and devoted Annamites to dream of methods of struggle which correspond to present needs, and to organize a resistance which can combat oppression.[16]

As Nguyen viewed the situation, Sarraut had seduced the intel-

16. *Cloche fêlée,* Nov. 26, and Dec. 3, 1925. The article was entitled "La France en Indochine."

lectual youth of Vietnam with his hypocritical promises, and so they still preferred peaceful reform to revolution. But, he warned, "if in two or three years they see the futility of their efforts, they will tire and cede a place to those who will be more useful to the Annamite race." Only vast economic and political reforms could preserve French rule and avert rebellion in Indochina.

The French administration was aware of Nguyen's challenge, for Nguyen An Ninh's fiery speeches and articles had earned him an impressive reputation among the youth of Saigon, and an informal party began to grow around him, sometimes named The Hope of Youth after the title of his most famous address.[17] It was not a formal party, for Nguyen did not believe in organized political action, and it had no regulations, but it rapidly became a political force in Cochin China.

With the rising tensions in and around Saigon in the mid-twenties, other parties similar to Nguyen An Ninh's began to sprout up, reformist in tone, calling for collaboration with France, but often characterized by a growing dissatisfaction with conditions in Vietnam and often possessing a potential for violence. Perhaps the most important of these small groupings was the *Dang Thanh Nien* (Youth Party) which began to coalesce around a group of lower middle class merchants, students and minor officials in the late months of 1925. Apparently the original stimulus for the group was to protest the arrest and then the trial of the old patriot Phan Boi Chau. When the trial took place in Hanoi in November 1925 two young nationalists, Tran Huy Lieu and Bui Cong Trung, organized massive demonstrations in Saigon demanding his release, and even sent a letter to the League of Nations.[18]

17. This party should be distinguished from the Dang Thanh Nien (Youth Party) of Tran Huy Lieu. Nguyen had already been punished by Governor Cognacq for his speech of October 1923. The latter had called him into his office to reprimand him and had forbade the *Salle* from inviting him to participate in future conferences. See *Cloche fêlée*, Jan. 7, 1924.

18. The two were editors on the newspaper *Dong Phap Thoi Bao*. Tran Huy Lieu later became a member of the VNQDD and ultimately the communist party, and until his recent death was a well-known historian in the Democratic Republic of Vietnam. See his "Phan dau de tro nen mot dang vien cong san" [How I became a member of the communist party] *NCLS*, no. 10 (Jan. 1960), pp. 77–90. Bui Cong Trung came from a mandarin family attached to the Hué court. In the 1920s he studied in the Soviet Union and became a journalist in Vietnam as well as a member of the

By the next March, the party began to take on a more formal organizational existence. After a series of meetings at a hotel on the Rue d'Espagne in Saigon, the party was officially formed before a group of three thousand in a village not far from the city. The new Youth Party had no formal ideology or program and no regulations. As Tran Huy Lieu commented in his brief history of the party, the group considered itself "constitutionalist" but without much enthusiasm.[19] Its propaganda organ was *Jeune Annam,* edited by Lam Hiep Chau. Once organized, the Youth Party began to cooperate informally with other similar groups in the Saigon area and managed to achieve a tentative unity around a central committee with Nguyen Trong Hien as chairman and Tran Huy Lieu as secretary. The provisional alliance had no definite program except, according to one source, a vague commitment to Sun Yat-sen's Three People's Principles.[20]

The Appointment of Alexander Varenne

Sparked by the return of Phan Chu Trinh, the trial of Phan Boi Chau, and antiforeign riots in China, the atmosphere in Cochin China continued to heat up in late 1925 and early 1926. Then a factor was added in Paris, with the appointment of a new and promising governor-general to head the French administration in Indochina. In 1924, a leftist government had taken office in France, and the next summer the relatively conservative governor-general Martial Merlin was recalled and replaced by the Socialist Party lawyer and journalist Alexander Varenne. Because of Varenne's reputation, there was considerable optimism among nationalist groups in Vietnam that his appointment might signal a new era in Franco-Vietnamese relations, and many journals began to prepare lists of demands for his arrival. There was, of course, corresponding concern among the French in Vietnam that he might sell out their own interests.[21]

Indochinese Communist Party. See the article of April 23, 1931 in *Ami du peuple* in AOM Carton 326, Dossier 2639.

19. Tran Huy Lieu, *Dang Thanh Nien* [The Youth Party] (Hanoi, 1961), p. 23.

20. Suren A. Mkhitarian, *Rabochii Klass i Natsional'no-Osvoboditel'noe Dvizhenie vo Vietname* [The Working Class and the National Liberation Movement in Vietnam] (Moscow, 1967), p. 183.

21. For a discussion, see William H. Frederick, "Alexander Varenne and

When Varenne landed in Saigon in November he was met by massive crowds and petitions demanding the release of Phan Boi Chau. He reacted quickly in a move that met with general approval, sending a telegram to Paris asking for, and receiving, clemency for the old rebel. He was also presented with a petition by Nguyen Phan Long of *Echo annamite,* the first of the famous "Cahiers des Voeux Annamites." Nguyen Phan Long had issued a call for reform proposals through his newspaper and they were ultimately condensed by an organizational committee of Vietnamese journalists and middle-level officials into a set of demands presented to Varenne by a crowd of six hundred on the latter's arrival on November 27, 1925. Claiming to represent all the people and not just the urban intellectuals, Nguyen's cahier called for a variety of political, social, and economic changes to be instituted in Vietnam.[22]

Varenne was somewhat noncommital and cautious in his respouse, but shortly afterward he attempted to show that he wanted to inaugurate a new era in Franco-Vietnamese relations. In his maiden speech before the Conseil du Gouvernement on December 21, 1925, he made a clear inference that the legitimate goal of the Vietnamese people should be independence. For, as he viewed the role of France: "Her mission achieved, it is possible to believe that she will leave nothing in Indochina but the memory of her labor, that she will demand no role in the life of the peninsula, either to direct or to advise, and that the peoples who will have profited by her tutelage will have no other ties with her but those of gratitude and affection."[23]

In effect, Indochina "could aspire to a fuller and higher life, to become one day a nation." Vague promises, of course, had become devalued currency in Vietnam since the days of Sarraut. As a Socialist, Varenne was aware that Vietnam required more than platitudes, and in his speech he alluded to several areas where improvements were needed: (1) in public education, where more schools and teachers were needed, and higher quality education at

---

Politics in Indochina," in Walter F. Vella (ed.), *Aspects of Vietnamese History* (Honolulu, 1973), pp. 108–109.

22. The cahier was eventually reprinted in a pamphlet, which can be found in AOM, Carton 331, Dossier 2677.

23. *AF,* March 1926, p. 156.

the university level; (2) in local representation, where he envisaged an enlargement of the electoral college for local consultative bodies; (3) in local administration, where he foresaw a rise in local participation; and (4) in the area of liberty, where he spoke vaguely of an extension of personal freedom.

But Varenne was in a difficult position, having to balance native aspirations with colonialist suspicions, and these irreconcilable elements soon surfaced to sabotage the optimism of the moment. The vagueness of some of his proposals stirred resentment among nationalists. Phan Van Truong of *Cloche fêlée* observed that, in the end, all governors-general were alike, speaking in clichés, rather than in specific ideas. We had hoped for more, he said sadly, but "it is just a repetition, in different terms, of the same ideas, the same prejudices, and the same sophisms."[24] Even the Francophile Nguyen Phan Long said that he was waiting for action, not words. Trouble also appeared from the French contingent. Varenne's comments about possible independence created dismay in French circles, and by the spring of 1926 he was forced to state: "It is possible to predict that in the indeterminate future Annam will become a strong nation, free of all ties with the protectorate-nation other than that of gratitude. But it can also be predicted (and this is the conviction of the governor-general) that the ties uniting French and Annamites will become sufficiently solid so that nothing will ever break them."[25] Only the future, he hedged, would decide which of these two hypotheses would come true.

In order to satisfy the rising chorus of demands for change in Saigon, Bui Quang Chieu decided to go to France to plead for reforms from the French government. He had asked Varenne for a constitution, and the latter had demurred, saying that only Paris could decide such questions. On his arrival in Paris, the Vietnamese journalist published an open letter, citing a series of reforms that, in his view, required immediate attention. While praising the French policy of association, he complained that Indochina, with

24. *Cloche fêlée,* Dec. 7, 1925.
25. *AF,* June-July 1926, p. 238. He had been chastened by the Minister of Colonies for his gratuitous remarks earlier and had been directed not to intervene in questions of basic policy. See AOM Carton 276, Dossier 2426, Minister of Colonies to the Governor-general, Jan. 16, 1927.

its thousands of years of history, was then one of the most back-
ward and unhappy societies in Asia. Paris might be unaware of
this, for the government in Indochina does not send the truth back
to France. But reforms were vitally needed if France was to preserve intact her rich colony in the Pacific. Vietnamese demands
were not incompatible with the French presence or French interests, he insisted, as he trotted out a familiar list of reforms: (1)
liberty of thought and press in quoc-ngu, (2) liberty of association
and assembly, (3) liberty of travel, (4) modernization of the educational curriculum, (5) equal pay for equal work in the administration, (6) greater representation for Vietnamese in political
affairs, (7) improved social and working conditions, (8) broader
suffrage, and (9) the end of the monopolies.[26] He concluded his
letter with a plea and a warning: We recognize the benefits of
French tutelage, he said, and we wish to see its continuation and
consolidation, but it must take larger account of our aspirations.
But, he warned, if Indochina does not receive reforms, it will be
lost to France in fifteen years. For the first time since the French
set foot on Vietnamese soil, he said, the possibility exists of an
alliance between revolutionaries and reformists. But Quang Chieu
had gone about as far as a Francophile could go in jolting the
smugness in Paris.

As Bui Quang Chieu prepared to return, the tension was growing in Saigon. Young Vietnamese, spurred on by the increasingly
inflammatory talks and editorials of Nguyen An Ninh and like-
minded nationalists, took to the streets to protest conditions. On
March 20, Nguyen and his colleague at the *Cloche fêlée,* Dejean
de la Batie, issued tracts calling for demonstrations the next day

26. The list of demands is located in Garros, pp. 183–187. Bui's activities
in Paris are well documented in SLOTFOM materials. See SLOTFOM,
Series III, Carton 3, dossier entitled "Notes de l'agent Désiré concernant
l'Association Constitutionaliste Indochinoise." For information on the banquet given to Bui Quang Chieu before his departure for Vietnam, see
SLOTFOM, Series III, Carton 31, note of Jan. 31, 1926. At the banquet,
Bui was critical of past French behavior, but indicated his confidence that
it would improve as a result of Varenne's appointment. This material provides rich sources for an understanding of Bui's own attitudes. At one point
he indicated that he was sometimes compelled to be more critical of the
French than he would like, because he would lose credit among his compatriots if he appeared too pro-French. See SLOTFOM, Series III, Carton
3, Report of Governor-general to Ministry of Colonies, Jan. 6, 1925.

against French policies, and the next day demonstrations took place as scheduled.

Inflammatory speeches were given. One speaker demanded an end to governmental tyranny and threatened that if no satisfaction were given, the only answer would be found in Moscow. Nguyen himself made a speech which, in the words of a contemporary French journal, "eclipsed in its violence as in its success all the others." It is you who are responsible for the events that are occurring, he told his audience. Your sufferings are due to you alone, because "you have not been able to impose your ideas, you have not dictated to the government your will." We have been enslaved for seventy years, and no improvements have taken place.

Charging that the collaboration France had offered Vietnam was of the nature of that which occurs between the buffalo and the laborer, he concluded:

Do not place too much hope in the socialist governor-general that has been sent you; he has come to cheat you, he has much to say, but he will give you nothing. There is no collaboration possible between French and Annamites. The French have nothing more to do here. Let them give us back the land of our ancestors, let them give us the floor and let us control ourselves.

Our country has given birth to innumerable heroes, of men who knew how to die for their land. Our race is not yet extinguished.[27]

Not since the glory days of Phan Boi Chau's propaganda tracts from Japan had there been such a voice of resistance in the Vietnamese wilderness. And, of course, the French had to react. They had been informed of Nguyen's desire to hold an inflammatory meeting on the twenty-fourth of March, so on that morning they arrested him, along with Dejean de la Batie and Lam Hiep Chau, editor of *Jeune Annam*.[28] On the same day, the funeral of Phan Chu Trinh took place, and thousands of Vietnamese were out lining the procession route from Saigon to Tan Son Nhut, where he was to be buried. Thousands of others, including members of the only labor union of note in the Saigon area, went to the port of Saigon to greet the Amboise, the ship bringing Bui Quang Chieu back from Paris. Not only Constitutionalists, but members of vari-

27. Garros, p. 241.
28. AOM, Carton 276, Dossier 2429, Report of Governor-general ad interim to Ministry of Colonies, Dec. 22, 1926.

ous other parties were there, and even the reactionary French journalist de la Chevrotière, president of the Colonial Council and
director of *L'Impartial,* came out to organize a counterdemonstration.[29] On his arrival early in the afternoon, Bui Quang Chieu,
who had been mollified while in Paris, made a speech praising
Franco-Vietnamese friendship, and went off to meet privately with
moderate French journalists like Arden of the *Saigon Republicain*
and Sée of *Opinion.* At a reception he did promise to request the
release of Nguyen An Ninh, but it was done without enthusiasm,
and as time went on, he made no move, despite demonstrations in
front of his publishing office. This inspired an open letter from
Dejean de la Batie printed in *Cloche fêlée* asking the Constitutionalist leader why he had tea with French journalists who were encouraging legal action against the three arrested reformists. As
for Bui Quang Chieu's call for Franco-Vietnamese harmony, the
letter concluded with a rhetorical question, how can any collaboration exist between conqueror and conquered?[30]

The crisis of 1926 proved to be evanescent. With Nguyen An
Ninh and his colleagues still in jail, student strikes broke out at
scattered schools around the country, notably in My Tho, at the
Lycée Chasseloup-Laubat in Saigon, and at the Protectorate School
in Hanoi. But there was no response from the mass of the population. Bui Quang Chieu remained silent, and by the end of April,
the crisis of Cochin China was over.

Interregnum

The social unrest of 1925 and 1926 in Cochin China had ended
in frustration for the nationalists. The more discontented elements
around Nguyen An Ninh and the Youth Party were scattered and
only the Constitutionalists remained as a political force. Rather
surprisingly, perhaps, Varenne settled down to a relatively un-
eventful and not overly productive reign as governor-general. He

---

29. According to communist sources, most participants went not to greet
Bui Buang Chieu but to ask for his intercession in the arrest of Nguyen
An Ninh. The French say that the counterdemonstration fomented by de
la Chevrotière created most of the disturbance. See AOM Carton 276, Dossier 2429, Report of Governor-general to Ministry of Colonies, Dec. 22,
1926.

30. *Cloche fêlée,* April 8, 1926.

had, in the words of a nationalist, shown the imperialist wolf under the socialist clothing. Material dealing with this period in the French archives reveals that Varenne was somewhat petulant that the progressives had not appreciated his efforts to help them, and he gradually lost sympathy with their aims. Under his leadership, some quiet changes were instituted, however, which alleviated some of the grosser sources of Vietnamese dissatisfaction. For example, a regional constituent assembly was established in Central Vietnam to match a similar one earlier founded in the North, and the Colonial Council in Cochin China. Like its counterparts, the new assembly had only limited powers and franchise, and was not permitted to discuss political questions. In February 1927, Varenne also granted equality of titles in the French administration—although salaries remained unequal. A few social reforms were initiated, including creation of an office to inspect labor conditions, and rural agricultural credit.[31] A major source of concern was in the realm of education. Most Vietnamese children were still not in school, and the vast majority of villages lacked a school of their own, a source of considerable grumbling among the rural populace. Varenne proposed that each village or group of villages be encouraged to develop its own elementary school. If local financing was not feasible, the government would attempt to provide budgetary assistance. Improvements were also instituted at the university level, the quality of the University of Hanoi was raised, and equivalence of its degree with those of institutions in France was granted.

On the whole, however, the Varenne era was a disappointment to progressives, particularly in the light of the extravagant hopes that had attended his arrival and his early statements about autonomy. In matters of substance, Varenne proved himself to be extremely cautious, especially when it came to granting Vietnamese increased freedom to participate in political affairs.

Discontent with French policies showed up in a number of areas, including Vietnamese exile groups in Paris, where students of varying political persuasions began to entertain hopes in 1925 of a nationalist alliance. In that year members of the Constitutionalist Party in France, including Duong Van Giao, Diep Van

31. *AF,* Jan. 1927, p. 16.

Ky and, for a short period, Bui Quang Chieu, met with more radical elements clustered around Nguyen The Truyen, a Tonkinese who had come to Paris in the early 1920s and soon became involved in radical activities.[32] Meeting in cafés, the Vietnamese called themselves the Association Constitutionaliste Indochinoise and for several months attempted to reach an accord. Disagreements over tactics ran too deep, however, and at the end of 1926 attempts at agreement were abandoned, after radicals began leaving joint meetings in disgust.

After the split, each group went its own way. The radicals, forming their own party in the summer of 1927 (called the Parti Annamite de l'Indépendance, or PAI) continued to struggle for unity among the Vietnamese exile groups in France, and proposed the establishment of a commission composed of prominent members of a number of reformist groups that would be charged with presiding over an evacuation of Indochina by French forces.[33] Receiving no answer from the French authorities (who, according to archival sources, thought it wiser to ignore the suggestion), they continued their political activities. They achieved a degree of influence among exile groups before they were banned by the French government for taking part in political demonstrations in March 1929.[34] As for the Constitutionalists in Paris, their level of activity declined in the late 1920s as some of their more prominent members returned to Vietnam. They ceased to play a role in the nationalist efforts in France.[35]

Within Vietnam, similar problems hindered efforts by nationalist groups to forge an alliance against the colonial authority. In Annam, reform-minded intellectuals attempted to obtain permission for the formation of a political party which would operate in all three areas of Vietnam. In the summer of 1926, meetings were held in Hué and Tourane to discuss a program, and delegates were sent to Hanoi and Saigon to get the advice and support of Pham

32. Nguyen will be discussed in further detail in part III of this work.
33. A copy of the petition, and indications of the French attitude, are found in SLOTFOM, Series III, Carton 39, report of Ministry of Colonies, April 2, 1927.
34. Material on their activities can be found in *ibid*.
35. This decline is reflected in Sûreté Générale reports, which cease to devote attention to them after the mid-1920s.

Quynh and Bui Quang Chieu. Bui Quang Chieu, however, refused to join, allegedly in the belief that the Constitutionalists were more effective alone,[36] and Pham Quynh apparently preferred not to cooperate with any group that had a potentially anti-French orientation.[37] Undismayed, the group held a convention at Tourane in September 1926 in order to draft a program. With forty people in attendance, they called the new party Viet Nam Tan Bo Dan Hoi or the Parti Progressiste du Peuple Annamite (Vietnam People's Rally for Progress). Ultimately, the program came to naught, for Varenne refused to grant official recognition to the party on the grounds that liberty of association had not yet been granted.[38]

The results were predictable. Some of the planners in the abortive party became disgruntled with reformist efforts and turned to revolution; others, like the recently pardoned Huynh Thuc Khang, turned to peaceful pursuits. Huynh himself resorted to journalism and became a member of the consultative assembly in Central Vietnam. Meanwhile, in Cochin China the only existing legal party continued its own activities. Bui Quang Chieu, leader of the Constitutionalists, was briefly piqued at the French and supported a proposed boycott of French goods, but by the late 1920s turned to a policy of Franco-Vietnamese collaboration (a stance accentuated in 1930 when other nationalist groups had turned to violence) and settled down to day-to-day concerns such as attempting to dominate the Colonial Council.[39] Nguyen An Ninh, released from prison in 1927, soon returned to politics after a brief bout with Buddhism in his home village, and attempted to round up supporters for a party in the rural villages around Saigon. He also travelled to Paris and discussed cooperation with leaders of the PAI. In late 1928, however, he was arrested after an altercation with the authorities in Cochin China and his inchoate party disintegrated.[40]

36. Gouvernement-Générale de l'Indochine (Direction des Affaires Politiques et de la Sûreté Générale), *Contribution à l'histoire des mouvements politiques de l'Indochine Française*, 6 vols. (Hanoi, 1930–1933), I, 17–18, hereafter cited as *Contribution*.

37. Frederick, pp. 145–146.

38. Philippe Devillers, *Histoire du Viet Nam* (Paris, 1952), p. 44.

39. *Tribune indochinoise*, Nov. 10, 1926, discusses the boycott.

40. According to Jean Dorsenne, *Faudra-t'il évacuer l'Indochine?* (Paris, 1932), his party had seven hundred to eight hundred members at the time of his arrest in 1928; see p. 63. He was arrested in October on the charge

In summary, the Varenne years, after the crisis of 1926, lapsed into a period of relative tranquillity and political quiescence. Political radicals were either quelled, in jail, or were working quietly beneath the surface of daily life. The moderates were still in evidence but posed no threat to French rule. As one frustrated nationalist of the day cried out: "Have we all forgotten Phan Chu Trinh?"

---

of assaulting a local militiaman and was sentenced to three years for clandestine activities. See AOM Carton 327, Dossier 2644, telegrams of Dec. 22, 1928, Jan. 11, 1929, and April 15, 1929. Details on his activities can be found in SLOTFOM, Series III, Carton 48, dossier enclosing report entitled "Les Associations anti-Françaises en Indochine et la propagande communiste: Historique," pp. 20–21.

Chapter 8

The Turn to Radicalism

As the French authorities were soon to find out, Phan Chu
Trinh and the spirit of resistance had not been forgotten. Forces
were still covertly at work undermining the colonial apparatus.
Resentful young nationalists, disillusioned by the meager results of
the Varenne years, began to turn to more radical solutions, and to
political organizations that were less hesitant to use insurrectionary
tactics as a means of obtaining independence.

First of these covert organizations to be formed was a political
party which was formed in Annam in the mid-1920s and was
known variously as the Tan Viet Cach Menh Dang, the Phuc Viet,
the Hung Nam, the Viet Nam Cach Menh Dang, and the Viet
Nam Cach Mang Dong Chi Hoi.[1] There is some disagreement
about the origins of the group, but it appears likely that members
were students from the Cao Dang Su Pham Ha Noi (Hanoi
Higher Normal School), or returned political prisoners from Con
Lon island.[2] Composed of both moderates and radicals, the new
party immediately became involved in late 1925 in a movement all
could agree upon: it demanded the release of Phan Boi Chau
after his arrest in Shanghai in the summer. During the hectic days
of fall the party members held meetings, distributed tracts, and appealed for mass demonstrations. Because the party became well
known to the French through its handbills, it was forced to change
its name from Phuc Viet to Hung Nam (Revive the South). At

1. For the sake of convenience, this party will be called the Revolutionary Party throughout this study.
2. For opposing views, see *Contribution*, I, 1–13; *Giai Cap*, pp. 397–398.
Apparently the genesis of the party was among prisoners at Con Lon and
intellectuals such as Ton Quang Phiet and Dong Thai Mai in Hanoi.

the same time, moderates within the party also began to pressure for a more moderate program of activities. Reformist elements around Le Huan and Tran Mong Bach were able to achieve consensus that independence was to be achieved by peaceful means if at all possible. Violence would be used only as a last resort. There was a vague commitment to communism, but it was assumed that Vietnam would not adopt a communist form of society until it was adopted by the Great Powers as well. Emphasis was on moral improvement, family reform, opposition to superstition and vice, and the development of commerce, industry and agriculture.[3]

Nguyen Thai Hoc and the VNQDD

A more important new party in the nationalist movement was the Viet Nam Quoc Dan Dang (Vietnamese Nationalist Party, or VNQDD). The VNQDD was a product of the post-scholar-patriot generation. In late 1925, a small group of intellectuals in Hanoi, led by a teacher named Pham Tuan Tai and his brother Phan Tuan Lam, formed a small publishing house, the Nam Dong Thu Xa (Southeast Asia Publishing House) with the dual aim of achieving commercial success and promoting revolution.[4] In the beginning, the organization concentrated on editing books and brochures on the Chinese revolution and forming a free school to teach quoc-ngu to workers. Soon it began to attract the support of other progressive youth in Tonkin, including a group of students and school teachers led by Nguyen Thai Hoc, a former student at the Commercial School in Hanoi who had lost his scholarship, allegedly because of poor grades.[5]

Born of a peasant family in Vinh Yen province in 1904, Nguyen Thai Hoc had earlier been inclined toward moderate reform, and in 1925 had written a letter to Varenne suggesting reforms in labor and commerce and the establishment of an industrial school in

---

3. Details can be found in *Contribution*, V, 12–13. Cleavages over strategy and doctrine were never resolved, leading to a permanent split personality in the party.

4. Materials on the formation of the VNQDD can be found in *TLTK*, vol. V.

5. Hoang Van Dao, *Viet Nam Quoc Dan Dang* (Saigon, 1970), pp. 26–29.

Hanoi. He had not received a reply, however, and in June 1927 he sent a petition to the resident superior of Tonkin asking permission to publish a monthly magazine with the aim of raising the educational level of the population and building its interest in commerce and industry. Once again, his request was not approved. Disillusioned with the possibilities of peaceful change, Nguyen Thai Hoc turned to the idea of armed revolt.

Because of harassment by French authorities, and censorship of its publications, the Nam Dong Thu Xa failed commercially, and in the fall of 1927 it become more politically minded. By making contact with other radical elements in Tonkin, the Nam Dong Thu Xa group began to add members. It managed to form eighteen cells in fourteen provinces throughout North and Central Vietnam, with a total of two hundred members.[6]

Late in December of 1927, a plenary meeting was held in Hanoi to establish a new revolutionary organization, the Viet Nam Quoc Dan Dang. There was considerable discussion of the general aims of the party; many wanted to combine the goal of establishing a democratic republic with promoting world revolution. Others were suspicious of the communist implications of such a program and felt that the aim of the party should be restricted to national independence. The final statement was a compromise: "the aim and general line of the party is to make a national revolution, to use military force to overthrow the feudal colonial system, to set up a democratic republic of Vietnam. At the same time we will help all oppressed nationalities in the work of struggling to achieve independence, in particular such neighboring countries as Laos and Cambodia."[7] Regulations on party organization, which resembled that of the Kuomintang in China, provided for several administrative levels from the basic unit, the cell, up through province, regional and central committees. The new party's strategy was patterned after that of Sun Yat-sen: first there would be a military takeover, then a period of political tutelage, and, finally a constitutional government.

With the party officially established, its members began in earnest to seek support from the general population and assistance

6. TLTK, V, 32–33.
7. *Contribution*, V, annex I.

from abroad. The new organization concentrated its activities among students, minor government employees, soldiers, urban petit bourgeoisie and women. There were few worker or peasant members. The VNQDD also began fashioning alliances with other nationalist factions in Vietnam. In a meeting of July 4, 1928, the Central Committee appealed for the unity of all revolutionary groups in Vietnam, and delegates were sent to talk with representatives of the two major existing revolutionary parties, the Revolutionary Party and the League, as well as with smaller groups such as the party of Nguyen An Ninh in Saigon.[8] Some contacts were made with all groups, but no concrete alliance resulted.

In the meantime, money problems were plaguing the new organization, and to raise funds the leadership decided to arrange for the establishment of a commercial enterprise which could at the same time serve as a headquarters for party members to meet and discuss revolutionary activities. Thus, in September 1928 a hotel-restaurant, the Vietnam Hotel, was opened. The French were aware of its real purposes and put it under observation, but took no immediate action. At the same time, the party underwent its first major reorganization. In December 1928, a new executive committee was elected, with Nguyen Khac Nhu replacing Nguyen Thai Hoc as chairman. Also, three new protogovernmental organs were created (legislative, executive, and judicial), and these became an embryonic government. In size and complexity the party was growing. According to estimates of the French secret service, by early 1929 the VNQDD consisted of one thousand five hundred members in one hundred twenty cells, mostly in provinces around the Red River Delta. Most of the members were students, petty merchants, and low-level bureaucrats; some were landlords and rich peasants. Few had scholar-gentry backgrounds.[9]

Alongside the VNQDD and the Revolutionary Party arose the first wholly Marxist organization in Vietnam, the Revolutionary Youth League. Like the Revolutionary Party and the VNQDD, it was an outgrowth of the rising nationalist sentiment in post-World War I Vietnam and drew its early support from frustrated urban intellectuals. Because of its importance and its distinctive character

8. *TLTK*, V, 40.
9. *Ibid.*, V, 38.

within the nationalist movement, it is treated separately in Part III of this work.

The Yen Bay Revolt

The gathering waves of resentment in Vietnam would ultimately break over Varenne's successor as governor-general, Pierre Pasquier. In November 1927, Governor-general Varenne left Indochina for France and resigned his post. He was succeeded a few months later by Pasquier, an old colonial hand, a former resident superior of Annam, and a writer who had demonstrated his familiarity with Vietnam in his well-known book *L'Annam d'autrefois,* which had earned praise from Pham Quynh. Pasquier prided himself on his pragmatism, and under his regime the old meaningless slogans of assimilation and association were replaced by a new "politique d'adaptation," by which the Vietnamese would be treated in accordance with the maturity of their own behavior.[10] It was also part of his self-image that he combined firmness with magnanimity, and he expressed himself willing to consider broadening Vietnamese participation in the political life of the country, in particular by presiding over the creation of a new Grand Conseil des Interêts Financiers et Economiques de l'Indochine. (Of the fifty-one elected members of the council, which held advisory powers in the area of budget and economics, twenty-three were Vietnamese.) He also issued directives aimed at reforming and strengthening the mandarinate, in order to arrest the decline in authority and quality of Vietnamese public officials and the corresponding rise in power of French provincial residents. At the same time, he made clear that French sovereignty in Indochina was not negotiable, and that the direction of Indochina should not be toward independence, but toward a confederation of Indochina under a French protectorate, with direct administration only in primitive areas.[11]

Such modest promises were hardly calculated to disarm some of the more perceptive critics of French rule, however. As even relatively detached French visitors were able to discern, the reality of French rule was far from idyllic. Jean Dorsenne, author of *Faudra-*

10. Pham The Ngu, *Lich Su Van Hoc Viet Nam* [A History of Vietnamese Literature] (Saigon, 1961), p. 162.
11. *AF,* Oct. 1928, pp. 316–317.

t'il évacuer l'Indochine? and a relatively sympathetic observer of the French system (Nguyen Phan Long commented that a book with a brutal title had come to singularly modest conclusions), pointed out that "we may talk of collaboration, but the word corresponds poorly to reality."[12] Press freedom was severely limited, liberty of assembly and association nonexistent, and the regime reeked of a heavy-handed authoritarianism. What was more, punitive regulations were compounded by the outright contempt displayed by many French colonialists for Vietnamese of all classes. Even after Pasquier prohibited the French custom of addressing Vietnamese by the familiar form in French (thus treating them as inferiors or as children), the practice was still employed regularly by nearly all of the French population. As for French observance of the protectorate, former Governor-general Varenne stated in France that the government, "despite treaties, thinks it necessary to assume almost all charge of public affairs in Indochina, reducing the indigenous adminstration to a humiliating and subordinate role." Traditional authority was flouted or ignored. As Bui Quang Chieu put it, Vietnamese mandarins were just clothes hangers for multicolored robes, the emperor simply a "mannequin doré."[13]

In the economy, too, major problems existed: the government monopolies in opium, salt, and alcohol irritated the local population because they combined financial hardship with social injustice; the practice of labor recruitment continued to arouse complaints despite half-hearted government attempts to mitigate its more brutal manifestations; high taxes were resented, particularly the capitation tax which hit the poor the hardest; and, for the workers, long hours, low wages, and poor working conditions were causes of dissatisfaction. The coming of the Great Depression at the end of the decade only exacerbated the national malaise. To general discontent was now added the impetus of worsening economic conditions. Middle-class interests were affected as many local firms were driven into bankruptcy. Rice farmers were hurt by a catastrophic fall in the price of rice. The incidence of hunger began to rise, particularly in the traditionally poor areas of Annam, and led to the danger of peasant revolt. In the big cities, economic doldrums led to falling salaries and rising unemployment.

12. Jean Dorsenne, *Faudra-t'il évacuer l'Indochine?* (Paris, 1932), p. 36.
13. *Tribune indochinoise*, Sept. 23, 1930.

An isolated event in Hanoi in early 1929 set in motion circumstances that would destroy the growing influence of the VNQDD
in Tonkin. In February of that year a Frenchman by the name of
Bazin was assassinated on a street in Hanoi. Bazin, a graduate of
the Ecole Coloniale in Paris, was a supervisor of labor recruitment
in Indochina. Under his direction, Vietnamese foremen were hired
to recruit laborers to work on plantations. In some cases, the hired
labor would be utilized in rubber or tea plantations in Cochin
China, while in others the laborers were sent off to distant French
colonies such as the New Hebrides. The conditions surrounding
this employment had become scandalous—at least among the Vietnamese who were victims of the process. Often the methods of
recruitment were accompanied by unnecessary brutality, with
peasants being beaten or coerced into joining (foremen received a
commission for each recruit). Conditions on the plantations were
notoriously bad, and pay was low. The Vietnamese believed that
those recruited never returned home again.[14] The government refused to take action, claiming on the one hand that recruitment
"had no official character" and on the other that recruitment was
beneficial, since it redistributed the population and alleviated pressure in the crowded delta areas of North Vietnam.

In desperation, a group of workers approached the VNQDD
leadership to suggest the assassination of Bazin in an attempt to
strike back at those responsible, but Nguyen Thai Hoc felt that
terrorism achieved nothing, that it would only result in the seizure
of party members by the French Sûreté Générale, and thus weaken
the party. Far better, he felt, to concentrate on overthrowing the
French colonial regime itself. Bazin, he opined, is just a twig; the
tree must be cut down, and then the twig itself would wither and
die. Turned down by the VNQDD leadership, one of the instigators of the plan, who may or may not have been a party member,
drew up a plan of his own and with the help of an accomplice shot
and killed Bazin outside the home of his mistress on February 9,
1929.[15]

The French authorities reacted by rounding up all the VNQDDs
they could find, including a young naturalized Frenchman by the

14. See Paul Monet's *Les Jauniers* (Paris, 1930).
15. *TLTK*, V, 49; Hoang Van Dao, pp. 51–58; SLOTFOM, Series III,
Carton 39, Case III, Dossier 2, telegram of Feb. 10, 1929.

name of Leon Sanh, who confessed to the crime. Sanh later retracted his original confession, and claimed to have been only a bystander. He did implicate an alleged accomplice, Nguyen Van Vien, who was captured and later died in prison. Out of three or four hundred arrested, seventy-eight were finally convicted by a tribunal and given sentences of from five to twenty years in prison.[16] Leon Sanh was acquitted.[17] As a result of the arrests, the VNQDD leadership was badly hurt. Most of the Central Committee was captured, and Nguyen Thai Hoc and Nguyen Khac Nhu were among the few who were able to escape from their hideout at the Vietnam Hotel without being seized. With the decimation of the party, those VNQDD leaders still at large became increasingly desperate.

An opposition group led by Ngugen The Nghiep had refused since early 1929 to follow party directives, and had been driven from the Central Committee. As a result, according to some sources, Nguyen The Nghiep's group had established its own party and made secret contacts with the French.[18] Disturbed by the problem of traitors who had betrayed party members after the Bazin affair, Nguyen Thai Hoc convened a meeting at the village of Lac Dao along the Haiphong-Gia Lam railway in the summer of 1929 to establish tightened regulations, which essentially were copied from those of the Revolutionary Youth League.[19] At the same meeting another break over strategy occurred, when Nguyen Thai Hoc, citing the rising discontent of Vietnamese troops in the French colonial army, called for a general uprising as soon as possible. Moderates such as Le Huu Canh and Tran Van Huan disagreed and felt that a revolt was premature. Nguyen Thai Hoc's prestige carried the meeting, however, and the party entered into a period of preparation for violent struggle. The plan was to provoke a

16. The various sources consulted give different figures on the total number arrested, but the total convicted was apparently between seventy and eighty. Of those seized, 36 were government clerks, 13 were officials in the French government, 36 were teachers, 39 were merchants, 37 were landlords, and 40 were military men.

17. French sources eventually decided that the crime was related to rivalry between groups involved in recruiting coolies for work on plantations. See SLOTFOM, Series III, Carton 39, Case III, Dossier 2, telegrams of Feb. 16 and 25, 1929.

18. *TLTK*, V, 46.

19. *Contribution*, II, annex 2, has the regulations.

series of uprisings at military posts scattered around the Red River Delta in early 1930, with partisan VNQDD forces joining in from the outside in an attack on the major cities of Hanoi and Haiphong. Uprisings would necessarily be limited to Tonkin because the party was weak elsewhere.[20]

During the remainder of 1929, the party concentrated on preparations for revolt; they located and manufactured weapons and hid them in clandestine depots. But planning was hindered by the activity of the French police, in particular its confiscation of hidden weapons. On January 28, 1930, a final meeting was held in the village of Vong La in Phu Tho province, where Nguyen Thai Hoc declared that the situation was becoming desperate, and asserted that if the party did not act immediately, its forces would be scattered. Whipped up into a peak of enthusiasm, the majority at the meeting went along, and the reluctant were coerced into approval. The uprising was set for the night of 9 February. Nguyen Thai Hoc was given the lower delta provinces around Haipong, Nguyen Khac Nhu was assigned the upper delta around Yen Bay, and Pho Duc Chinh would attack the military post at Son Tay. Nguyen The Nghiep, who had retreated beyond the border to Yunnan, said that he had the support of local soldiers at Lao Cay garrison and would strike at French posts along the border.

The uprisings were supposed to take place simultaneously, but at the last minute Nguyen Thai Hoc sent a request to Nguyen Khac Nhu to postpone action until the fifteenth. Unfortunately for the rebels, the messenger was apparently arrested, and Nguyen Khac Nhu was unaware of the change in plans.

Yen Bay was a military post consisting of over six hundred troops in four companies of infantry, commanded by twenty French officers and noncommissioned officers. VNQDD members had been promoting revolutionary feeling in the area for several months, and on the night of 9 February there was much tension in the camp town.[21] A number of revolutionaries had come to town that day with weapons in their baggage. The local French commander Le Tacon had been informed of suspicious circum-

20. Many of the discussions among the leaders are recollected in Hoang Van Dao, pp. 89–92.
21. AOM Carton 323, Dossier 2626, report by resident superior of March 9, 1930.

stances. Though he gave them no credence he did take minor precautions. At nightfall, the conspirators held a last-minute meeting on a nearby hill. Among the forty who attended some were frightened and wanted to postpone action, but zealots drew their guns and threatened to shoot anyone who attempted to back down. The uprising was to begin inside the camp at 1:00 A.M. Rebel forces were to divide into three groups—one to infiltrate the infantry, kill French NCOs in their beds and raise support among the indigenous troops; a second group including partisans from the outside and rebel infantry was to fight its way into the post headquarters, while a third detachment would enter the officers' compound.

Fighting broke out on schedule and sixty rebels broke into the French headquarters area. As it turned out, however, many of the local troops were reluctant to follow the partisans and ran instead to the headquarters where they gave support to the French and prevented its fall.[22] Other areas were seized during the night, and a few French soldiers were killed, but the French struck back and seized some participants, while the others fled. By 9:00 A.M. order had been restored. On the same night, other key targets in the delta area erupted as VNQDD units under Nguyen Khac Nhu took action at Hung Hoa and Lam Thao in Phu Tho province. Nguyen was scheduled to lead the attack on Hung Hoa, but when he observed how lightly armed and ill prepared his troops were he retreated without inflicting casualties.[23] At Lam Thao, local French units took no offensive action. Retreating from Hung Hoa, Nguyen Khac Nhu's forces helped secure the post, but the French arrived shortly thereafter and captured many of the partisans, including Nguyen who committed suicide. Appraised of these events in the upper delta, Pho Duc Chinh abandoned plans for an attack on Son Tay garrison and fled, but he was taken a few day later.[24]

Five days after Yen Bay, one final outbreak occurred—the seizure of the district of Vinh Bao in Hai Duong province, in preparation for an attack on Haiphong. The sub-prefect there was detested

22. *Ibid.* Perhaps one reason for the failure to achieve support among the soldiery was that the local leader Quang Can became ill and was sent to a hospital in Hanoi. When he heard the results of the attack at Yen Bay, he committed suicide.

23. Hoang Van Dao, p. 114.

24. *TLTK*, V, 76; AOM Carton 323, Dossier 2626, report of March 9, 1930.

by the local citizenry, who were zealous in support of the revolutionary cause. News of the Yen Bay defeat had reached the area, but was garbled, so attacks opened in the village of Co Am, where the planning had taken place, and the partisans headed toward the capital of Vinh Bao district. The sub-prefect Hoang Gia Mo went to Co Am to observe the situation and was seized (while hiding in a haystack) and executed. The government responded by bombing Co Am village on the sixteenth and the partisans fled in disorder.[25] On the twentieth Nguyen Thai Hoc himself was arrested.

The failure of the Yen Bay mutiny was a disastrous and nearly fatal blow to the VNQDD. Almost all the top leaders were in prison, and most were executed in mid-June. Before his own execution, Nguyen Thai Hoc made a last plea to the French in the form of a letter to the authorities, claiming that he had always wanted to cooperate, but that French obstinance had forced him to turn to revolt. If you want to stay in Indochina, he contended, you must abandon your brutal policies and become our friends, give us the basic liberties—universal education, and training in commerce and industry—and end the corrupt habits of the local mandarins.[26] In the aftermath of defeat, the moderate Le Huu Canh, who had unsuccessfully attempted to postpone the Yen Bay uprising, tried to reunite the party under the banner of peaceful reform as the *trung lap* (neutralist) faction. Other remnants carried on the work of Nguyen Thai Hoc and reformed the organization in the Hanoi-Haiphong area. After an unsuccessful attempt on the life of Governor-general Pasquier, however, they were suppressed in 1931 and 1932. The survivors fled to Yunnan in South China, where other elements under Nguyen The Nghiep were still active.

Nguyen had been briefly imprisoned by Chinese authorities in Yunnan province, but had continued to direct the local VNQDD group from prison. When he was released in 1933, he arranged a consolidation of his party and other groups in the area, including a few followers of Phan Boi Chau who had formed their own

25. AOM Carton 322, Dossier 2614, has the telegrams reporting the incident to Paris.

26. Louis Roubaud, *Vietnam: La Tragédie indochinoise* (Paris, 1931), pp. 147–148.

Canton-based Viet Nam Quoc Dan Dang. In July 1933, this party fused with Nguyen The Nghiep's organization in Yunnan.[27] In 1935, Nguyen The Nghiep surrendered to the French consul in Shanghai.[28] The remaining elements in the VNQDD, afflicted with factionalism, were only moderately active in the 1930s, attempting to organize workers along the Yunnan railroad, and threatening occasionally to make border attacks. They were not effective, and were closely watched by Yunnan warlord Lung Yun. For all practical purposes, the VNQDD ceased to exist as a potent political force from the Yen Bay disaster until World War II.

In a sense, the VNQDD can be seen as a transitional stage between the Phan Boi Chau style of anticolonial resistance and the relatively modern nationalism of the 1930s. Members of the VNQDD were often the products of French schools, and sons of peasant families. School teachers, government clerks, and petty merchants, they were a distinctly post-Confucian generation, with few of the intellectual inhibitions that affected earlier movements. Yet, significantly, they suffered from some of the same limitations that had hampered Phan Boi Chau's generation—an inability to avoid that dangerous taint of reckless impetuosity that was so characteristic of early nationalism in Vietnam, a lack of understanding of how to involve the masses in the struggle for independence, and an insufficient realization of the economic basis of discontent in Vietnam. Although the VNQDD leaders were certainly more conscious of socialism than earlier revolutionaries, and although they attempted to pattern themselves after Sun's movement in China, they did not seem to be interested in adapting his theories of land revolution to Vietnam, and they made no attempt to work among the peasantry. Consequently, the VNQDD remained essentially a movement of urban intellectuals, with some support coming from Vietnamese troops in the French army, but little from the countryside. If in some respects they were more modern than Phan's party, they were no more effective.

27. Information on post-1930 activities of the VNQDD is contained in the monthly reports of the Sûreté Générale in SLOTFOM, Series III, Carton 48, 1930–1936.
28. AOM Carton 329, Dossier 2659, report of July 1935.

Chapter 9

The Reynaud Visit

The reaction of the moderates to the uprising at Yen Bay was ambivalent. The Constitutionalists in Cochin China, for example, were not in favor of violence (indeed, they rejected it under any conceivable circumstances) and Bui Quang Chieu vociferously denied French colonialist de la Chevrotière's charge that the Constitutionalist Party had supported the VNQDD uprising.[1] At the same time, many of the moderates were irritated by the French attitude and, specifically, by the ruthless French reaction to Yen Bay, which included widespread and arbitrary arrests, and the bombing of the village of Co Am. Obviously, the Francophiles were anxious to make common cause with the French, but they found French policies difficult to defend. Bui Quang Chieu complained publicly that claims in the French press that "Bolshevism" was behind the events of 1930 were unwarranted and said that the real problem was "a moral repression that no dignified people could accept." Conceding the fact that Vietnam was prosperous (he must have been thinking about himself), he complained about the "lack of simple rights, the harsh treatment, the violations of individual liberties. . . . You have the duty to maintain public order," he concluded, "but this doesn't imply the right to spill the blood of innocents to achieve revenge on the guilty."[2] In mid-June of 1931, Bui began demanding governmental and social reforms in the *Tribune indochinoise,* the newspaper which had replaced *Tribune indigène* after his return from Paris in 1926. He complained that the French idea of progress was to repeat "marchons, marchons" while walking around in circles.

1. *Tribune indochinoise,* Sept. 23, 1930.
2. *Tribune indochinoise,* Feb. 14, 1930.

The government finally responded in late 1931. After a long period of hesitation, during which left-wing members of parliament in Paris argued unsuccessfully for the creation of a Commission of Inquiry to look into conditions in Indochina, Minister of Colonies Paul Reynaud finally agreed in the summer of 1931 to visit Indochina on an inspection trip. Upon his arrival in mid-October, the minister was met by a virtual cacophony of demands for reform from the various sectors of the progressive community. On the right, Duong Ba Trac, in a letter to Reynaud in *Nam Phong*, demanded that the French firmly suppress youth activities and revolutionary groups and introduce some men of real talent (presumably himself) to cooperate with France.[3] From the pages of his own newspaper *Annam nouveau*, Nguyen Van Vinh called for the dismantling of the protectorate system and the institution of direct rule throughout Indochina by the French. Huynh Thuc Khang, graduate of Con Lon prison and now editor of the moderate progressive journal *Tieng Dan* in Hué, wrote a letter praising French contributions to the modernization of Vietnam, but complained about the "incomprehension of the government toward the profound changes that are so silently taking place in the domain of the intellect, changes which the transformation of our material existence have rendered inevitable."[4] Huynh compared Vietnam to a sick man whose disease is in his internal organs, and asserted that any medicine treating only the exterior symptoms would fail.

The most prominent of the petitions to the minister, however, came from the pens of Bui Quang Chieu in Saigon and Pham Quynh in Hanoi. In a long speech of welcome to the minister at a banquet in Saigon, Bui issued a new list of minimum demands— the famous "cahier des voeux Annamites"—demands for administrative reform and social improvements that the Constitutionalists had been making for years.[5]

The message from Pham Quynh in Hanoi, not surprisingly, was somewhat different. Now assistant professor of Chinese and Vietnamese language and literature at a French lycée in Hanoi, and a member of the Grand Conseil, Pham in his own open letter to

3. *Nam Phong*, no. 67 (Nov. 1931).
4. *Tribune indochinoise*, Nov. 20, 1931.
5. The list is reminiscent of the earlier cahier of 1925. See *Tribune indochinoise*, Oct. 21 to 26, 1931.

Reynaud focused on the restoration of monarchial powers and the need for national identity.[6] The problem, in his view, was not simply one of equal representation, or more schools, or equal pay for equal work. The problem, rather, was one of permitting the Vietnamese to live their own national life, and to develop their own cultural personality. Conceding that Vietnam was "indissolubly tied to France" and the Vietnamese "do not complain of our condition," he added that under the beneficent rule of France the personality and the national sentiment of Vietnam had begun to revive and to become "une idée force"; the confrontation of this idea with the reality of French control had created "an indefinable malaise." The problem with Vietnam, according to Pham, was that she was suffering from a personality crisis as much national as individual: "We are a people who are searching for a country but haven't found it." That country, he assured the minister, could not be France, because the Vietnamese already have a country of their own.

What Pham Quynh went on to demand was a political constitution that would permit the Vietnamese "to develop their own personality as a nation and to assure them a national life dignified of the name within the body of the French empire." By granting this, France could become the eternal benefactor of the Vietnamese people. What Vietnam desired was a national constitution to permit it to integrate into a French Union—a Vietnamese monarchy with a constitution in a federal Indochina. Pham Quynh pointed out that Reynaud's predecessor as Minster of Colonies, Pietri, had already indicated a willingness to establish a modern adaptation of the 1884 treaty of protectorate between the French and the Vietnamese emperor in order to satisfy national aspirations. As Pham Quynh envisaged it, the young monarch Bao Dai could become Vietnam's first modern king—advised by the French, but given considerable powers to govern his own kingdom.

Minister Reynaud was not unaware of the dilemma that faced the French in Indochina. At base, the Vietnamese elites wanted independence above all, and it was only because the alternatives were anarchy or conquest by another acquisitive power that they were

6. Pham Quynh, "Letter ouverte á son Excellence le Ministre des Colonies," p. 3, in *Nam Phong*, no. 166 (Oct. 1931).

willing to tolerate the necessity of French rule. Yet it was difficult for France to exploit that sentiment, because, as the Morché commission (established in 1931 to investigate conditions in Vietnam) had concluded in its report: "The French love the country [Vietnam] more for the material advantages that they find there than for itself." In Reynaud's estimation, the government had to establish a policy that would satisfy the demands of French and Vietnamese elites, and that would be beneficial to the mass of the population.[7]

Reynaud was thus inclined to give serious consideration to the reform proposals of Bui Quang Chieu and Pham Quynh, for some reforms were clearly necessary. In a formal speech on 13 November he promised a series of reforms conforming in many respects to Bui Quang Chieu's "cahier des voeux Annamites": he agreed in principle to the concept of equality of representation and promised to meet it wherever possible; he agreed to provide for a permanent representative from Vietnam to the Conseil Superieur des Colonies in Paris; he promised educational reforms, an end to the alcohol monopoly, and revisions in monopolies of salt and opium.[8]

To Pham Quynh, he sent an indirect message. In a speech in Hanoi in early November, he stated publicly that a "marriage of the two civilizations" was the best possible solution to the problem of synthesizing French and Vietnamese cultural traditions, and on 1 November he told the Council of Ministers in Hué that he would permit the return of Emperor Bao Dai to Vietnam and that he would support the restoration of the principles of 1884 in Central Vietnam.[9]

Upon his return to Paris, Reynaud put the machinery of reform in motion, calling for, in addition to the points listed above, a reduction of the rice export tax, an extension of the long-term agricultural credit arrangements, an abrogation of imprisonment for debt, and reforms in the mandarinate. In effect, as he put it, he

7. See the report written at the end of his visit in AOM, Carton 54, Dossier 635, p. 7.

8. *Tribune indochinoise,* Nov. 13, 1931.

9. Tran Huy Lieu, *Lich Su Tam Muoi Nam Chong Phap* [A History of 80 Years of Resistance to the French] (Hanoi, 1958), II, 100. Hereafter this source will be referred to as *Lich Su.*

would follow a "politique d'égards" toward the people of Vietnam. Much of his program seemed patently designed to placate Bui Quang Chieu and Pham Quynh. In one area, however, he instituted fewer changes than they would have desired. As had Governor-general Pasquier and others, Minister Reynaud felt that there were too many intellectuals in Vietnam, and that emphasis on education should be concentrated at the primary level. However, in response to complaints from Vietnamese parents that too much French lan-gauge and too little traditional morality was taught in the Franco-Vietnamese school system, he placed greater emphasis on quoc-ngu and on Vietnamese tradition in the curriculum.[10]

If Minister Reynaud did flout Bui Quang Chieu's advice in specific areas, he was apparently going in the right general direction. Before Bui left for Paris to become the new Cochin Chinese representative to the Conseil Superieur, he remarked that the de-mands that the Constitutionalist Party had been making since 1917 were finally beginning to come true.[11]

The Return of Bao Dai

Paris also began to make tentative moves in the direction of reviving the monarchy in response to Pham Quynh's insistent proddings. The question of imperial authority stemmed from the original Treaty of Protectorate of 1884 by which the French had taken over some of the authority of the emperor in Central and North Vietnam. A parallel structure of administrative authority had been established, with French residents in an advisory capacity to assist indigenous province chiefs in the outlying areas, and ad-visors in the ministries to counsel the cabinet officials. At the top, a French resident superior presided over the old imperial council and advised the emperor. In time the royal authority and that of the mandarins began to decay. First the position of imperial repre-sentative in Tonkin was abandoned and his great powers were given to the French resident superior. Then, up and down the administrative hierarchy, the French began to take over major

10. For some of these complaints, see AOM Carton 332, Dossier 2684, report of De Letie, June 10, 1931; also see Resident Superior Le Fol's comments in AOM Carton 332, Dossier 2684, report of June 6–10, 1931.

11. *Tribune indochinoise,* April 29, 1932.

decision-making powers, the emperor and his bureaucracy becoming increasingly irrelevant.

The weakness of the imperial authority was magnified in 1925 when Emperor Khai Dinh died and was succeeded by the twelve-year-old Bao Dai, who was then studying in Paris. There were demands in some anticourt circles for the French to institute direct colonial rule over Central Vietnam, since the more directly controlled areas, Tonkin and Cochin China, were more advanced in a number of respects than Annam, the area still under court supervision.[12]

The French, however, preferred to maintain the emperor as the symbol of Vietnamese authority in Annam while holding the substance of power. In a new agreement between the French and the court, called the Convention of 1925, the few powers the emperor in Annam had retained were stripped from him and given to the local French resident superior. All that rested in the hands of the emperor were ritual duties and other minor formalities. As the new statute stated: "(1) only rules concerning rituals and the constitutional rules of the empire will be the subject of imperial decrees. Direct intervention of the sovereign is limited to the exercise of the right of grace and the attribution of posthumous honors, etc. All other questions relating to justice and the administration of the empire, the organization of service, and the appointment of Vietnamese functionaries will be handled by the Protectorate, (2) civil and military administration expenses of the government of Annam will be incorporated into the general budget of Annam, (3) the Council of Ministers will be presided over by the Resident Superior."[13] If the emperors before 1925 had been scarecrows, now even the straw had been picked clean.

During the adolescence of Emperor Bao Dai, little was done to alter the status quo, and Bao Dai continued his education in France.[14] By 1930, however, Pham Quynh was beginning to agitate for the formal restoration of the 1884 treaty and for the

---

12. For examples, see *AF,* Dec. 1926, p. 378.
13. AF, Jan. 1926, p. 41.
14. At that point, Bao Dai wanted to continue his studies in Paris until 1932, so the French decided to maintain the 1925 regulations until his return. See AOM Carton 332, Dossier 2684, report of Le Fol, June 6–10, 1931.

restoration to Bao Dai of his legal authority. In a series of famous articles entitled "Vers une Constitution" he repeated his proposals for the establishment of a constitutional monarchy. Labeling the present situation "a bastard regime which satisfies no one" he asked that the government either establish a true protectorate or impose direct rule. Some Vietnamese, he conceded, would prefer direct administration, since it is already that way in practice in much of Indochina. But, he asked rhetorically, does France really want to make Vietnam an integral part of France, or would it prefer the formation of an autonomous Annamite nation within the French empire? Assimilation, in other words, or true association? Assimilation, he contended, ran counter to good sense. Cochin China was a colony, of course, but that was a special case, a Vietnamese frontier area, and such a system would never succeed elsewhere.

A true protectorate, on the other hand, would be legal, it would suit Vietnamese aspirations as well as satisfy French requirements, and it would not overthrow existing institutions like the court and the mandarinate, but would simply reform and modernize them. He admitted that these institutions as now constituted were unpopular and corrupt. But it was the abuses, not the institutions in themselves, that were the problem, and if the monarchy could be solidly based on the 1884 treaty, with the Protectorate government having only limited advisory powers, and with the emperor retaining considerable executive power, and assisted by the Council of Ministers responsible to him as well as to an assembly and to the Protectorate, the system might be effective. The people would have limited democratic rights through a single-chamber parliament based on limited suffrage (depending on the evolution of society). The parliament would have the power to initiate laws, but final decisions would be made by a council of state composed of French and Vietnamese specialists. French interests would be represented by a resident superior in Hué and a representative in Hanoi. As the 1884 Treaty specified, the resident superior could demand the dissolution of the parliament in case of disagreement with the government, with Paris as the court of final appeal. The mandarinate itself would be reorganized, and furnished with French advisers. In the field of education, he suggested that secondary education and higher education remain a French responsibility, but that elementary education should be placed in Vietnamese hands, and should emphasize nationality and morality, based on the ancient traditions and those Western ideas which favored the development of individual dignity. Universal education would be the goal, but with a practical bias.[15]

Reaction to Pham Quynh's proposal in the nationalist community was generally unfavorable. One newspaper opined that "in our opinion, it is better to let the administration of the Protectorate preside over our destinies. A very bad French bureaucrat is better than a very good Annamite mandarin." Nguyen Van Vinh, now editor of the Tonkinese newspaper *Annam nouveau,* waged a frontal attack on any attempt to modernize the feudal regime. In his view, the old system was dead, and there was no point in attempting to revive it. As for the sovereign himself, he was powerless, lacking both in finances and in an army. The mandarinate was an anachronism. The best solution would be a new-type mandarin who had a clear idea of his duties as a bureaucrat and was not indebted to the ruler for his continuance in office. Such training could better come from the French.[16]

Pham Quynh had been whistling the same tune for over a decade without much effect. Now, however, he apparently had an ally in the governor-general's office. Governor-general Pasquier himself was of the opinion that the monarchy could become an effective ally in maintaining French presence in Indochina, and by late 1930 he had given advance notice of reforms which would be "the modern adaptation of the internal sovereignty of Annam to the Treaty of 1884."[17] On September 7, 1932, Bao Dai, who was nineteen years of age and highly Western in his dress and outlook, returned to Vietnam to put the new system into effect. On the tenth, the old convention of 1925 was abolished and a royal decree issued with the benign approval of Governor-general Pas-

---

15. *Tribune indochinoise,* Oct. 24 to Nov. 3, 1930, carries the text.

16. I have not seen the original article. Excerpts are located in *AF,* May 1931, pp. 172–173. Pham Quynh was undaunted, and replied in *Nam Phong,* no. 160 (March 1931). See the article, "Serai je ministre?" pp. 21–32; and "Opinions d'un lettré campagnard." The text is in *Tribune indochinoise,* Sept. 28 to Oct 5, 1931.

17. Pham The Ngu, *Lich Su Van Hoc Viet Nam* [A History of Vietnamese Literature] (Saigon, 1961), p. 167.

quier.[18] In the decree, Bao Dai listed the various reforms that he would eventually set forth—in justice, education, and the mandarinate, and a broadening of the powers of the consultative chamber, the Chambre des Représentants du Peuple. At the same time he stated that the spirit of the reforms (and how dear to Pham Quynh's heart this statement must have been) would be to preserve the best of traditional morality while building a modern society. He cautioned against excessive haste—such reforms would take time—and then departed on a long imperial journey through his domain.

By early May of 1933 the emperor was ready to take action. In a surprise move, but with the behind-the-scenes approval of Pasquier, he dismissed the old Council of Ministers, including its president, Nguyen Huu Bai, suppressed the functions of the prime minister held in the Council by that official, and said that he would take over these functions himself. He then appointed a new five-man cabinet, composed of Thai Van Toan for Works, Arts, and Rites; Pham Quynh for National Education and Director of the Cabinet; Ngo Dinh Diem for Interior; Ho Dac Khai for Finances and Social Welfare; and Bui Bang Doan for Justice.[19] At the same time a mixed commission consisting of both French and Vietnamese was established to watch over the reforms promised in September of 1932, with Pham Quynh as president and Ngo Dinh Diem as secretary.

The new government did not receive a very happy welcome in nationalist circles. Nationalist feeling, even among moderates in Saigon, was that the whole matter had been manipulated by Pasquier, with Pham Quynh as his stooge. The appointment of the thirty-five-year-old Ngo Dinh Diem, a former province chief in Phan Thiet province, was given general approval, for he was considered honest, popular, and capable.[20] There was some disgruntled feeling about the abrupt dismissal of the old cabinet, however, particularly of Nguyen Huu Bai, a Roman Catholic who had filled the office of prime minister since 1930.[21] The attack on

18. *Tribune indochinoise*, Sept. 14, 1932.
19. *Tribune indochinoise*, May 10, 1933. For more detailed information on the case of Nguyen Huu Bai, see *AF*, Feb. 1935, p. 43.
20. *Tribune indochinoise*, July 21, 1933.
21. *Tribune indochinoise*, July 24, 1933. Some felt that Ngo Dinh Diem,

the reforms in the Center was led by Nguyen Phan Long, who, with Bui Quang Chieu in Paris, had become chief editor of *Tribune indochinoise*. In a series of editorials, Nguyen criticized the move as a subterfuge and a delusion. The emperor was no more powerful than before, either in the Center or the North, so the virtually direct control by France would continue. Governor-general Pasquier was accused of being a tyrant, a "smiling but tenacious old reactionary." But the journalist reserved his most venomous criticisms for Phan Quynh, a man who "had no qualification to be director of the imperial cabinet," a man "without profundity," a "local curiosity" who played "a decorative role" for the French, "a cultivated spirit, seductive but without vitality and without originality, and of a disquieting flexibility."[22] In effect, said Nguyen Phan Long, nothing had really changed, except that the young emperor had been discredited. There were ministers as before, he contended, but they still served the interests of the resident superior, and no reform could take place without his permission. True, the emperor had some formal powers in the Council of Ministers since the post of prime minister has been eliminated, but the resident superior presided there also and would prevent any decisions unwelcome to the French.

As it turned out, the mixed commission did recommend some changes in administration and justice, as well as a broadening of the powers of the Central Vietnamese deliberative chamber. But although these reforms were put into effect, they were paltry in comparison with the hopes that had been aroused, and it soon appeared that the court was no more independent of the French than before. Nor had the court's authority in the North increased. By mid-Summer the last saving grace of the cabinet was removed when its most popular member, Ngo Dinh Diem, resigned.[23] The resignation caused a furor. Rumors had it that Diem's resignation was caused by his disgust at the failure of the commission to con-

---

also a Catholic, was to be his replacement as the Christian member of the council. Some French sources opposed Nguyen Huu Bai's dismissal, including Resident Superior Le Fol, who said it might alienate traditional elements in Annam. AOM Carton 330, Dossier 2664, report of Le Fol of March 31, 1933, p. 7.

22. *Tribune indochinoise*, July 21, 1933.
23. *Tribune indochinoise*, Aug. 25 to 28, 1933.

sider meaningful changes.[24] Emperor Bao Dai resigned himself to the inevitable, and Pham Quynh stayed on, thus eclipsing his already waning reputation as a nationalist figure. As one bitter observer said, the Bao Dai reforms had the head of an elephant, and the tail of a mouse.[25]

Bao Dai and Pham Quynh did not abandon their hopes, however, and continued to press for a "return to 1884." In 1939 they journeyed to Paris to request that the French move in that direction, and rumors flew that the Daladier government was going to decree the return of Tonkin to court control.[26] The news caused a considerable stir, and progressive journals hastened to register their opposition, until Minister of Colonies Mandel declared that the rumor was without foundation. Archival sources indicate that the French had no intention of loosening their control over Indochina, at least under the shadow of Japanese expansionism. Bao Dai reluctantly accepted a postponement of reforms, and upon his return to Hué wrote to Mandel suggesting some minor changes which would increase his prestige and the presence of the court in the North. The French replied, with no more than a hint of condescension, that no reforms could be considered until after the war crisis was over.[27]

24. French sources say his dissatisfaction was motivated more by personal than by ideological reasons. Khoi was Nguyen Huu Bai's son-in-law. Ngo Dinh Diem knew that his brother was angry and was persuaded by the latter to resign. AOM Carton 330, Dossier 2664, resident superior's report of March 31, 1933.

25. Pham The Ngu, p. 169.

26. *Giai Cap*, pp. 416–417.

27. His reform proposals are located in AOM Carton 132, Dossier 1190, letter of Bao Dai of Aug. 27, 1939 to Minister of Colonies Mandel. He suggested that the position of *kinh luoc* be reinstated under a new name, that the powers of the Privy Council in Tonkin be broadened, and that Central and North Vietnam each be given a representative in the Conseil Superieur des Colonies in Paris.

Chapter 10

The Decline of the Moderates

The decade of the 1930s, beginning with the violent events of 1930 and 1931, saw a perceptible decline in the influence of moderate elements in the nationalist movement. In part this was due to the fact that some of the more prominent Francophiles were no longer active. Nguyen Van Vinh died of illness in 1936. Pham Quynh, now a court official in Hué, no longer played the role of journalist-adversary to the government. Bui Quang Chieu was also co-opted by the French; during his stay in Paris as representative to the Conseil Superieur his influence in Vietnam declined. When he returned to Saigon in June 1935 he found that younger elements in the Constitutionalist Party no longer followed him.[1] In addition, a split developed among the old leadership, always prey to the personality conflict between Nguyen Phan Long and Bui Quang Chieu, the chief egos of the party. In the late 1930s, Nguyen formed his own slightly leftist faction in the party and left the *Tribune indochinoise* to form a new newspaper, the *Vietnam Bao,* with Le Quang Liem. Bui managed to recover sufficient influence to obtain reelection to the Colonial Council, but his dominance was at an end.

With the old figures ineffective or absent, new groups began to emerge to fill the gap. When Minister of Colonies Marius Moutet permitted Vietnamese to form political parties in Cochin China, a number of moderate groups appeared, although they seemed to lack the bite of the parties of earlier days. Typical was the Dang Dan Chu (Democratic Party) of Doctor Nguyen Van Thinh,

---

1. For French comments see AOM Carton 329, Dossier 2654, monthly reports of July and November 1935.

former Constitutionalist from Cochin China.[2] Composed of reformist French and Vietnamese intellectuals, its message was strongly middle class, aimed at the achievement of political freedoms, admission of more Vietnamese to administrative posts, broadening of representation in the consultative assemblies, and dominion status.

Perhaps a more basic reason for the decline of the Francophiles was the fact that with the reforms of the 1930s the French administration had met their minimum demands; they ceased to stand forth as promoters of social change. While the Constitutionalist leadership had cause for dissatisfaction in the 1930s, those issues which excited their concern—the establishment of a progressive income tax, the policies of the Bank of Indochina, the enrichment of the *chetty* moneylending class at the expense of the Vietnamese bourgeoisie—usually threatened their own interests rather than the population as a whole. Where broader issues were at stake— reform of the labor laws, or the convening of an Indochinese Congress to consider the demands of the people for social and political reform—the Constitutionalists remained silent. In short, the Francophiles had been effectively seduced by the French, and they ceased to count as a force in the nationalist movement. Indeed, it might be said that they ceased to be nationalists at all, for they clearly feared their more radical compatriots more than they feared the French.

The vacuum left by the Francophiles on the right created an opportunity for a centrist, national reformist group of the Nguyen An Ninh stripe to take the lead in the Vietnamese nationalist movement. Curiously, however, the national reformists had almost disappeared as a political force in Vietnam—having either lapsed into inactivity or drifted toward more radical solutions. Nguyen An Ninh was in and out of jail, and in his political views had moved closer to the rising Indochinese Communist Party. Other than him, there was no potentially charismatic force on the horizon.

2. Nguyen Van Thinh (1884–1946), first joined the Constitutionalist Party in 1926, then founded his own organization in 1937. A landlord as well as a physician, he supported Cochin Chinese autonomy in 1946 against unity with the North, and committed suicide the same year. See R. B. Smith, "Some Vietnamese Elites in Cochin China, 1943" *Modern Asian Studies,* 6, part 4 (Oct. 1972), 469.

Some of the slack in the South was taken up by the rise of two syncretist religious movements, the Cao Dai along the Cambodian border, and the Hoa Hao in the Mekong delta. More of a regional than a nationalist character, and comprised predominantly of rural Vietnamese whose sense of national awareness was not well developed, the new movements gained considerable strength in limited areas of Cochin China. The Cao Dai in particular was harassed by the French for allegedly anticolonial activities and its support for the restoration of Prince Cuong De, one-time colleague of Phan Boi Chau and now a pro-Japanese figure in Tokyo.[3] In Annam and Tonkin, freedom to form political parties did not exist as in Cochin China, so there were no formal political organizations. Activities were either carried on clandestinely, or through informal alliances in the consultative assemblies.

Some moved into the cultural field and tried to express their political frustrations in ways that would not attract the attention of the ubiquitous French censors. As we have seen, Vietnamese culture began to undergo a form of revival at the end of World War I as a result of the importation of Western ideas. This cultural revival, under the leadership of Pham Quynh and *Nam Phong* journal, had little specific political orientation and lacked any central direction except for a desire to promote a sense of cultural unity through the development of a national literature in quoc-ngu. To the degree that this movement possessed any political direction at all, it followed the ideas of Pham Quynh himself. It was neotraditionalist and dedicated to the revival of traditional classics and values. Climaxing Pham Quynh's campaign was an attempt to promote the famous quoc-ngu classic, Nguyen Du's *Kim Van Kieu,* as a model for the moral and philosophical training of young Vietnam.

Eventually, a reaction against the neo-traditionalists began to surface in the late 1920s and early 1930s. During this period new attitudes were already beginning to develop among the Vietnamese youth who were products of the Franco-Vietnamese school system. A growing sense of individualism, a gradual loss of interest in the Confucian classics and in the past, and a strong admiration for all

3. According to some sources, there were about three hundred thousand followers of the Cao Dai in the prewar period.

things French and Western became "cultural chic" in leisurely circles in Saigon and Hanoi. French language and literature began to replace Chinese studies, and few young Vietnamese expressed any interest in Confucian learning.

But there was also a frustrated, bitter quality to this new mood —centered on the irritation felt by young middle-class youth at the tenacity of traditional values and practices, and at the failure of the French administration to realize reforms in the political and social fields. The first manifestation of this attitude had appeared in the 1920s with a growing interest in literary romanticism. For a while works like Dumas' *La Dame aux camélias* were highly popular with young Vietnamese. Frustrated at the failure of reformism, they sought "an escape for their disappointment" in romantic love stories.[4] Eventually the desire for escape in romanticism and reverie led to the creation of new works in quoc-ngu, and in the 1920s two novels appeared which took the educated public by storm—*To Tam* (To Tam) by Hoang Ngoc Phach, a teacher at a secondary school in Hanoi, and *Qua Dua Do* (The Watermelon), by Nguyen Trong Thuat.[5] *To Tam* dealt with the problem of thwarted love (he was a commoner, she was of a noble family), whereas *Qua Dua Do* was an escapist adventure novel about a Vietnamese Robinson Crusoe, who maintained a strong sense of Confucian loyalty to his ruler even during an extended period of exile. The French were anxious to encourage this new trend, hoping to siphon off discontent from the political realm, and AFIMA, the Francophile cultural organization formed by Pham Quynh in Hanoi, granted *Qua Dua Do* a literary prize as best novel of the year.[6]

This new mood began to move into the quasi-political field by the end of the decade. In 1930 Hoang Tich Chu started a new magazine, *Dong Tay* (East and West) with the aim of promoting quoc-ngu as the national language, but without the accompanying Chinese influence so prevalent in the writings in *Nam Phong*.

4. Hoang Ngoc Thanh, "The Social and Political Development of Vietnam as Seen through the Modern Novel" (Ph.D. Dissertation, University of Hawaii, 1969), p. 136.
5. Hoang, pp. 129–136; Le Van Dam, "Vingt années de littérature franco-annamite," *France-Asie* 7 (Oct. 15, 1946), 358.
6. *Ibid.*, p. 130.

While Hoang's effort failed, he set the course for the cultural trend of the ensuing decade, and in 1932 the major publishing event of the period took place with the establishment of the daily newspaper *Phong Hoa* (Manners). *Phong Hoa* and the literary group which coalesced around it in March 1933, the Tu Luc Van Doan (Self-Reliance Literary Group), was founded by the Vietnamese writer Nhat Linh, a former student of physics in Paris who returned to Hanoi in 1930 to follow a literary career.[7] Refusing to join the government, he gathered around him a group of Vietnamese anxious to create a Westernized literature and, indeed, a new society. Through his writings and those of his collaborators in *Phong Hoa,* a frustrated generation managed to hint at the nature of their dissatisfactions.

In quoc-ngu novels, often published by Doi Nay (the group's own publishing house), and in short stories in *Phong Hoa,* the young writers declared cultural war on the old society and voiced their determination to help build a new nation. In their popular works of the 1930s, they reflected the changing spirit of the times, and angrily described the agonizing problems of a rapidly changing society.

In several novels and short stories Nhat Linh was the leader of the group and probably the most vociferous critic of the past. In *Doan Tuyet* (Ruptures), written in 1935, he preached active struggle against social evils and the past. In *Doi Ban* (Two Friends), written three years later, he praised the courage of a wealthy young Vietnamese who abandoned a life of leisure to follow the revolutionary path. Other novels and stories promoted emancipation of women, the joys of physical love, individualism, the need to abandon the old concept of filial piety, and reforms to alleviate the conditions of the rural poor.[8]

Two other prominent members of the group were Khai Hung and Hoang Dao.[9] Khai Hung, son of a mandarin province chief, a

7. Nhat Linh, real name Nguyen Tuong Tam, was born in 1906. Once a member of the VNQDD, he became Minister of Foreign Affairs in the Vietnamese Provisional Government in 1946. He committed suicide in 1963, allegedly in protest against the policies of President Ngo Dinh Diem. See Dao Dang Vu, "Le Roman vietnamien contemporain," in *France-Asie* 27 (June 1948), 737.

8. Hoang Ngoc Thanh discusses these novels in some detail.

9. Khai Hung's real name was Tran Khanh Du, Hoang Dao's was

graduate of the lycée Albert Sarraut, and, in the 1930s, a teacher at a private school, added his own more moderate criticisms of the status quo. More inclined to write about the wealthy than Nhat Linh was, he nevertheless mirrored the latter's concern for social reforms and Westernization. Later he became a publisher of the VNQDD journal *Viet Nam* and an active opponent of communism.[10]

Hoang Dao was a judicial officer at the French court of justice in Hanoi. Most famous of his novels was *Bun Lai Nuoc Dong* (Slums and Huts), in which he flailed at mandarin and landlord corruption, excessive taxes and the French monopolies; demanded judicial and administrative reforms; and called attention to the need for improvement of rural conditions. Like Nhat Linh, he was strongly critical of the continued use of the Confucian classics as a basis for training the governing class.[11]

All in all, the literary group reflected a new mood. If some writers, like Khai Hung, tended to concentrate on the problems of the young and affluent, others wrote about social classes previously ignored in Vietnamese literature—rickshaw drivers, urban workers, and prostitutes. Family problems, and the question of sexual equality, were discussed. Focus of the writers' concern were the old evils of traditional society—landlordism, rural poverty, obscurantist educational practices. On the positive side, they reflected a determination to rise against the old society and build a new one, based on science and democracy. In their preoccupation with youth, action, health and physical activity, the validity of Reason, and love of life, they are strongly reminiscent of the devotees of the New Culture movement in China two decades earlier. Like such New Culture leaders as the philosopher-educator Hu Shih and Peking University chancellor Ts'ai Yuan-p'ei, they appeared to feel that the attention of progressives ought to be directed primarily at cultural reform—at building new habits and values, at constructing a new educational system—rather than at active political work.

Nguyen Tuong Long. Others in the group were Ho Trong Hieu, Nguyen Thu Le, Ngo Gia Tri, and Nguyen Tuong Lang.

10. *Ibid.*, p. 273.

11. Le Huu Muc, *Luan De ve Hoang Dao* [Talks on Hoang Dao] (Hue, 1957), pp. 46–49.

Yet they were unable to avoid political entanglements. In 1936, *Phong Hoa* was closed for attacks on the prominent mandarin Hoang Trong Phu, and a new magazine, *Ngay Nay* (Nowadays), was established by Hoang Dao. *Ngay Nay* was similar to, if slightly less aggressive than, *Phong Hoa*. The suppressed political ambitions of the group began to boil over by the late 1930s as some of them moved toward more active political work. Nhat Linh set up a political party, *Hung Viet* (Revive Vietnam), which was quickly suppressed by the French. Hoang Dao and Khai Hung were sent to concentration camps as the war approached, and Nhat Linh fled to China where he joined the pro-Japanese *Dai Viet* party. The arrests and the breakup of the embryonic party were symbolic, for the group had lost its vital force in the last years of the 1930s, as the literary mood itself changed to one of decadence and debauchery.

In summary, the decade of the 1930s saw the growing bankruptcy of reformist nationalism in Vietnam. Irreconcilable differences played a part in weakening the reformist cause; personality clashes and minor tactical squabbles created schisms even within the Francophile camp. Aware of the opportunity, the French government deliberately attempted to detach such relatively collaborationist figures as Bui Quang Chieu and Pham Quynh from the more radical elements; they were successful, but in the process destroyed whatever credibility the two had within the nationalist movement. Satisfying Bui and Pham Quynh did not destroy the nationalist movement, but merely removed its most moderate figures.

Some Characteristics of Urban Nationalism

How should we evaluate the performance of this first generation of urban nationalists? On the positive side, they improved on the record of their predecessors in many respects. Their goals were more precise, and they had a deeper understanding of the nature of Western civilization, and its implications for Vietnam. With this understanding came a more sophisticated attitude toward the mechanics of building a resistance movement in a colonial society.

It is equally clear, however, that the urban nationalists had some grievous weaknesses. They suffered seriously from factionalism and were unable to achieve even a semblance of unity. Moreover their organizations were often restricted to an elitist urban membership. A few, such as Nguyen An Ninh, occasionally made efforts to enlist the support of the mass of the population, but as a rule the nationalist leaders seemed unconscious of a need to tap the potentially powerful force in the countryside. As a result, the new nationalists, although more sophisticated than their scholar-patriot predecessors, were no more successful.

There also was no central focus to the urban nationalist movement. Where other Asian colonial societies often formed united nationalist movements embracing reformists as well as radicals, in Vietnam there were only a few uncoordinated groups, which lacked power and cohesion, between the collaborationist efforts of the Constitutionalists and the insurrectionary mentality of the VNQDD. What could have been the vibrant center of a nationalist movement was almost totally unoccupied territory. National reformists of the Phan Chu Trinh and Nguyen An Ninh stripe had the appeal, but seemed to lack the political ability.

One reason that has been advanced to explain the weakness of national reformism in Vietnam is the pitiless suppression of Vietnamese political parties by the French, a suppression which could only be overcome by clandestine organizations totally dedicated to the forceful overthrow of colonial authority.[12] There is validity in this point of view. French suspicion of the motives of even the most moderate elements in the educated community was an obstacle to any form of Franco-Vietnamese cooperation and it must have driven many moderates to despair.[13] The French treatment of the Vietnamese moderates improved somewhat in the 1930s after the Reynaud visit, but although they successfully detached the Constitutionalists from the rest of the movement, they had little effect on more progressive elements.

A major problem for the urban nationalists lay in their inability to cooperate with each other. One cause, of course, was the attitude of the Constitutionalists, who did not really want unity or the

12. For example, see Milton Osborne, "The Faithful Few: The Politics of Collaboration in Cochinchina in the 1920s," in Walter F. Vella, ed., *Aspects of Vietnamese History* (Honolulu, 1973), pp. 163–166.

13. At one point Governor Pagès of Cochin China even expressed his irritation that Vietnamese teams were beginning to defeat the French in soccer. AOM Carton 329, Dossier 2654, governor's report of Nov. 1935.

departure of the French. As Milton Osborne has pointed out, the Francophiles were caught in a paradox. Liking French civilization all too well, they often seemed closer to the French than to their Vietnamese compatriots.[14] The affluent leadership of the Constitutionalist Party, living in French-style houses, going to French schools, eating French food and drinking French wine, did not really want the French to go, and rationalized to themselves that the presence of the French was of ultimate benefit to Vietnam. Convinced that Vietnam was bound to be the client state of one nation or another the Francophiles acquiesced to French rule as the least unattractive of alternatives.

Given this fact, some facets of the behavior of the Constitutionalists are easier to understand. With the exception of a brief period in the mid-twenties, when they toyed with the idea of alliance with more radical groups in Paris, the Constitutionalists preferred to maintain an independent posture. Nor, of course, did they attempt to establish a mass-based political party capable of pressuring the French to grant major reforms. Such activities went beyond the goals of the inner leadership. Suspicious of the possible consequences of relying on mass support, perhaps even distrustful of the masses themselves, they preferred to make small gains in the relatively secure and tranquil atmosphere of the Colonial Council than to compete with more radical elements for the allegiance of the populace.[15] In that sense it is irrelevant to say that they did not understand how to achieve their goal through mass political action, for their goal was more limited—their goal was simply to attain a share of power and wealth within the scope of French rule.

To this degree, in terms of their own goals, they did not really fail. They succeeded, at least by the 1930s, in achieving some of their most cherished aims—educational opportunities, participation in consultative bodies, relative equality in the professions and the bureaucracy—a variety of small favors without the reality of

14. Osborne, p. 170.
15. Osborne gives an example of the party's fear of the masses. Vella, pp. 174–175. A similar example is located in SLOTFOM, Series III, Carton 3B, dossier entitled "Notes de l'agent Désiré concernant l'Association Constitutionaliste Indochinoise" (note of Jan. 14, 1926), which states that Bui Quang Chieu demanded to see all speeches in advance to avoid the possibility of excessively radical statements.

power. Where the Constitutionalists failed, of course, was in the larger sense of not seeing the fundamental issues at stake in Vietnam, and the shape of the future.

But if the Francophiles' seemingly inept political tactics can be ascribed partly to the nature of their goals, this does not help us to explain the failure of other, more radical nationalists to establish a nationwide movement with a mass base. Why could they not unite against their common enemy? Why were they unable to follow the example of their counterparts elsewhere in Asia by founding a united nationalist party with a mass base in the rural villages? Part of the answer may lie in the distinctive geographical and political character of colonial Vietnam. Separated from each other by distance, tradition, and administrative fiat, the people of the three regions of Vietnam had physical and emotional difficulties in communicating with each other, obstacles that remained even in the face of a common adversary.

But if mutual distrust, caused by a tradition of regionalism, can be offered as a partial answer to the inveterate factionalism of Vietnamese nationalism, it cannot wholly satisfy, for a greater degree of nationalist unity was established in other colonial societies with similar problems and less national awareness than Vietnam. Nor does it explain the curious inability of the urban nationalists in Vietnam to project their message beyond the cities to the rural villages. Although urban-rural distrust existed elsewhere in Asia, nowhere did the gap seem so wide as in Vietnam.

The answer, perhaps, lies in the cultural differences between Vietnam and its Asian neighbors. For in many Asian colonial societies religion formed an emotional link between city and village. Hinduism, Theravada Buddhism, or Islam knitted society together in common resentment against the cultural challenge of Western civilization, and provided a strong sense of cultural solidarity to the native population, rural and urban alike. The earliest anticolonial resistance movements in many Southeast Asian societies were strongly religious in nature. And although the religious character began to give way to the modern nationalist movements in the mid-twentieth century, religion still often formed an ideological bond within the movement.

But does Vietnam not have the equivalents of Islam, Hinduism, and Theravada Buddhism so useful to nationalist movements elsewhere in Asia? Vietnam certainly does not lack religious traditions. Mahayana Buddhism and Confucianism are two religious (or, in the case of Confucianism, quasi-religious) systems potentially useful as a focus for a resistance movement. Yet it is significant that neither in Phan Boi Chau's time nor later was either Buddhism or Confucianism successfully used as a cohesive force in the Vietnamese nationalist movement.

The failure of Buddhism or Confucianism to serve as an ideological symbol for the Vietnamese anticolonialist movement must be found in the role each played in society. Buddhism, for example, did not play the formative social role that it did in other Buddhist societies in Southeast Asia. Buddhist temples did not educate the youth of Vietnam, as they did in Burma and Thailand. Buddhist ethics and metaphysics did not permeate the thinking of Vietnamese elites, for they were impregnated with Confucianism. Buddhism, in effect, was not deeply enough rooted in Vietnamese society to furnish an ideological cement for the emerging nationalist movement.

Confucianism would seem to be a more likely source for the cultural symbolism so necessary to a mass movement because of its pervasive influence in education, and its stress on community cohesion. Yet with Confucianism there were also disadvantages. It exerted less emotional impact on the mass of the population than did Buddhism or Islam in neighboring areas. More a political ideology than a religion, it lacked the emotional appeal among the people, for whom it had relatively little personal meaning. It was perhaps not as potentially effective as a unifying force among the population as the more purely religious systems elsewhere in Southeast Asia.

Significantly, however, even among the scholar-gentry, Confucianism did not long survive as a cultural focus for the anticolonialist movement. The Can Vuong, of course, had relied on Confucian appeals. Within a generation, however, Phan Boi Chau and Phan Chu Trinh had virtually abandoned Confucianism as a tool for building a modern nation. Identified with reaction, with the court and the bureaucracy which slavishly followed the French, it soon lost its attraction to Phan Boi Chau, who began to rely on a simple appeal to patriotism. Later, among the urban nationalists, to be nationalist and modernist meant, almost by definition, to be anti-Confucianist. Under such circumstances, Confucianism, co-opted by the reactionary and collaborationist elements in the population, could hardly serve as a unifying force in the resistance movement. Instead, modern nationalists turned to Western ideas —to democracy and science. Later these would become important within Asian nationalism as goals for newly independent governments. In the interwar period, however, such Western imports had little meaning for the mass of the population. Nor did they express the primordial sense of identity so necessary in building up a mass movement for national liberation.

In Vietnam, then, cultural symbols were relatively absent from the nationalist movement. Nationalists were reduced to the appeal of foreign ideas, or a simple call to Vietnamese patriotism. After World War I, this absence of a cultural unifying factor contributed to the growing factionalism within the movement. Nationalist parties were based on regional, or even on personal loyalties. With Vietnam already administratively divided by the French, patriots in Hanoi, Hué, and Saigon found it difficult to communicate with each other, figuratively as well as literally. Only an organization which could offer an ideology to overcome such fissiparous tendencies would have an opportunity to knit together the forces of nationalism in Vietnam.

PART III

SOCIAL REVOLUTIONARIES

Chapter 11

The Revolutionary Youth League

The quickening pace of economic development that provided a springboard for the emergence of an indigenous middle class after World War I also led to the creation of a Vietnamese proletariat. While a local bourgeoisie began to appear in the big cities and provincial towns throughout the three areas of Vietnam, a semi-industrial proletariat that found employment in the industrial plants in and around big cities, in the mines at Hong Gay, and in the large French-owned rubber plantations in the plateau region in the South, also began to emerge. The figures tell the story: from 1919 to 1929 the number of workers in Vietnam more than doubled, from one hundred thousand to two hundred twenty thousand.[1]

In general, the working conditions for this new laboring class were not attractive. Indeed, they were almost uniformly bad, whether in the sweatshops of Haiphong, the industrial suburb of Ben Thuy, the mines along the Tonkin Gulf, or the rubber plantations of Cochin China. Recruitment of workers often involved coercion, and the means were frequently brutal. Salaries were low, and working hours sometimes extended more than twelve hours a day for a seven-day week.[2] Not a few French journalists visiting Indochina during the interwar years—Paul Monet, Louis Roubaud, Roland Dorgelès, Jean Dorsenne, Andrée Viollis—returned to publish shocking accounts of these conditions.[3]

1. Of this number, 39 percent were in commerce and industry, 37 percent in plantations, and 24 percent in mining. John T. McAlister, *Vietnam: The Origins of Revolution* (New York, 1971), p. 62.
2. For one account of working conditions, see *Buoc Ngoat Vi Dai cua Lich Su Cach Mang Viet Nam* [A Great Step Forward in the History of the Vietnamese Revolution] (Bureau on the Historical Research of the Party, n.d.), pp. 124–136.
3. Roland Dorgelès, *Sur la route mandarine* (Paris, 1929), criticized

In February of 1924, workers at a weaving factory in Nam Dinh in the North went on strike to protest low wages and management's treatment of them. Strikes then occurred at other factories in the Nam Dinh area, where a number of light industries had been established around a working population of fifty thousand Vietnamese.[4] The activity was basically spontaneous, with little organization, however.

The first organized workers' union was founded in 1920 by Ton Duc Thang. Ton, who had attended a technical school in Saigon before the war, participated in a strike at the Ba Son arsenal in 1912. He then went to France and worked as a naval mechanic until 1918, joining in the famous sailors' strike at Toulon.[5] Returning to Vietnam in 1920, he brought with him a lifelong commitment to Marxism. He had no immediate idea of forming a workers' party, but he organized a secret labor union in Saigon. The union did not have written statutes, nor a fixed headquarters, but meetings took place once a month at the house of a member under false auspices. As a result, the union's area of influence was limited to a few private enterprises and public services in the Saigon-Cholon region, and its membership totaled less than three hundred workers.[6]

By 1925, the union had gradually become involved in the politics of the period, and it promoted a strike at the Ba Son arsenal in August in support of anti-imperialists in China (the strike would delay the departure of a French cruiser from Saigon harbor to Shanghai). Because pay and working conditions were relatively

conditions for cement workers; Paul Monet, *Les Jauniers* (Paris, 1930), discussed recruitment policies. Louis Roubaud, *Vietnam: La Tragédie indochinoise* (Paris, 1931), and Andrée Viollis, *Indochine S.O.S.* (Paris, 1935) deal with the general situation.

4. Tran Van Giau, "Phong trao dau tranh cua giai cap cong nhan tu 1919 den 1929" [The struggle movement of the working class from 1919 to 1929] in *Hoc Tap* [Study] (Sept. 1929), p. 51.

5. Tran Van Giau, "Nhung anh huong dau tien cua cach mang thang muoi Nga den thoi cuoc chinh tri Viet Nam" [The early influence of the Russian October revolution on Vietnamese politics] in *Hoc Tap*, Aug. 1957, pp. 53–54. He joined the Revolutionary Youth League in 1926 and since 1969 has been the president of the Democratic Republic of Vietnam.

6. Phan Than Son, "Le Mouvement Ouvrier de 1920 a 1930," in Jean Chesneaux, ed., *Tradition et Revolution au Vietnam* (Paris, 1971), pp. 169–170.

good at the arsenal, the strike was difficult to set up, but a stoppage finally took place in early August, with demonstrators demanding increases in salary and shorter hours. Their demands were met, but more importantly the departure of the ship was delayed until late November.[7] In 1925, Ton's union also had its first imitator: Hoang Quoc Viet, a former student at the Industrial School in Haiphong, established a union at the Mao Khi anthracite mines north of the Red River delta.[8]

The rise of the workers' movement coincided with the first appearance of Marxist ideas in Southeast Asia. By 1920, Marxist ideas were beginning to trickle into Vietnam, chiefly by word of mouth and through a few journals, such as *l'Humanité* and *La Vie ouvrière,* illegally smuggled in from France. Contrary to Marxist orthodoxy, however, it was not primarily within the emerging working class that Marxist doctrine had its greatest earlier success in Vietnam, but rather among the urban intelligentsia, the same element that had taken the lead in building a new nationalist movement after World War I. By the early 1920s, references to Marxism and the Bolshevik revolution began to appear in newspapers and journals smuggled in from the outside world. French colonial authorities attempted to counter the dangerous doctrine by censorship and by compelling friendly Vietnamese publications like *Avenir du Tonkin* and *Nam Phong* to include anti-Bolshevik articles in their columns. The technique was not universally successful, it appears. One student at the Hanoi Normal School was quoted as saying to another as early as 1918: "If the Westerners don't like them, the communists must be good."[9]

Until 1925, however, the concrete results of Marxist activity were minimal in Vietnam, and it was in France that the first steps toward building a communist movement were taken. The French Communist party (FCP), established after a split between moderate and radical socialists at a conference in Tours in 1920, had been given primary responsibility by the Comintern to promote the development of communist movements in the French colonies.

7. *Ibid.,* pp. 167–168.

8. Hoang joined the League in 1928 and organized communist cells in a variety of industrial and mining establishments. *Ibid.,* p. 175.

9. Tran Van Giau, "Nhung anh huong," p. 51.

The FCP became particularly active among Vietnamese sailors and mechanics working in the shipyards of Bordeaux and Marseilles, and a number of Vietnamese nationalists living in France became active members of the FCP in its early years. Among the Vietnamese who turned to communism while in France was the founder of the Vietnamese communist movement, Ho Chi Minh.[10]

Ho Chi Minh

By birth and native origins, Ho Chi Minh carried a proud tradition. He was born Nguyen Sinh Cuong on May 19, 1890, in Kim Lin village, Nam Dan district, Nghe An province.[11] Young Ho's family was of Confucian gentry status, but had fallen on hard times. His father, Nguyen Sinh Sac, had been orphaned at an early age but had studied with a local scholar and had eventually gone to Hué to enter the Quoc Hoc (National Academy). Eventually he took the civil service examinations and received a master's degree in 1901. Four years later he accepted a governmental post at Hué. He found government service unattractive, however, and returned to his village—where the local citizens had built him a house on a small plot of land—and became a local schoolteacher.[12]

The influence of father on son was significant, for Nguyen Sinh Sac had come to detest the traditional system of education, even though he had profited by it. He became a wandering scholar, he often deprecated the civil service system and the old literature, and he vowed that he would never teach his own children to follow that

10. Besides Ho Chi Minh there were Ton Duc Thang, Duong Bach Mai, and Nguyen Van Tao. The latter later became a member of the Central Committee of the ICP and a delegate to the Sixth Congress of the Comintern.

11. He has had many names. At age ten he took the name Nguyen Tat Thanh. In early adulthood he chose the pseudonym Nguyen Ai Quoc (Nguyen the Patriot). Although he chose many aliases to keep secret his identity, it was as Nguyen Ai Quoc that he gained fame as a Vietnamese revolutionary. After World War II he used the Chinese name Ho Chi Minh (he who enlightens). To avoid confusion, he will be referred to as Ho Chi Minh throughout this book.

12. *Ho Chi Minh: Notre camarade* (Paris, 1970), says that Nguyen Sinh Sac refused to accept government employment because of his disgust with the mandarinate system. See page 17. A bit later Nguyen allegedly became a drunk and a destitute. One French report says that his drinking and brutality led to his dismissal by the court in 1910. See AOM Carton 326, Dossier 2637. Ho's mother died in 1900, a brother died poor in 1950, and his sister died in 1954.

route. Young Ho understandably applauded his father's attitude, for Nguyen apparently made little attempt to apply a regimented discipline to young Ho's training, although he did eventually send his son to study with a local scholar.

When Ho was in adolescence, Phan Boi Chau, who had achieved considerable renown in Nghe An province for his revolutionary activities as well as for his success in the 1900 examinations, returned from Japan to look for potential candidates for study in Japan. As a friend of Nguyen Sinh Sac, Phan came to ask his two sons to return with him to join the exiles in Japan. Young Ho had considerable respect for Phan Boi Chau, but he refused the offer, allegedly stating that he could not leave without his father's permission, and his father was away at the time.[13] There is little evidence but much speculation as to why Ho decided not to follow Phan Boi Chau. Some sources contend that he did not like Phan's reliance on the royal family and on aid from Japan. One quotation has him saying that relying on Japan was like "driving the tiger out the front door while welcoming the wolf in through the back."[14] On the other hand, Ho was no more enamored of Phan Chu Trinh's ideas of using the French against the feudal monarchy. Whatever his inner feelings, Ho's real desire was to go to France, presumably to see Western civilization at its heart, and then return to help Vietnam.[15]

When he was about twenty, Ho entered the National Academy at Hué, where he studied French, history, geography, and natural science. After about a year, however, he decided to go south, where he first got a job teaching French and Vietnamese in Phan Thiet province, and then, in Saigon, as a cook on the United Transport line Admiral Latouche-Treville.[16]

Young Ho evidently spent several years at sea, visiting a number of countries, including, so rumor has it, the United States. Then, after a few years in London, where he worked at odd jobs

13. When the local governor of Nghe An arrested some of the local gentry in connection with Phan Boi Chau's visit, the young Nguyen Tat Thanh went to Vinh and demanded their release. *Nash President Ho Shi Minh* [Our President Ho Chi Minh] (Hanoi, 1963), p. 34.
14. Van Tan, "Lanh tu cua dang" [The party leadership], *NCLS*, no. 10 (Jan. 1960), p. 38.
15. *Ibid.*
16. *Ibid.*, pp. 167–168.

(as a snow-sweeper and cook's helper at a restaurant in London), he went to France. Shortly after the end of World War I, he organized an Association of Vietnamese Patriots in Paris, and drew up a list of eight demands to be presented to the representatives of the Great Powers convening at Versailles. Because his own knowledge of French was insufficient, he had a recent acquaintenance, the lawyer Phan Van Truong, compose the list in acceptable French. His demands consisted of Vietnamese autonomy, freedom of association, of religion, of the press, of movement, the granting of amnesty to political prisoners, equal rights between French and Vietnamese, abolition of forced consumption of alcohol and opium, of forced labor, and of the salt tax. The petition, entitled *Revendications du peuple annamite,* was sent to all allied delegations and to all deputies of the French National Assembly.[17]

Through this one brazen act Ho became suddenly notorious among the Vietnamese community in Paris, and the more prudent began to avoid his company. By 1921, now going under the name Nguyen Ai Quoc (Nguyen the Patriot), he was becoming increasingly active in French politics. Through his friend Jean Longuet, editor of *Le Peuple,* a socialist member of parliament and a nephew of Marx, he joined the French Socialist Party and studied the techniques of political journalism. He began writing articles for *l'Humanité* and *La Vie ouvrière*—usually about the life of the worker in Paris. He became an avid reader, frequented the Bibliothèque Nationale and left-wing literary clubs, and eventually produced a play, *Le Dragon de Bambou,* which achieved some success in progressive circles, but was banned by the government during the visit of Khai Dinh in 1922.[18] To support himself he learned photo retouching from someone who had become proficient at it—Phan Chu Thinh—and once did a portrait of the socialist leader Jean Juarès. Whenever he had the time and the funds he traveled widely, to Italy and Switzerland, and came to the

17. A copy of the petition is located in SLOTFOM, Series III, Carton 3, Dossier III 2–1. There was little response to his petition. A few recipients, including the American delegation, sent a formal acknowledgment without comment.

18. Tran Dan Tien, *Nhung Mao Chuyen ve Doi Hoat Dong cua Ho Chu Tich* [Glimpses of the Life of Ho Chi Minh] (Hanoi, 1960), p. 33.

conclusion that Europeans were nicer in Europe than in Asia: "All are human beings: everywhere we met good and bad people, honest and crooked people. If we are good people, we will meet good people everywhere."[19]

Eventually Ho found the French Socialist Party inadequate for his political needs. His major interest in politics, then as always, was the colonial question and the liberation of Vietnam, but he found that many members of the FSP were fundamentally uninterested in the colonial problem, and some were even ambivalent about their position regarding colonialism. At about this time, a friend gave him a copy of Lenin's "Theses on the National and Colonial Questions," which had appeared in *l'Humanité*. He had had some trouble in understanding the debates over the Second and Third Internationals in party meetings, but, as he later reminisced, he understood Lenin's "Theses" and was deeply moved. Here, it occurred to him was Vietnam's road to liberation.[20] Having become an instant convert to Lenin, he began to talk incessantly about the colonial problem to comrades, insisting that it was impossible to be a true revolutionary without simultaneously being anticolonialist.[21] Chosen a delegate to the FSP conference at Tours to discuss possible adhesion to Lenin's Third International in 1920 he teamed up with French revolutionaries like Paul Vaillant-Couturier and Jacques Duclos, and spoke on the colonial problem at the congress. Moderates passed off his arguments and said that parliament was considering the question. On the final vote he sided with the radicals and became a founding member of the French Communist Party.

During this period, Ho also continued his journalistic career, and while supporting himself as a photo retoucher he founded the radical anticolonialist newspaper *Le Paria* (The Pariah), a self-styled "Tribune des populations des colonies." Ho was not only chief editor, he also did most of the writing, producing articles on colonial problems in Africa as well as in Indochina. The magazine

---

19. *Ibid.*, p. 38.

20. "Ho Chu Tich noi ve chu nghia Le-nin va cach mang Viet Nam" [Chairman Ho discusses Leninism and the Vietnamese revolution], in *Hoc Tap*, March 1970, p. 2.

21. *Ibid.* It is not hard to imagine French socialists running for cover to avoid Ho's lectures on colonialism.

did not sell particularly well; many Vietnamese, feeling that he was a "wild animal," continued to avoid his company, so most of the subscribers were French workers and intellectuals.[22] Eventually he began giving issues away and relying on contributions.

There was nothing theoretical about Ho's writings in *Le Paria* and other journals of the period. Unlike his contemporary Mao Tse-tung, whose writings sometimes had a philosophical vein, Ho was always most concerned with the specific problems of people. His articles were characterized by a strong sense of sympathy for the oppressed, and a typical essay would deal, in sometimes melodramatic tones, with such problems as the condition of the Chinese peasants, atrocities committed by French troops in Indochina, or lynchings perpetrated by the Ku Klux Klan in the southern United States. In their entirety, his essays comprise a scathing indictment of the colonial system of oppression throughout the world, occasionally moderated by an article in praise of life in Soviet Russia. Ho was by no means without humor, and often he relied on rather heavy-handed sarcasm to make a point. On one occasion he wrote a public letter to Albert Sarraut referring to the watchdogs that Colonial Minister Sarraut was placing on suspicious Vietnamese, and including his own daily schedule so that the government could save money on this unnecessary expense.[23]

At the same time, Ho occasionally allowed himself some bitter criticism of his own colleagues. In an article published in the May 25, 1932, issue of *l'Humanité,* he wrote: "Since the French party has accepted the twenty-one conditions and adhered to the Third International, it has undertaken, among other duties, a particularly delicate one: the colonial policy. It cannot afford to content itself, like the First and Second Internationals, with purely sentimental and inconsequential statements, but it must have a precise plan of action, an effective and realistic policy." The trouble is, he added,

22. Most of the subscribers were members of Ho's Union Intercoloniale, composed of Moroccans, black Africans, and Vietnamese. One Vietnamese member was Phan Van Truong. Born in 1878 in Hanoi, he became a naturalized Frenchman and a lawyer. He was imprisoned in 1914 with Phan Chu Trinh on suspicion of anti-French activities. Released in 1915, he became a lawyer at the Court of Appeals in Paris. Information on Union Intercoloniale activities can be found in AOM Carton 109, Dossier 1035, reports.
23. This comment appeared in *Le Paria,* Aug. 1, 1922.

the French proletariat is essentially indifferent to the colonial problem, and thinks that a colony "is nothing but a country full of sand below and sun above, with a few green palms and a few brown natives, and that's all and they are completely indifferent."[24]

Ho remained in France for about four years, building his knowledge of French civilization and his reputation as a major Asian figure in the world communist movement. In mid-1923, he was called by the Comintern to Moscow. He left by rail for Berlin, traveling first class and gleefully imitating the regal behavior of a rich tourist on a world tour. From Rostock he took a Russian ship to St. Petersburg, where, since he had no papers and was without acquaintances, he was forced to remain for several months "in an atmosphere of tension." Finally verified, he left for Moscow at the end of the year. He lived in a hotel near the Kremlin that was frequented by Asians, and one day at breakfast he learned of the death of Lenin. As a Vietnamese he soon found himself a member of the Peasant International (the Krestintern) and studied Marxism at the Lenin School of Oriental Peoples. All told, he was in Moscow for about a year. While there he found the time to serve in July 1924 as a delegate to the Fifth Comintern Congress, at which he demanded that the world communist body devote more time to colonial matters, on the grounds that a European revolution could succeed only after a revolution had taken place in the colonies.[25]

Late in 1924, Ho arrived in Canton, China.[26] Ostensibly he had been sent from Moscow to be an interpreter for the Comintern mission to the Kuomintang (the Chinese Nationalist Party). In actuality, Ho's duties were only indirectly related to the Comintern delegation in South China, for the Comintern had apparently assigned him two other responsibilities: (1) to establish a liaison between all communist organizations in Southeast Asia with the Comintern headquarters in Moscow, and with its bureau in the Far

24. *Ho Chi Minh: Notre camarade,* pp. 29–30.
25. Ho's speech at the congress is in *International Press Correspondence* (Inprecor), July 17, 1924, p. 424. See also AOM Carton 109, Dossier 1035, note of August 31, 1924.
26. There is some disagreement over his arrival date, some saying December 1924 and others early 1925. I am inclined to accept the earlier date.

East, centered at Shanghai, and (2) to supervise the founding of the first communist organization in French Indochina. Such duties were obviously more appropriate for a man of his stature in the communist movement.

Whatever the precise instructions given to Ho on the eve of his momentous journey to China, it is certain that among his intellectual baggage was the Leninist theory of the nature of colonialism and nationalism in Asia. Lenin had been one of the first Marxists to see the importance of utilizing nationalist movements in Africa and Asia as an ally of the communists in the struggle against capitalism and imperialism, and he had outlined the tasks of the communist movement in colonial areas in the famous "Theses on the National and Colonial Questions" presented to the Second Comintern Congress in 1920.[27] In at least two respects, Lenin's theories would be applicable to Vietnam. Of basic importance to potential Asian communist movements was Lenin's assertion that nationalist movements in colonial areas, though often led by the local bourgeoisie rather than the tiny proletariat, could and should be an ally of the proletariat in the struggle against the common enemies—Western imperialism and Asian feudalism. In Lenin's view, Asian communists should attempt alliances with all progressive bourgeois nationalists (that is, those opposed to the presence of imperialists on native soil), while at the same time preserving their independence within the nationalist movement. In the second place, and perhaps more important in Vietnam's own situation. Lenin advised Asian communists to view the peasantry not as an inert mass, but as a basic force to be reckoned with as a potential ally in the struggle against the forces of reaction and the status quo in Asia.

In some areas of East and Southeast Asia, the application of Leninist principles of the United Front led communists to join mass nationalist movements under middle-class leadership. In Indochina, however, Ho's problems would be complicated, for the only movement of national proportions, Phan Boi Chau's old Restoration Society, was in the process of disintegration as a consequence of repeated failure. Other political groupings were either regionally limited or were at least semi-collaborationist in na-

27. For a discussion of Lenin's theories, see Charles B. McLane, *Soviet Strategies in Southeast Asia* (Princeton, 1966), pp. 11–27.

ture.[28] Presumably Ho's instructions were to set up the nucleus of
a communist movement in Vietnam within the small but growing
proletariat, and then to attempt to bring together the scattered
progressive elements in the country in a broad united front of all
forces opposed to feudalism and the preservation of imperialist
authority.[29]

The Formation of the League

Ho's first move after arriving in Canton was to establish contact
with Vietnamese exile groups in the area. In late 1924 he held
talks with Phan Boi Chau and gave the old patriot some random
advice about how to bring his moribund party back to life.[30] At
the same time he got in touch with the small radical group, the
Tam Tam Xa (Association of Like Minds), one of whose members, Pham Hong Thai, had recently startled Vietnam with his
assassination attempt on Governor-general Merlin. The Association, made up in part of remnants of Phan Boi Chau's old Restoration Society, had orginally been formed in 1923.[31] Many of its
members apparently had vague socialist leanings but, in the Phan
Boi Chau tradition, they were little concerned with ideology, believing that politics would be a divisive force. The overriding goal
of the group was to unite all resistance elements and, through acts
of assassination and propaganda, to wage a violent revolution
against the French. The future system of government would ultimately be decided by a congress elected by majority vote throughout the nation.

It was out of the Association of Like Minds that Ho in June
1925 created the nucleus of the Viet Nam Thanh Nien Cach Menh
Dong Chi Hoi (Revolutionary Youth League of Vietnam), the
first truly Marxist organization in Indochina. The new revolution-

28. There is some indication that Ho wrote the Comintern in Moscow
sometime in 1925; he allegedly sent an analysis of Vietnamese nationalist
parties. I have been unable to obtain a copy.
29. Ho was already conscious of the problem of building a united front
in Vietnam, and had raised the question at the Fifth Congress of the Comintern. See Jane Degras, ed., *The Communist International: Documents*
(London, 1960), II, 156.
30. *Nien Bieu,* p. 201.
31. The major source for information on the Tam Tam Xa is To Nguyet
Dinh, *Pham Hong Thai* (Saigon, 1957).

ary group was not designed as a formal communist party, but as a nursery for the training and education of committed Marxists who would later form the core of a full-fledged Marxist-Leninist organization. Ho's reluctance to promote the immediate formation of a communist party seems to be based on his belief that such a move would be premature in Vietnam, where "no one yet understood the meaning of the word communism," and where the working class was still infinitesimal.[32]

The aims of the new organization were deliberately kept general in order to appeal to a wide audience; they were national revolution, overthrow of the French, and restoration of independence through the organization of an anti-imperialist front of all progressive factions in Vietnam. World revolution and the realization of a communist society were soft-pedaled.[33] Membership was open to all those of both sexes seventeen years and over who accepted the aims of the organization. Control was to be vested in a central committee located at Canton. When sufficient members had been trained in China and dispatched back to Vietnam, regional committees would be established in Tonkin, Annam, and Cochin China, and similar committees would be set up at province, district, and village levels.[34] All levels would have elected assemblies, but the organization as a whole would be run on a basis of democratic centralism.[35]

To give structure to his conception of gradually educating the people to an understanding of communism, Ho established three separate levels of organization. With the aid of Kuomintang party man Liao Chung-k'ai and the Indian communist M. N. Roy he set up the short-lived Hoi Dan Toc Bi Ap Buc The Gioi (League of Oppressed Peoples of Asia) in Nanking, made up of Koreans, Indonesians, Indians, and Chinese, as well as Vietnamese.[36] At the heart of the Revolutionary Youth League itself was a third level, which was designed as the nucleus of a future communist party,

32. *Contribution,* IV, 15.
33. This did not demand much ideological contortion, for Ho already accepted the concept of a two-stage revolution, from a bourgeois democratic first stage to a socialist final stage.
34. For the organization and statutes, see *TLTK,* IV, 132–133 and 137–142.
35. *Giai Cap,* pp. 389–390.
36. For why it was abandoned, see *Contribution,* IV, 16.

the Thanh Nien Cong San Doan (Communist Youth Group), made up of nine leading members of the organization.[37]

Ho took advantage of the environment in South China to establish training facilities for his young disciples. Until 1927, Canton was the headquarters of both the Kuomintang and the Chinese Communist Party, and Vietnamese revolutionaries were enrolled in local training schools under Communist or Kuomintang direction. Among those schools attended were the Communist Party Peasant Seminar, Sun Yat-sen University and, in particular, the military school at Whampoa where a special section was set aside for Vietnamese students.[38]

Vietnamese participation at the Whampoa military school was on a relatively formal basis. Instructors were chosen from among the leading members of the League. Courses were offered on capitalism, on the history of the liberation movements of Asia, and on the fall of Vietnam. There were also courses in critical study of other political philosophies such as Gandhism, Sun's Three Peoples' Principles, and anarchism, and there were more specific courses on Marxism-Leninism and the Bolshevik revolution, the organization of the Comintern, agit-prop work, and the organization of the masses.[39] One of the basic texts was Ho's *Duong Cach Menh* (The Road to Revolution), in which, for the first time, the specific tasks of the Vietnamese revolution were set forth. Written at the end of 1925 or early the following year, the aim of the booklet was to give Vietnamese revolutionaries a greater understanding of Marxism and its applicability to Vietnam. The author was particularly anxious to eliminate the most obvious failures of past nationalist movements. Ho contended that (1) reliance on reformism should be strongly opposed—the Russian revolution got rid not only of the king, but of capitalists and landlords as well,

37. Those mentioned include Ho Chi Minh, Ho Tung Mau, Le Hong Phong, Le Hong Son, Truong Van Lenh, and Luu Quoc Long. See Suren Mkhitarian, *Rabochii Klass i Natsional'no-Osvoboditel'noe Dvizhenie vo Vietname* (Moscow, 1967), p. 195. *Contribution*, IV, 15, mentions six members. Eventually the group was expanded to twenty-four members.

38. It was called the Vietnamese Revolutionary Special Political Training Department. See *Giai Cap*, p. 392.

39. Vu Tho, "Qua trinh thanh lap dang vo san o Viet Nam da duoc dien ra nhu the nao" [How did the process of forming a proletarian party in Vietnam take place?], *NCLS*, no. 71 (Feb. 1965), p. 18.

(2) revolutionary unity should be stressed as all-important (regionalism and racism were strongly condemned, and it was emphasized that the final revolution must be led by a highly disciplined and united Marxist-Leninist party under the leadership of the Comintern), (3) revolutionary work itself should not consist of the haphazard efforts of a few isolated heroes engaged in a romantic but quixotic struggle against the forces of evil (an obvious slap at Phan Boi Chau); it should instead be a carefully organized struggle based on the firm support of the masses and an understanding of revolutionary theory and practice.[40]

All in all, the League's training program became a relatively sizeable operation. A total of about three hundred young Vietnamese were eventually sent to Canton, of whom approximately one hundred studied at the Whampoa Academy. A few of the more promising students, such as Tran Phu, Le Hong Phong, and Ha Huy Tap, were sent on to Moscow's University of the Toilers of the East to study Marxist-Leninist theory at its source.[41]

By the end of 1925, the first recruits were being returned from Canton to initiate activities in Vietnam—in commercial enterprises and factories, in the rubber plantations, and in the schools, where discontent with French colonial authority was likely to be high and rising. Unlike its predecessors, the new movement was strongly determined to grow roots among the masses. In his primer on Marxism, Ho emphasized that the proletariat and the peasantry, the most alienated elements in society, were the key to the success of the revolution.[42]

Because many of the original founders of the League were from Central Vietnam, particularly from the provinces of Nghe An and Ha Tinh, it is not surprising that the early strength of the organization was located in Annam, which set up the first regional com-

40. This book is not available to me. It is discussed in *Giai Cap*, pp. 380–386.

41. The most useful source for information on the activities of the school and its leaders is League member Nguyen Dinh Tu's confession to the Sûreté Générale. See AOM, Carton 335, Dossier 2690, "Déclarations dernières de Nguyen Dinh Tu, dit provisoirement Phan Van Cam, dit Van Cam, sur sa vie depuis Juin 1925 jusqu'à son arrestation en date du 5 Août 1929 à Ha Tinh." I am grateful to Martin Bernal for pointing out this source to me.

42. *Giai Cap*, p. 383.

mittee, and which alone had attracted two hundred members by 1926.[43] Soon, provincial committees were formed in several provinces in the North and Center, as were city committees in Haiphong, Hanoi, Saigon, and My Tho and Can Tho in the Mekong Delta. By 1928, red unions had started to organize in factories, mines, plantations, and commercial establishments, as the League attempted to "proletarianize" in line with directives of the Sixth Comintern Congress. All this League activity among workers is somewhat misleading, however, for ninety per cent of the active members were supposedly from petty bourgeois intellectual families, as compared by only ten per cent from worker or peasant backgrounds.[44] The League had not yet created a movement with its roots imbedded deeply among the masses.

A major part of the work of the League was propaganda. League members strove to build up among the populace an acquaintance with Marxism and a desire for social revolution. To provide an organ for the dissemination of Marxist ideas, Ho established at Canton as official League journal, *Thanh Nien* (Youth). Published weekly from July 1925 until April 1927 (eighty-eight issues in all), the journal was smuggled by ship into Vietnam. The message of the journal was half nationalist and half watered-down Marxism as it attempted to inculcate a sense of Vietnamese identity and to introduce new Marxist terminology and theory.[45] In addition, a number of small books and pamphlets on Marxism and revolutionary theory were published.

Attempts at United Front

Perhaps the major task the League set forth was to bring some order into the nationalist movement and, if possible, to establish its own leadership over other resistance elements, in line with the Leninist strategy of participating in alliances with bourgeois or peasant parties based on opposition to colonial rule. This would be no easy task, for the existing parties in Vietnam were already hav-

43. *Ibid.,* p. 394.
44. *Contribution,* V, 19–20, says that most Tonkinese members were workers, while the membership elsewhere was mixed. Tran Van Giau disputes this, and asserts that most of the members in the North were petit bourgeois. He appears to be correct. See *Giai Cap,* p. 395.
45. *Ibid.,* p. 375.

ing difficulties in overcoming obstacles to unity. Perhaps the most promising prospect for alliance, because of the shared commitment to Marxist ideals, was the Revolutionary Party.

By 1926, the Revolutionary Party had become aware of Ho's movement in Canton, and had begun to make tentative offers of alliance. Early contacts with the League achieved few results, in part because of the League's criticism of the "utopian" nature of the Revolutionary Party's program, and of its insistence that alliance could take place only if the members of the Revolutionary Party entered the League as individuals. By mid-1927, however, a tentative agreement was reached regarding the formation of a unity committee. The Revolutionary Party changed its name to the Viet Nam Cach Mang Dong Chi Hoi (Vietnamese Revolutionary League), and its ideology and program were revised to coordinate more closely with the League's own program. National revolution was seen as a step toward world revolution, and there was a clear expression of the desire to move Vietnam toward a communist society.[46]

Problems soon arose, however. The Revolutionary Party wanted to reserve all the major posts in the projected regional committees to itself. Within the League, a radical faction under Tonkin regional committee secretary Tran Van Cung considered the Revolutionary Party too imbued with "petit bourgeois" nationalism, and the accord was thereupon rejected. The Revolutionary Party found it suddenly had considerable competition—from the nationalist but noncommunist Viet Nam Quoc Dan Dang (VNQDD) in the North, and from the League in the South. Losing strength, particularly among workers, it sent a representative, Nguyen Si Sach, to China in 1928 to try again to reach some understanding with the League.[47] He returned in April with a letter which appears to have been deliberately insulting. The League, claiming that it was not only larger but also more advanced than the Revolutionary Party, said that an alliance could take place only if members of the Revolutionary Party joined already functioning cells of the League.

46. The regulations can be found in *TLTK*, V, 14–17. Details on the negotiations are in AOM, Carton 335, Dossier 2690, "Déclarations dernières," *passim*.
47. Nguyen Si Sach later joined the League, was arrested, and died in a French prison in 1929.

As a sop it offered two seats on one of its regional committees.[48] Not surprisingly, the offer was spurned, but the Revolutionary Party continued to lose members to its more dynamic competitor. By 1929, there was still no alliance.

Negotiations with the VNQDD were even more difficult. From the beginning, the two organizations found themselves competing for followers in Tonkin. Strongly nationalist and determined to promote an armed insurrection against the French, the VNQDD did not at all tend toward Marxism, and some of the leaders had even developed an aversion to socialism.[49] It had been formed at a time when communists in Asia were beginning to view alliances with middle-class parties with caution. The League reflected this distrust and made only a few half-hearted gestures toward cooperation. By 1928, ill feeling was on the rise as the VNQDD relied increasingly on Chiang Kai-shek and his Nationalist Party in China, now the archenemies of the Chinese Communist Party. As a result, serious negotiations between the two never took place.[50]

In any event, the Comintern was beginning to have second thoughts about the wisdom of encouraging alliance with bourgeois nationalist parties in Asia. The Sixth Congress, meeting in the summer of 1928, initiated a major change in the direction of communist strategy in Asia. The united front concept was now to be more narrowly defined, and alliances with bourgeois parties were acceptable only under stringent conditions. Petit bourgeois attitudes within communist parties were criticized, and instructions were issued to increase the "proletarian" character of organizations by recruiting more in working class areas.[51]

48. *Contribution,* I, 35.

49. The ideology of the VNQDD is discussed in Tran Huy Lieu, "Chu nghia dan toc cach mang va su chuyen bien cua no trong giai doan lich su giua hai cuoc chien tranh the gioi" [Revolutionary nationalism and its evolution between the two world wars], *NCLS,* no. 151 (July-Aug. 1973), pp. 6–25.

50. There is some disagreement over whether negotiations were spurned by the VNQDD or the League. See Hoang Van Dao, *Viet Nam Quoc Dan Dang* [Vietnamese Nationalist Party] (Saigon, 1970), p. 43; *Contribution,* I, 9; and *Giai Cap,* p. 425. Actually, neither side was prepared to make major compromises.

51. The Sixth Congress and its attitude with regard to colonial questions is discussed in Kermit McKenzie, *The Comintern and World Revolution, 1928–1943* (New York, 1964).

During the lifetime of the League, then, the concept of a Leninist united front never became operant in Vietnam. This is not to say that the League's policies were a total failure. The League had considerable success in stealing support from its rivals, and a high proportion of its membership had earlier belonged to other organizations. That it was not successful in forging a united front of all nationalist groups is in part a reflection of the highly divisive and competitive character of the anticolonialist movement itself.

The League Breaks Up

The events of the late 1920s present a mixed picture as far as the growth of the revolutionary movement is concerned. The League itself was obviously gaining in strength and numbers. By 1929, there were over one thousand adherents, half in Tonkin.[52] At the same time the worker movement was on the rise. Red unions were being established at key industrial centers around the country, and the number of strikes had increased markedly since 1925. By 1929, League members began to organize peasant associations, mainly in the rural areas of North Vietnam.[53] These recruiting effects did not substantially change the basic middle class character of the League, however.

The events in Vietnam and abroad began to have their effect among certain elements in the League, particularly in Tonkin, where the desire to set up a true communist party led to the creation in early 1929 of the first communist cell (*chi bo*) made up of seven members.[54] The impetus for the new cell came from Tran Van Cung, a League member from Annam who had become secretary of the Tonkin regional bureau. In Tran's recollection, he and like-minded League members in Tonkin had grown to feel that the League as constituted was too weak, lacking in leadership

52. *Giai Cap,* p. 431; SLOTFOM, Series III, Carton 48, dossier entitled "Les Associations anti-françaises en Indochine et la propagande communiste: Historique," p. 40. This is the first of a series of classified reports issued by the Sûreté Générale over a period of ten years. Hereafter these reports will be cited as *Note périodique.*
53. For some of their activities, see *Giai Cap,* pp. 410–416.
54. Members were Tran Van Cung, Ngo Gia Tu, Trinh Dinh Cuu, Duong Hac Dinh, Nguyen Van Tuan, and Nguyen Duc Canh. *TLTK,* VI, 45. Tran Van Cung (Quoc An) has discussed this period in his brief memoirs. See *Buoc Ngoat,* pp. 105–119.

and ideologically flabby. In late 1928, he had told League chairman Lam Duc Thu that a communist party should be established,
but the latter brushed him off. The cell formed in early 1929 under
his leadership also served as the nucleus of the Tonkin regional
committee of the League, and in that capacity Tran Van Cung and
his disciples called a conference of the Tonkin members of the
League in late March to discuss the need for creation of a communist party and to choose representatives to send to the forthcoming League conference in Hong Kong. At the meeting, all
twenty representatives approved of the proposal to establish a
communist party, and four delegates, led by Tran Van Cung, were
elected to attend the Hong Kong meeting.[55]

At the end of April, delegates from all three regions and from the
emigré Vietnamese group in Thailand gathered in Hong Kong for
the League's first plenary meeting.[56] Prior to the formal convening
of the conference, Le Hong Son of the Central Committee called a
preliminary meeting of the delegates from all areas to see if the
forthcoming Tonkin proposal could be worked out in advance.
There was general agreement on the need for creation of a formal
communist party, but disagreement on how to go about it. Some
wanted to abandon the League entirely, others wanted to make it
the umbrella of the new organization, and still others wanted to
create communist support groups (*nom trung kien cong san*) to
carry out preparatory work before a final decision.[57] Lacking
agreement at the preliminary conference, the question was left for
the plenary session to decide.

At the plenary meeting, held May 1–9, 1929, the Tonkinese
delegates immediately complained about the manner of determin-
ing representatives, contending that they should have the largest
number of delegates, since there were many more League members
in the North. Whether or not their contention was justified, the

55. Mkhitarian says thirty representatives met in April. See page 225.
Other delegates were Ngo Gia Tu, Duong Hac Dinh, and Nguyen Van
Tuan.
56. There is some divergence on the number of representatives. For various treatments, see *Giai Cap*, p. 433; *Contribution*, I, 56–57; Mkhitarian,
p. 226; SLOTFOM, Series III, Carton 48, *Note périodique* "Historique."
57. Mkhitarian, p. 226. Much new information on this period can be
found in SLOTFOM, Series III, Carton 48, *Note périodique*, no. 4 (Jan.
1930).

proposal was rejected, and when the Tonkinese delegates demanded that immediate consideration of the creation of a communist party be placed first on the agenda, they were rebuffed by the full conference.[58] The chairman of the League, Lam Duc Thu, retorted that such a matter could not be discussed at a meeting of the League, but should be brought up separately. There was some sentiment among other delegates in favor of creating a communist party, but for various reasons, they were reluctant to voice support of the proposal. Some were afraid to antagonize Lam Duc Thu, some felt that hasty action would be unwise, and others believed that creation of an open communist party would invite retaliation from the increasingly anticommunist Kuomintang government in Nanking.[59] Deprived of official support from the conference, although with considerable covert sympathy, Tran Van Cung announced the withdrawal of the Tonkinese delegates; he and two others left the meeting and returned to North Vietnam.[60]

After the departure of the delegates from Tonkin, the conference turned to the original purpose of the meeting and discussed a new program of action and new statutes, in the light of decisions taken at the Sixth Comintern Congress. A new program was drawn up which showed a considerable advance over the 1925 version, at least from a Marxist point of view: it was strongly anti-imperialist and antifeudal in tone, calling for the confiscation of landlord land and the eventual creation of a proletarian dictatorship.[61] As far as united front policy was concerned, the conferees decided to pursue

58. There is no indication how the voting went. For details, see SLOT-FOM, Series III, Carton 48, *Note périodique*, no. 4 (Jan. 1930).

59. There are a number of unfavorable references to Lam Duc Thu (real name Nguyen Cong Vien) in the literature on the period. For example, King Chen, *Vietnam and China, 1938–1954* (Princeton, 1969), pp. 25–26, refers to his "luxurious living." *Giai Cap*, p. 433, asserts that other members "lacked confidence" in him. Curiously, SLOTFOM materials seldom refer to him, and designate Hong Son (Le Hong Son) as League chairman at the time. There is no doubt, however, that Lam was an important figure in the movement. Later he left, or was expelled, and is considered a traitor in most nationalist circles.

60. Duong Hac Dinh stayed to report events at the conference to the renegades. A communist source reports that he was later purged from the League. *Buoc Ngoat*, p. 117.

61. *TLTK*, IV, 143–169, has the Vietnamese version. SLOTFOM, Series III, Carton 48, *Note périodique* "Historique," discusses the conference in detail.

an alliance with the Revolutionary Party, but to open attack on the VNQDD. Finally, the conference agreed that the Vietnamese proletariat was still too weak and unaroused to justify the immediate formation of a communist party. The League, however, would make advance preparations for the ultimate changeover.[62]

Communism in Disarray

Upon their return to Tonkin, the three renegade delegates immediately issued a statement asserting that capitalism and the workers' movement were rapidly gaining momentum in Vietnam, and that the League was a group of "false revolutionaries" who "have never carried their efforts to the proletarian masses or adhered to the Comintern."[63] In their view, it was high time to form a communist party, including willing members of the League and the Revolutionary Party. After convening a preliminary meeting at a temple in Hanoi to discuss the issue, a Hanoi conference of representatives officially established the Communist Party of Indochina (ICP) in mid-June and chose a provisional central committee of seven men. The program of action strongly reflected the decisions of the Sixth Comintern Congress, calling for a proletarian-peasant alliance and reliance on the aid of progressive elements of the petty bourgeoisie.[64]

The establishment of the new party had an immediate disintegrating effect on the other radical organizations in Vietnam. In the North, almost all League members joined the new ICP. In the Center, Revolutionary Party influence continued strong, but some members in Quang Nam and Quang Ngai turned to the new communist organization. In the South, the old League continued to maintain its strength; only when Ngo Gia Tu arrived in Saigon did the ICP begin to build its influence there, primarily through red

62. The current view in Hanoi (as of the Comintern in Moscow at the time) was that the renegades were correct in feeling that the time was ripe for creating a formal communist party. *Giai Cap,* p. 439.

63. For the quoc-ngu version, see *TLTK,* IV, 170–173. A French version is located in *Contribution,* I, annex 2. SLOTFOM, Series III, Carton 48, *Notes périodiques* nos. 1, 3, and 4 ("Historique", Dec. 1929, and Jan. 1930 respectively), have details on the ongoing controversy between the two factions.

64. The manifesto, and other details about the new party are in SLOTFOM, Series III, Carton 48, *Note périodique* "Historique."

cells in commercial enterprises.[65] ICP influence had begun to penetrate all three areas of Vietnam, but was dominant only in the North.

In the meantime, the rump conference in Hong Kong had elected a new central committee comprising almost all the members present and had expelled the Tonkin delegates as "unworthy to represent the masses." Upon their return to Vietnam, however, delegates from the Center and the South reported that competition from the new ICP was stiff, and after an apparently hasty meeting in Hong Kong, the League's central committee decided to set up a competing communist party, the An Nam Cong San Dang (Annam Communist Party).[66] The new party issued a declaration criticizing the ICP as Menshevik and drafted a program and statutes conforming to Comintern directives. The new leadership was apparently carried over intact from the old League, for the latter's central committee became the governing body of the new ACP.[67] By late 1929 the two parties were actively competing with each other, exchanging insults, and, in some cases, even establishing competing cells in the same enterprise.

In the Center, the Revolutionary Party gradually began to feel the effects of the formation of the ICP and membership dropped by half. Some members wanted to create a purely national organization that would disown any connection with the new parties, but most continued to favor a merger. In the meantime the Revolutionary Party leaders responded in their timeworn fashion by renaming their own organization. It now became the Dong Duong Cong San Lien Doan (Indochinese Communist League). The ICP, however, still refused the newly named organization's demand for fusion of the two organizations and offered acceptance of Communist League members only on an individual basis.

---

65. An extended discussion of this period is located in Nguyen Nghia, "Cong cuoc hop nhat cac to chuc cong san dau tien o Viet Nam va vai tro cua dong chi Nguyen Ai Quoc" [The unification of the first communist organizations in Vietnam and the role of comrade Nguyen Ai Quoc], *NCLS,* no. 59 (Feb. 1964), pp. 3–4.

66. There is disagreement on the date. *Giai Cap,* p. 457, mentions November 1929. *Contribution,* IV, 22, and Nguyen Nghia, p. 3, take August as the founding date.

67. For the members of the new committee, see SLOTFOM, Series III, Carton 48, *Note périodique* "Historique."

The Unity Conference

When the Executive Committee of the Comintern heard about the events in far-off Indochina it was obviously displeased. In October 1929 it sent off a blistering letter criticizing the factionalism of the Indochinese revolutionary movement. According to the Comintern, the lack of a united party was a real danger to the development of communism in Vietnam and was "entirely mistaken".[68] It asserted that the objective conditions for a capitalist revolution were already present in Vietnam, and that "the development of the independent workers movement and the existence of a communist organization in the country create the essential urgency of the creation of a communist party in Indochina." It criticized the League faction for showing "indecisiveness and indifference" and called for the immediate formation of a united communist party based on proletarian leadership. It stressed the necessity of increasing worker representation in the party, and suggested that a unity conference be convened, chaired by a representative of the Comintern who would be sent as a mediator. Presumably as a result of the letter, the first serious attempt to achieve unity of the various revolutionary organizations occurred in December 1929 when members of the rival organizations met with a delegate from the Comintern. Although the Hong Kong meeting failed to produce final agreement, conditions were destined to improve.[69]

Earlier in 1929, Ho Chi Minh, who had been active in Europe and among Vietnamese emigres in Siam, was instructed to return to South China as the Comintern's official representative at unity talks.[70] Under his chairmanship a new unity conference was convened on February 3, 1930, with one representative from the ICP and two from the ACP. A member of the Communist League was

68. A French version of the letter is located in *Contribution*, IV, annex 7. Comments are found in I. A. Ognetov, *Komintern i Vostok* [The Comintern and the East] (Moscow, 1969), pp. 430–431.

69. Evidently the split was not considered total by all parties. Le Hong Son, in charge of the League at the time, said he would not fight the ICP, since it was "working for the cause." SLOTFOM, Series III, Carton 48, *Note périodique*, no. 1 (Jan. 1930). The representative from the Comintern was Le Hong Phong, a League member who had been studying in the Soviet Union since 1927.

70. Information on his activities in Siam can be found in *Nash President*, pp. 135–157.

invited but did not appear.[71] Ho Tung Mau and Le Hong Son, representing the old League but apparently taking part as intermediaries, also participated.

The meeting took place in a small house in a village near Kowloon. Ho began by lecturing the delegates for their laxity in permitting the break to take place. Apparently sensing that the difference between the two parties was based less on major issues of doctrine than on the question of tactics and personal pique, Ho suggested that what was needed was not the absorption of one party by the other, but an entirely new party, with a new program and statutes, and into which all who approved the aims could be accepted as members. There was a quick and probably relieved acceptance of the suggestion by both sides. Symptomatically, the main remaining bone of contention was the question of the name. The ICP wanted to keep the name Dong Duong (Indochinese), which the ACP categorically rejected. Ho soothed the delegates by saying that neither Indochinese (because it implied all of Southeast Asia) nor Annam (because it was reminiscent of the Chinese way of referring to the "pacified South") was an appropriate name for the new organization. He obtained general agreement on a third name, the Viet Nam Cong San Dang (Communist Party of Vietnam). Remaining problems were solved without conflict. Temporary statutes and a new program were drawn up, and a provisional central committee was chosen, with two members from each side and Ho as mediator.[72] Other groups, the Communist League and a Chinese exile group in Saigon-Cholon, could enter when arrangements were complete. Eventually a provisional central committee of nine members was to be formed, and would request official recognition from the Comintern. On February 5, the conference adjourned and the members returned to Vietnam to begin the process of amalgamation and selection of a new provisional central committee until the convening of an official party congress.[73]

71. Mkhitarian, p. 248, says there were two delegates from the ICP, Nguyen Duc Canh and Trinh Dinh Cuu. Nguyen Nghia has information on ACP activities during this period. See pages 5–6.

72. Details are in SLOTFOM, Series III, Carton 48, *Note périodique*, no. 6 (April 1930). *TLTK*, VI, 134–140, has the texts in quoc-ngu.

73. The text of the declaration issued at the close of the conference is in *Buoc Ngoat*, pp. 75–77.

Chapter 12

The Red Soviets of Nghe-Tinh

The Vietnamese communist movement began to consolidate during the first year of the new decade. It had endured a perilous period of factionalism and had achieved a delicate unity. To this degree it had overcome, at least temporarily, the problems that had proved such an obstacle to earlier movements of national resistance in Vietnam. There were signs, too, that the new party might be able to avoid other serious deficiencies which had so limited the effectiveness of its predecessors. The League, during its short years of existence, had followed Ho's advice and avoided the kind of ill-conceived attacks on French authority which had characterized Phan Boi Chau's old nationalist organization, and which had led to a brutal French response. By its attention to organization and discipline the League had managed to build up an extensive network of supporters throughout the country and had established itself as the best disciplined and most effective anti-French political organization in Vietnam. Then, too it had made a serious if not always successful effort to build up support among the urban and rural masses—something that earlier groups had not even attempted. True enough, the League had been essentially an elitist group, comprised primarily of intellectuals. But under constant prodding from the Comintern, it made a strenuous attempt to broaden the base of its support among workers in factories and the mines, on the rubber plantations in the South, and among poor peasants in the rural areas throughout the country. In 1930, the communist movement was in a relatively secure position. The Yen Bay revolt had destroyed the influence of the VNQDD apparatus in Tonkin, and the communists had no serious rival within the resistance movement. If it could avoid internal squabbles and an adventuristic outlook, it might hope to build its strength and form the nucleus of a nationwide anti-imperialist movement that would eventually sweep the French into the sea.

The Party Emerges

In October 1930, the temporary committee chosen by the three regions met officially in Hong Kong for the first plenary meeting of the central committee of the new Communist Party of Vietnam.[1] The major items discussed were an official name for the party, the acceptance of a new political program and regulations, and the establishment of mass organizations. The need for a new name had been created by Comintern displeasure with the existing name as expressed in a letter earlier in the year.[2] In Moscow's view, Vietnam, Laos, and Cambodia were linked by economic ties despite cultural differences, and activities in the three areas should therefore be directed by a single party.[3] The name Vietnamese Communist Party was obviously too restricted. Some local communists complained that there was little communist activity in Laos and Cambodia, but in the end the party dutifully changed its name once again, this time to the Dang Cong San Dong Duong (Indochinese Communist Party, or ICP). At the same time, decision had little more than academic meaning, for what little communist activity existed in the two non-Vietnamese areas—one small communist cell in a rubber plantation at Chup in Cambodia and another at a tin mine in Laos—was initiated almost entirely by Vietnamese.

Of more immediate importance was the question of the party's front policy, and here there were indications of a significant change of direction. The Sixth Comintern Congress (of 1928) had called for a narrower interpretation of the United Front than had hitherto existed, and for more emphasis on class struggle and increased

1. Two delegates did not attend the meeting. Nguyen Phong Sac was sent to Annam as a liaison with the soviet leadership, and Tran Van Can got lost in Hong Kong and missed the conference. "Cac co so bi mat cua co quan lanh dao dang cong san dong duong." *NCLS,* no. 37 (April 1962), p. 22.

2. Details on Comintern instructions, brought by Le Quang Dat from Shanghai, are located in SLOTFOM, Series III, *Note périodique,* no. 13 (Jan. 1931), p. 8.

3. Tran Huy Lieu, *Lich Su,* II, 36–37.

work among the urban proletariat. The new party formed a front organization entitled the Phan De Dong Minh (Anti-imperialist Front), but its composition was to be restricted to the proletariat, the rural poor, and only the most revolutionary elements among the petit bourgeoisie. Under the prodding of Moscow, the new party was moving decisively away from the nationalist orientation of the League and in the direction of Marxist orthodoxy.[4]

In order to facilitate the building of a mass base, the Hong Kong conferees also moved toward the establishment of mass organizations under party direction: unions (*tong cong hoi*), peasant associations (*nong hoi*), communist youth leagues (*thanh nien cong san doan*), red assistance associations (*cuu te do*), and women's leagues (*phu nu lien hiep hoi*). As for the party's domestic apparatus, new regulations, following existing administrative divisions, set up regional bureaus in each of the three sections of Vietnam as well as (where feasible) in Laos and Cambodia with branches at lower levels extending down to cells in factories, mines, villages, and schools. Because French suppression hindered ICP activities throughout the country, the immediate establishment of a fully elected Central Committee operating within Vietnam was considered impossible, so a three-man Standing Committee was established to act temporarily in the name of the Central Committee.[5]

Beginnings of Revolt

The formation of the new communist party in 1930 came at a

4. There are vague references in Sûraté Générale materials that the League and Ho Chi Minh were criticized by the Comintern for their "nationalist" tendencies during the early 1930s. For example, see SLOTFOM, Series III, Carton 52, *Note périodique*, no. 33 (fourth trimester 1934), annex 9, translation of article in *Revue Bolchevique*. For a contemporary criticism, see *Lich Su*, p. 33.

5. Members of the Standing Committee were Nguyen Phong Sac (later replaced by Ngo Duc Tri), Nguyen Trong Nha, and Tran Phu. It was first located at Hanoi, but soon moved to Saigon for better links with China and France. Tran Phu, son of a mandarin from Central Vietnam, had become one of the leading figures in the party after studying at the Stalin School in Moscow, and drafted the party program of October 1930. Early the next year, however, he was seized by the French and died—whether of disease or torture is not certain—in prison. For a biographical sketch, see Ton Quang Duyet, "Mot vai y kien bo sung ve lich su hai dong chi Tran Phu va Nguyen Thi-minh Khai" [A few additional opinions on the history of Tran Phu and Nguyen Thi-minh Khai], *NCLS*, no. 139 (July-Aug. 1971).

crucial time in the history of Vietnam. By the late 1920s, worsening economic conditions throughout Indochina had led to growing unrest, not only in urban working areas, but on rural plantations and in the rice-farming countryside as well. As we have seen, the size of the Vietnamese proletariat had continued to increase, reaching over 200,000 in 1929. This was a four-fold increase since the beginning of the century. Working conditions and salaries were as unsatisfactory as ever, and had not been substantially alleviated by the minor reforms during the liberal regime of Governor-general Varenne. In the last years of the decade, the number of strikes began to increase—from seven in 1927, involving 350 workers, to 24 in 1929 comprising over 6,000 workers, to 98 in 1930, with a total of 31,680 participants.[6] These strikes occurred throughout the three zones of Vietnam, although they tended to be concentrated in the big urban areas of Hanoi-Haiphong in the North, Ben Thuy and Vinh in the Center, and Saigon-Cholon in the South, as well as in the rubber plantation areas in the Terre Rouge near the Cambodian border.

The strike movement probably began as a spontaneous response to conditions, but in late 1927 and 1928 the League began to send its own militants into urban areas to form illegal workers' unions. At the end of 1928, as the League attempted to "proletarianize" its operation, it moved into factories throughout Vietnam, and to the mines north of the Red River Delta. For the first time, industrial workers' unions were formed in Tonkin. The League's activities were taking place at a crucial time, for the world economic crisis of the late 1920s was beginning to have serious effects on the Indochinese economy. As the depression worsened, French capital fled the country, leading to a rapid increase in unemployment; in some enterprises over half the workers were laid off.[7]

Such sporadic strike activity was undoubtedly disquieting to the French, but in itself was no cause for alarm. Discontent was growing in the rural areas of Central Vietnam, however. Unhappiness about high taxes and high rents, and about the venality and corruption of local mandarins, coupled with resentment of the French monopolies, led to riots in the late 1920s. To these chronic condi-

6. Other figures can be found in *Giai Cap,* p. 83; and *Lich Su,* IIB, p. 16.
7. *Lich Su,* p. 12. Salaries were down by 30 to 50 percent, and employment by one-third.

tions were added the disastrous consequences of flood conditions
in Central Vietnam and a severe fall in the price of rice. Land
values tumbled as rice lost its value and countless acres of land
were simply abandoned by their peasant owners. In late spring of
1930, food riots in the countryside provided a dismal counter-
point to the work stoppages in urban areas.[8]

The economic dissatisfaction in rural areas marked the first
time in two decades that the Vietnamese peasantry showed the
potential to become an active force in the nationalist movement.
Had the sporadically active urban resistance groups been able to
unite forces and take advantage of the crisis conditions in the
countryside, a serious threat to French rule might have resulted.
On the whole, however, the Vietnamese nationalist movement was
unprepared for the opportunity. Moderates occasionally called for
urgent attention to bettering economic conditions for workers and
peasants, but took no further action. The VNQDD prepared to
strike at French rule in the North but its plans ignored the seething
unrest elsewhere in the country. Other urban groups were in a
state of disintegration. Only the new ICP seemed to view the signs
of discontent as an opportunity.

To see the rising wave of protest and to know how to handle it
were two different problems, however. Since its Sixth Congress, the
Comintern had recognized the existence of a rising revolutionary
wave throughout the world for which communist parties should be
preparing. But the congress was not specific about which areas
were ripe for an armed uprising, nor about the tactics to be followed in case a spontaneous rebellion occurred. Such decisions
could only be made by the party on the spot.

In the early months of 1930 a series of strikes broke out in
French Indochina—at the Phu Rieng rubber plantation near Bien
Hoa in Cochin China, where thousands struck, demanding salary
increases and shorter working hours; at a match factory at Ben
Thuy; and at a textile plant at Nam Dinh in Tonkin. While not

8. Tran Van Giau, *Giai Cap Cong Nhan Viet Nam, 1930–1935* [The
Working Class of Vietnam, 1930–1935] (Hanoi, 1962), p. 12, has figures
on the drop in the price of rice. French reports concede that 30 percent of
the people were hungry in Annam. See the report of M. Faure in AOM
Carton 333, Dossier 2686. Tran Van Giau's work cited here is a sequel to
Giai Cap. Hereafter it will be cited as *Giai Cap (1930–1935).*

exceptionally important in themselves, these strikes were stimulated in part by communist activists and can be seen in retrospect as the opening shots in a year of rebellion.[9] From the point of view of the ICP, the strikes were important because, for the first time, the participants were willing to make political demands as well as economic ones. By mid-April workers had left their jobs at several industrial centers in Hanoi and Haipong, while unrest at Ben Thuy continued. Workers at the Ba Son arsenal in Saigon demanded a raise. Nervous, the French attempted to maintain order by prohibiting demonstrations, but the movement was begining to reach national proportions. By May and June, the situation had deteriorated so badly that opposition parties in Paris called on the Doumergue cabinet to form a commission of inquiry on Indochinese reforms.

From the government's point of view, the month of May witnessed an ominous new development—the appearance of jacqueries as peasants demanded an amelioration of their own economic conditions. On May Day, peasants joined workers in marches in Thai Binh province. The first major incident was in the Thanh Chuong district of Nghe An province where three thousand peasants raided the Ky Vien plantation, destroyed property, seized rice and tools, and planted the hammer and sickle flag on the main adminstration building.[10] Similar riots took place elsewhere in Annam and in Tonkin. Demands for lower taxes and the release of political prisoners were made. Many of the French in Indochina, who for years had been accustomed to putting a Bolshevik label on all forms of nationalism in Vietnam, were quick to point to communist leadership in the strike movement. And, indeed, superficial indications of communist involvement were everywhere. By 1930, red unions had been set up in a number of industrial and

9. Details on the Phu Rieng and Nam Dinh strikes are in AOM Carton 322, Dossier 2614, telegrams of February through April 1930. For information on the Ben Thuy uprising, see AOM, Carton 333, Dossier 2686, report of M. Petit, inspector of local militia at Vinh. The hyphenated phrase Nghe-Tinh is a short form for the adjoining provinces of Nghe An and Ha Tinh.

10. Reports can be found in AOM Carton 323, Dossier 2628, and Carton 332, Dossier 2684. Also see *TLTK*, VI, 62–63. The plantation was owned by a Cochin Chinese who allegedly had confiscated communal land and exploited workers. See AOM Carton 327, Dossier 2641, telegram of June 4, 1930.

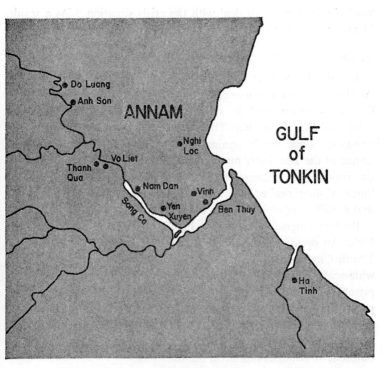

Map 2. Area of Nghe An–Ha Tinh revolts

commercial establishments. Red flags were conspicuous in peasant riots (although one observer noted that more than a few peasants thought that the hammer and sickle was the government's flag). And party activitists made a concerted attempt to bring out the workers in support of world proletarian solidarity by passing out leaflets calling for support of the Soviet Union.

In fact, however, the communist party was barely managing to keep up with events. Central Committee directives, reflecting orders from the Comintern and the Communist world syndicalist organization (the Profintern), stressed the necessity of organizing the workers, and regional and local committees made strenuous efforts to build up revolutionary organization in factories, villages, and schools as a means of asserting party leadership over the movement. But the party's organization at the local level was still woefully inadequate to deal with the crisis situation.[11] As a result, in many areas the strike movement was essentially spontaneous.

The Formation of the Soviets

In early September the disturbances began to reach their peak. At the center of the movement was the province of Nghe An in Central Vietnam, with its capital city of Vinh and the industrial suburb of Ben Thuy. Ben Thuy had been the scene of anti-French resistance since the beginning of the year, with the heart of the unrest at the Ben Thuy match factory. Since early May, farmers in the rural areas adjacent to Vinh had been involved in the resistance, rioting against the local authorities, pillaging plantations, and vocally supporting workers' demands.[12]

By late August, the alliance between workers and peasants in Nghe An province had been solidified. Peasants in the districts of Thanh Chuong, Nghi Loc, and Nam Dan, near Vinh, engaged in wide-scale rioting, looting, and building-burning. They released prisoners and drove the local governmental authorities to the provincial capital. There was little resistance from the notables, many of whom were frightened into inactivity. Higher mandarins, accustomed to giving little attention to the village level, were indifferent or powerless to affect the situation.

Meeting little resistance, local rebels began to expand their activities. Suicide troops ran from village to village to stir up trouble throughout the Center. Agitators called mass meetings to build up village support, and the calculated threat of violence intimidated reluctant elements. Local communist activists promised relief from poverty conditions, an end to oppressive taxes, and a more equitable distribution of local rice lands.[13] When the French attempted

11. French information indicated there were about three hundred active communists in the Nghe-Tinh area. See Billet report of June 27, 1931, in AOM Carton 333, Dossier 2686, p. 2. They estimated that about 10 percent of the peasants followed the rebels.

12. *TLTK*, VI, 62–67; Tran Huy Lieu, *Les Soviéts du Nghe Tinh* (Hanoi, 1960), pp. 18–26. During this period many of the workers at Ben Thuy, who often had kinship ties with villagers, went into the rural areas to drum up support. Reports of strangers in villages in the area were common; communist meetings were held in pagodas. See AOM Carton 332, Dossier 2684, report of Ho Doc Khai, June 10, 1931.

13. AOM Carton 333, Dossier 2686, report of Thai Van Giai, June 28, 1931.

to respond with military power, the incidence of bloodshed increased. On September 12, later called the "most critical day" by acting Governor-general René Robin, a mass riot broke out at the railway station of Yen Xuyen. Several thousand marchers moved toward the provincial capital of Vinh (apparently in the hopes of seizing the local branch of the Bank of Indochina). The French responded by dispatching troops to halt the advancing rioters and by bombing the crowds from the air.[14] One hundred seventy-four Vietnamese were reportedly killed; hundreds were wounded. The immediate crisis passed when the crowds dispersed, but attacks throughout the Center continued, and local authority simply vanished as notables and village gentry abandoned their posts or joined the revolutionaries.[15]

The peasant revolts were centered in the Central Vietnamese provinces of Nghe An and Ha Tinh (and, to a lesser degree, to the south in Quang Ngai). There was considerable historical precedent for rebelliousness in the area. Vietnamese in the Nghe-Tinh region had long been noted for their stubbornness, and were often described as the "buffaloes of Nghe An". Economic problems had simply made them more stubborn. Because of overpopulation, land was scarce; three-quarters of the people possessed less than one-half hectare of land.[16] Taxes and rents were unusually high in the area, and workers' salaries were low because of the availability of cheap labor in the surrounding countryside. Although some French sources insist that the area of the Song Ca was one of the most prosperous in Annam, the bulk of evidence indicates that it was not in 1930.[17]

14. *AF*, Nov. 1930, p. 354, has the French point of view. French strength was low, with less than a dozen French troops and about seventy-seven Vietnamese militiamen. Local authorities estimated that if the rioters had broken through at Yen Xuyen, they could have seized the provincial capital of Vinh. For details, see the report by the governor-general of Dec. 31, 1930, in AOM Carton 325, Dossier 2634.

15. *Ibid.*

16. Bui Huu Khanh, "Mot vai y kien ve van de phan phong trong phong trao xo viet Nghe Tinh" [A few opinions on the problem of anti-feudalism in the Nghe-Tinh Soviet movement] in *NCLS*, no. 34 (Jan. 1962), p. 32. Most of the unrest occurred in the valley of the river Song Ca, west of Vinh.

17. For example, a report of July 8, 1931 in AOM Carton 333, Dossier 2687, says 50 percent of the population in Nghi Loc, and 60 percent in Thanh Chuong, had no land; ninety percent of the population of Nam Dan

For the communists the distintegration of government power in the local areas was both an opportunity and a dilemma. The political vacuum created an almost unprecedented chance to seize power in the countryside. Yet the situation must have caused a certain amount of trepidation among the new provincial and regional leadership, since directives from higher levels were almost totally nonexistent. Lacking specific guidelines from the Central Committee (upon hearing of the revolt, the Committee sent Nguyen Phong Sac to act as a liaison officer with the Center, but he evidently arrived after the fact), the Annam regional committee decided on an activist policy designed to fill the vacuum left by the fleeing local officials and instructed the Nghe An provincial committee to organize revolutionary power in the villages. Local party organizations were to encourage the formation of peasant associations (*nong hoi xa bo*) and the institution of a village militia (*doi tu ve*). Local taxes were to be annulled, rents lowered, and communal land previously seized by rich landlords was to be confiscated and distributed to the poor peasants in the village. Excess rice was to be distributed to the needy.[18]

Evidently the first soviet to be formed was at Vo Liet village in Thanh Chuong district on September 12, 1930. Shortly thereafter, soviets were established throughout the Nghe An districts of

---

was hungry. Whether these worsening conditions can be seen as a direct cause of the revolt is a matter of debate. A number of recent studies investigating the causes of peasant revolt in Asia stress that poverty conditions, by themselves, do not necessarily lead to rebellion. For an interesting recent discussion of peasant revolt in the context of the Nghe-Tinh soviets, see James C. Scott, *The Political Economy of the Peasant Subsistence Ethic in Southeast Asia* (New Haven: Yale University Press, forthcoming). The causes of the uprising are extensively discussed in the Morché commission report located in AOM, Carton 333. Most observers agreed that hunger, anger over high taxes and the monopolies, and mandarin exactions and corruption were leading factors. Because of mandarin absorption of traditional village commune lands and because of disastrous weather conditions, it is likely that the peasants in the valley of the Song Ca could not fall back on traditional remedies to ease the pain. For an interesting analysis of these questions, see the articles in John W. Lewis, ed., *Peasant Rebellion and Communist Revolution in Asia* (Stanford, 1974).

18. For a directive of the Nghe An provincial committee, see *Lich Su*, p. 66. Circulars of the regional committee are in AOM, Carton 326, Dossier 2637, and SLOTFOM, Series III, Carton 48, *Note périodique*, no. 18 (March-April 1931), annex 7.

Thanh Chuong, Nam Dan, Hung Nguyen, Huong Son, and Nghi Loc.[19] The new soviets were comparatively simple organizations that took the form of typical communist peasant associations. To form an association, the drum of the village communal temple (*dinh*) was sounded to call peasants to gather in the village meeting hall. The proposed regulations were then read to all present and those who assented automatically became members of the association. The new organization and the local village party cell were then usually charged with forming an administrative committee to act as the executive body of the new soviet.[20] This executive committee (*ban chap hanh*) was chosen for a three-month duration to handle all major duties in the village. It was divided into several divisions: (1) secretariat (2) communications (3) organization (4) finance (5) verification (6) training (7) inspection, and (8) struggle.[21] The village soviet was essentially autonomous, for no organizational structure above the village level existed. For protection, each village formed a self-defense force, usually armed with sticks and spears or knives.[22] To maintain support for the new authorities, mass organizations for workers, women, and youth were formed. In a burst of zeal, the leadership attempted to reform peasant habits: useless ceremonies such as banquets for funerals and marriages were simplified or eliminated, and stiff penalties were imposed for gambling and stealing. Classes to teach quoc-ngu were opened.

The major cause for the soviet movement, of course, had been peasant dissatisfaction with economic conditions, and once in power the new leadership began to initiate steps to satisfy local demands for change. Since most of the new soviets were dominated by the poorer peasants in the village, there may have been considerable pressure, not only for a reduction of taxes and rents, but for a redistribution of land. The party leadership apparently insisted on a relatively moderate policy, however. Provincial party

19. Tran Huy Lieu, *Les Soviéts*, p. 26; *Lich Su*, p. 66.
20. Tran Huy Lieu, *Les Soviéts*, p. 27.
21. Trung Chinh, "Tinh chat doc dao cua so viet Nghe Tinh" [The unique character of the Nghe-Tinh Soviets], *NCLS*, no. 32 (Nov. 1961), p. 12.
22. This local force is now considered to be the first revolutionary military organization in Vietnam, and the precursor of the People's Army of Vietnam.

directives did not call for confiscation of all landlord land, but for only communal lands seized earlier by wealthy elements in the village. In general, this policy was observed, although in some areas where famine was high, peasants seized landlord land on their own initiative.[23] In a few cases, peasants set up producers' cooperatives (*hop tac xa*), but they were not encouraged and were abandoned. Most of the emphasis was put on tax elimination and rent reduction, as well as the distribution of the paddies of rich peasants to the poor. Rent was reduced rather than totally abolished, but, in practice, few landlords dared to claim it.[24]

As the land revolution proceeded, landlords and rich peasants who had not left the village were often mistreated. Village notables were evicted, their homes and property were destroyed, and in some cases they were forbidden to leave the village. In many areas, the rich and the powerful were actually executed, although accurate figures on the numbers killed are lacking.[25] At the beginning of the movement, it appears that some moderate elements—intellectuals, Roman Catholics, rich and upper middle peasants—joined the soviets, but most were eventually expelled or eliminated.[26]

It was at this stage that the party Central Committee held its

23. Earlier sources often said that much confiscation of landlord land took place. Modern sources in Hanoi deny this. See Tran Huy Lieu, "Van de chinh quyen xo viet" [The problem of soviet power], *NCLS*, no. 33 (Dec. 1961), pp. 1–2; Bui Huu Khanh, p. 29. A French archival source has a provincial circular of October 9, 1930, calling for continued distribution of landlord land with prior submission to the provincial committee. See AOM, Carton 326, Dossier 2637, translation of alleged provincial circular of Oct. 9, 1930.

24. Tran Huy Lieu, *Les Soviéts*, p. 28.

25. *Contribution*, V, contains a lengthy list of alleged communist atrocities, as obtained through interrogation of prisoners taken during the period. For a communist comment, see Trung Chinh, p. 13.

26. *Lich Su*, pp. 77, 81. According to French information, all Buddhist villages in Ha Tinh went over to the rebels, while Catholic areas remained loyal. SLOTFOM, Series III, Carton 48, *Note périodique*, no. 4 (May-June 1931). One source gives the total members of the soviet movement as 35,777; a French source estimated 40,000. See "L'Agitation politique en Indochine de 1929 à Mai 1931," p. 4, in AOM Carton 326, Dossier 2639. Provincial circulars authorized selected assassinations with prior approval by the committee. AOM Carton 326, Dossier 2637, circular of Oct. 9, 1930. Details on communist activities in Ha Tinh province can be found also in AOM Carton 335, Dossier 2690.

first formal session since the achievement of unity at the Hong Kong meeting in February. Undoubtedly the nationwide strikes and the formation of soviets in Annam were major topics of discussion, but the published documents of the conference mention surprisingly little about the events taking place in Nghe-Tinh. The party's political program was limited to generalizations about a revolutionary movement on the rise and about revolutionary forces preparing to seize power and establish worker-peasant governments. It did state that the party should make preparations to lead the masses in Vietnam toward the ultimate formation of a revolution government, but it refrained from predicting that the worker-peasant forces were in a position to take power in the immediate future.[27] The Central Committee realized the gravity of the situation, however, and issued a general directive to all levels, calling on party organizations everywhere to give maximum support to their comrades in beleaguered Nghe-Tinh. In response, sporadic worker and student strikes and peasant demonstrations took place during the last months of the year, particularly in Quang Ngai province in the Center, and in the delta cities in the South.[28]

The French Response

Until late summer, the French colonial authorities made little attempt to do more than put down each uprising as it occurred. Taken by surprise, plant managers and government officials in many areas were forced to grant concessions to striking workers or rioting peasants. By September, however, the protest movement had become too general to be given such casual treatment, and the government began to formulate more effective measures to deal with the rising wave of strikes and demonstrations. With less than three hundred troops available in the area (and they were local militia under French officers and NCOs), the government called in Foreign Legionnaires to deal with the rebellious provinces, and martial law was declared. French resident Le Fol was determined

27. The program is located in *Buoc Ngoat,* pp. 78–89.
28. The local Nghe An provincial committee decided in October 1930 to continue violent struggle despite growing problems. Otherwise, they estimated, the masses would lose faith in the party. See the provincial circular of Oct. 9, 1930, in AOM Carton 326, Dossier 2637.

to force the court administration to share responsibility for all actions taken in Annam, and the Privy Council was reluctantly compelled to sign all proclamations emanating from the government. The Minister of the Interior of the Hué court, Nguyen Huu Bai, was declared imperial viceroy to deal personally with the riot-torn provinces in the Center, and he devised a plan to combine military and political measures to pacify the troubled area: (1) local military forces would be reinforced by a system of military posts (*don*) manned by troops loyal to the court, and padded by local militia who were recruited in neighboring villages and headed by Vietnamese officials (*bang ta*), (2) population control would be achieved by making clan patriarchs responsible for the behavior of all members of the kinship unit;[29] parent-teacher associations were formed to control the behavior of school students, (3) local political authority would be strengthened by the creation of a political organization to operate at the village level; the organization would include all members of the community loyal to the colonial regime (it was called the Ly Nhan Dang, or Society of Right Minds). Finally, to prevent the epidemic from spreading to other areas, all citizens of the Nghe-Tinh region residing elsewhere were told to return to their native village.[30]

Ideally, the system was designed to permit Vietnamese local authorities to restore order and imperial control, while the French military units, with a policy of severe repression, would search out and capture the rebels, force the hostile villages to their knees, and quell the disturbances throughout the Central provinces. Where, as in Nghi Loc, villagers had taken the lives of government officials, reprisals would be the most severe.

In the short run, the political-military plan was only partially effective. Through the last months of 1930 the riots continued and many of the French-supported official groups were subverted or

29. Some of the local militia units were eventually dominated by the communists. See AOM Carton 33, Dossier 2686, report of M. Faure, special security commissioner at Vinh, June 27, 1931.
30. Tran Huy Lieu, *Les Soviéts*, p. 34; *TLTK*, VI, 70. There were sixty-eight such military posts in Nghe An and fifty-four in Ha Tinh. A Russian source says that many members of the Ly Nhan Dang were Catholics. See I. A. Ognetov, *Komintern i Vostok* [The Comintern and the East] (Moscow, 1969), p. 434.

existed only on paper.[31] By early 1931, however, a combination of military pressure and seductive policies designed to woo the undecided began to take effect. Because of the constant turmoil, the 1930 fall harvest was subnormal in Central Vietnam and by winter famine began to appear. To encourage submission the government issued identity cards with which the holder, upon indicating his loyalty to the authorities, received free food at specified locations in French-held areas.[32] As famine rose to serious levels, the communist party itself was forced to permit starving peasants to surrender in order to receive nourishment.

In other ways, too, the threat of famine served to destroy the shaky unity of the movement. Since Nghe-Tinh was an area with few landlords, the poorest peasants, desperate for rice, turned on the rich and even middle-level peasants to obtain food, thus alienating many of the potential allies of the movement. Because of this rice struggle (called in communist party histories the *lua gao dau tranh*), a period of almost blind violence began.

Another major problem faced by the communists was the ability of the French security police to harass and seize party leaders. After the Central Committee held its Second Plenum in Saigon in March of 1931, in order to consider policy regarding the Nghe-Tinh movement, one member, Ngo Duc Tri, was seized by the French. He not only confessed party secrets but also gave away the locations of many of the party leaders. As a result, during March and April, almost the entire Central Committee was seized.[33] Even the regional committees were dispersed. By spring, the soviet movement, torn by dissension and its leaders pursued by the authorities, began to subside. Intermittent riots took place during the spring and early summer of 1931. By early August, the last soviet (in the district of Anh Son) was forced to submit. Calm had returned to Indochina.[34]

31. *TLTK*, VI, 74.

32. Tran Huy Lieu, *Les Soviéts*, p. 37.

33. *Lich Su*, p. 31; and SLOTFOM, Series III, Carton 48, *Note périodique*, no. 18 (April-May 1931). Information on the arrest of Ngo Duc Tri was given in a telegram of April 8, 1931; see SLOTFOM, Series III, Dossier 44, "Note concernant Ngo Duc Tri" of Oct. 31, 1931, for further information.

34. A list of locations of unrest is given in *Contribution*, V.

The Lessons of Nghe-Tinh

The Nghe-Tinh revolt of 1930–1931 was perhaps the most serious uprising against the French since the Can Vuong movement before the turn of the century. It was the first major revolt by the peasantry since the tax riots of 1908, and it was the first time that rural discontent was coordinated and led by a nationalist party. In this sense it looked to the future more than it harked back to the past; it foreshadowed the strategy to be followed by the communists in the postwar period.

Historians in the Democratic Republic of Vietnam are well aware of the significance of the revolt. Communist historiography now views the soviet period as a glorious stage in the early history of the movement in Vietnam. There is no question of its importance in the history of the party, nor of the heroic determination of the peasant rebels' and leaders' suicidal struggle against great odds. At the same time, it was also a very nasty defeat for the young organization, and at least a temporary blow to its plan to overthrow the colonial government and put itself in power. As a result of the events of 1930–1931, virtually all of the major leaders of the party were arrested or killed. Not only the regional committees, but the party leadership in Saigon and most of the party professionals at the local levels were in prisons in various parts of Indochina. Moreover, other important communist operatives in Asia—including Ho Chi Minh, who was jailed in Hong Kong in June 1931—were seized in China; the Comintern's Far Eastern Bureau was broken up, and the Vietnamese party's contacts with Moscow were disrupted.[35]

Given the disastrous consequences of the revolt, and the untimeliness of its occurrence, what were the lessons to be learned from Nghe-Tinh?[36] Was the miscarriage of the revolt the result of the Comintern's miscomprehension of the situation—its mistaken notion that revolutionary potential lay in the deteriorating conditions

35. *Ho Chi Minh: Notre camarade*, p. 53. One was Serge La Franc, also known as Joseph Ducroix (Ducroux), a representative of the Comintern who had recently talked with ICP representatives in Saigon. He was arrested in Singapore.

36. For a more detailed discussion of these issues, see William J. Duiker, "The Red Soviets of Nghe-Tinh: An Early Communist Rebellion in Vietnam," *Journal of Southeast Asian Studies*, 4 (Sept. 1973).

in French Indochina? Or was the decision to resort to armed struggle the result of misinterpretation by the new and untried ICP leadership of the generalized statements about revolution that were emanating from Moscow? Or was the rebellion in Vietnam essentially a spontaneous uprising of peasants and workers, a disorganized jacquerie that the communists belatedly and unsuccessfully tried to control?

Given our present knowledge of the origins of the revolt, no categoric answer to these questions can be given. Even historians in Hanoi today appear to be uncertain about the precise role of the party in the early stages of the movement. Most of the leaders of the period have been long dead, and little primary material relating to party decisions is extant. Such material as does exist, however, appears to indicate that the decision to revolt was made by the provincial or regional leadership of the party in the Center on the basis of conditions in the area. The Comintern, of course, had seen the possibility of a new revolutionary wave in the world since 1928, and its directives to the infant communist party were replete with instructions to train the party and the masses for the period of revolutionary struggle ahead. On the other hand, Moscow was far from Vietnam, and was careful to warn the ICP leadership that any decision on an uprising had to be made by the party leaders themselves on the basis of local conditions.

For its part, the ICP central leadership apparently did not expect that its directives to lower organs to intensify activities would spark a major uprising in 1930. The party was organizationally and theoretically unprepared for a major confrontation with French power in 1930 and, from the scattered evidence available, the leadership was well aware that an uprising would be premature.[37] A Central Committee directive sent to the Annam regional committee immediately before the formation of the soviets made no reference to the formation of soviets nor to armed struggle.[38] When the Standing Committee met in Saigon in October, the soviets already existed; they simply tried to make the best of the situation, and to minimize the damage. One Standing Committee directive to the regional committee stated that "with things as

37. *Ibid.*, p. 197.
38. Tran Huy Lieu, "Van de," p. 6; Trung Chinh, pp. 3–4.

they are, we must behave in such a way as to reserve party and Soviet influence so that even if they are defeated, the meaning of the Soviets will penetrate deeply into the minds of the masses, and the influence of the party and the peasant associations will still be preserved."[39] At the same time, it indicated its disapproval of the adventuristic policies taken in the Center in a directive sent to all party levels.

Even in Annam, it is difficult to assess the responsibility. The regional committee's official journal *Nguoi Lao Kho* (The Toiler) allegedly said as late as October 5, 1930, that this was not the time for violence, because neither the party nor the masses were prepared. In the view of the editors, the best time for an uprising in Vietnam would be during a general world war.[40] If this is the case, it is possible the decision was made at a still lower level, in the Nghe-Tinh provincial committee.

In any event, it seems likely that the party hierarchy in the Center was faced with seemingly revolutionary conditions throughout the area and, adjusting as best it could to fast-changing events, simply tried to maintain its credibility among the masses by attempting to take the lead in an essentially spontaneous uprising. The central leadership did not initiate the soviets, nor did it approve of them when they appeared, but it felt that once they were under way they should be supported to the end. The central leadership recognized that French harrassment and insecure communications made difficult the exertion of their influence. In consequence, the regional committee was forced to a considerable degree to make decisions on its own. It attempted to maintain orthodoxy by following a simple soviet model and by interpreting Comintern strategy in the best way it could, but it was unable to keep events under control.

Whatever the failures of the ICP, the Comintern cannot be absolved of responsibility for the results. Its propaganda had consistently spoken of the imminent rise of a revolutionary wave throughout the world. It had abdicated responsibility by contending that only local party leaders could determine whether revolutionary conditions existed in a particular area. And, in a 1929

39. Trung Chinh, p. 5.
40. *Ibid.*, p. 4.

letter to the League, it had emphasized that the party need not be stable or well prepared before taking advantage of revolutionary conditions. Not surprisingly, the enthusiastic local cadres interpreted events in the Center as promising.

Their prognosis was mistaken. Conditions were not ripe for a revolutionary upsurge in 1930. Dissatisfaction with current conditions was relatively high among workers, but their demands were focused primarily on economic problems and few had reached the point of actively advocating the overthrow of the government. Similarly, the urban middle class was not, as a whole, in a revolutionary frame of mind. Some had joined the ICP or the VNQDD, but the general mood in the cities was one more of sullen discontent than of active opposition. Even among the peasantry, where discontent had reached a peak in late 1930, the feeling of desperation was overpowering only in Annam and in scattered parts of Cochin China.

In any event, the party was destined to pay a high price for its failure: years of persecution, isolation, and the near-extinction of its organizational apparatus would follow. Over one thousand accused communists were charged with complicity in the events, eighty were executed and nearly four hundred were deported for long-term sentences. The lessons that the party drew from the events, would, however, ultimately have beneficial effects on future behavior and strategy. From the debacle of the soviet movement emerged a revolutionary organization more united, better disciplined, and better able to utilize the appeal of nationalism. The memory of the Nghe-Tinh soviets would linger on through the 1930s and a decade later would become a major factor in persuading the party that the key to success in Vietnam lay in the villages, in the untapped potential of the millions of Vietnamese rice farmers. The party would not soon again exhaust its resources in a vain attack against vastly superior forces. If the soviets were a bitter lesson for the communists, it was a lesson well learned.

Chapter 13

Building the United Front

The euphoria of early 1930, when the new party looked forward to a revolutionary high wave in Vietnam, gave way to four years of patient and sometimes agonizing party-building, usually under the hostile scrutiny of the French Sûreté Général. With many of its leaders captured or executed, its local network scattered, and its communications with the Comintern disrupted, the party was forced to reassess its position, and to concede that the road to socialism in Vietnam would be a long and arduous one.

The party was by no means without resources, however. Although the internal leadership had been badly hurt by French arrests, it still had leadership of high quality outside the country—in South China, where the leaders of the old Revolutionary Youth League, Ho Tung Mau and Hong Son, were still active in support of party activities, and in Moscow, where a number of young Vietnamese revolutionaries were being taught at the Stalin School (also known as the University of the Toilers of the East). Beyond such human resources the ICP had one incalculable advantage over all other nationalist parties in Vietnam—the support of the world communist movement, headed by the Comintern. During the four years from the fall of the soviet movement until the First Party Congress in March of 1935, the Comintern provided ideological, financial, and educational support, by means of which the ICP was able to busy itself with reestablishing its base in Vietnam. Through its liaison office in the Colonial Section of the French Communist Party, which selected promising young Vietnamese nationalists, the Comintern was able to bring to Moscow for training in Marxist-Leninist doctrine and revolutionary techniques several dozen recruits for periods of from one to three years.[1] Graduates of the Stalin School were returned by circuitous routes to East Asia, from whence they were directed to rebuild the shattered apparatus of the party.

With the inner party leaders nearly all dead or in prison, and French security efforts hindering party work within the country, the new Moscow-trained leadership attempted to reconstruct the party from two bases outside Indochina—one in northeast Thailand and the other, under Le Hong Phong (now the recognized leader of the party, with Ho Chi Minh in prison) in Kwangsi province not far from the Sino-Vietnamese border.[2]

By 1932, the ICP was already beginning to attempt to revive its organizational apparatus within Vietnam. Stalin School graduate Tran Van Giau managed to reconstruct party organs in Cochin China despite sporadic harassment by local governmental authorities. In the Center and the North, revival was more difficult. In Tonkin, activity in the Red River Delta was almost totally absent, and the party had to establish the regional leadership in mountainous Cao Bang province under the Tay leader Hoang Dinh Giong. In the Center, French efforts hindered all attempts to organize at the regional level until 1934.

In the long run, however, the French security forces were fighting a losing battle against not only communist determination, but against policy decisions made by the French government in Paris. In the first place, replacements from the Stalin School returned to Vietnam as quickly as the French managed to arrest their predecessors. Second, periodic amnesties of political prisoners were declared by the French government, and arrested communist leaders were released, only to return to political activity. Finally, even imprisonment did not seem to solve the problem. Prisons, called "schools of Bolshevism," were hotbeds of communist activ-

1. The best information on these activities is in SLOTFOM, Series III, Carton 44, dossier entitled "Les élèves annamites a l'école Staline et le pacte franco-soviétique."

2. Le Hong Phong (real name Le Huy Doan?) was born in 1902 in Nghe An province. At first a member of the Tam Tam Xa, he joined the League in 1926, briefly attended the Whampoa Academy in Canton, and then was sent to the Soviet Union for further training. His activities in South China during the 1930s are discussed later in this work. Captured by the French in 1940, he was executed the same year.

ity; prisoners printed local newspapers, taught classes in Marxist-Leninist doctrine, and even directed communist party activities on the outside.[3]

The early 1930s can be accurately described as the "Stalinist years" of the ICP. For much of the new leadership of the party had been trained in Moscow at a time when his influence was paramount. And the imprint of his ideas is clearly visible on party strategy during this period. Surviving party programs and resolutions constantly emphasized the need for proletarianization of the party. Party cadres were instructed to put on blue denim and take jobs in industrial establishments and mines; workers were to be put in leadership positions whenever possible. Nationalism was condemned, and there was to be no attempt to ally with middle class elements against imperialism. Even the peasantry was considered suspect. Comintern directives criticized the ICP for its excessive reliance on peasant support, particularly in Cochin China where the party's strength lay primarily in the rural areas outside Saigon.[4]

While the official party leadership was under deep cover, the most visible form of communist activity in Vietnam was the newspaper *La Lutte* (The Struggle) in Saigon. *La Lutte* was established by Ta Thu Thau as a legal French-language organ of the Vietnamese working class in 1933. Ta Thu Thau was one of a number of Vietnamese intellectuals who had become attracted to the ideas of Leon Trotsky while in France in the late 1920s.[5] On his return to Vietnam, he became the leader of a small but vociferous Trotskyite group in Saigon clustered around the new journal. Although hostility between Trotskyites and the Comintern prevented formal cooperation between Ta Thu Thau's group and the ICP, a group of communists in the Saigon area joined the journal's edi-

---

3. AOM Carton 330, Dossier 2664, report of resident superior ad interim, March 1933.

4. SLOTFOM, Series III, Carton 48, *Note périodique,* no. 30 (first trimester 1934), p. 10, shows the worker emphasis. This stress on the proletarian character of the party is easily discernible in materials available on the period. For a provincial decree of Feb. 12, 1933, criticizing lower-level cadres for permitting too much peasant emphasis in the party, see AOM Carton 323, Dossier 2625, secret annex, first trimester, 1933, annex 5.

5. Ta Thu Thau began as a follower of Nguyen An Ninh. Joining Nguyen The Truyen's PAI in Paris, he probably became a Trotskyite in 1929 and was expelled from France in 1930 for rioting.

torial staff during the early 1930s, and for several years, an informal alliance existed between the two groups. Although documentation is lacking, there is some evidence that the Comintern tolerated this cooperation, at least until 1937.[6]

Having established an informal united front in Saigon, the revolutionaries at *La Lutte* concentrated on winning support for their programs from the Vietnamese populace.[7] The most concrete manifestation of their activity was their participation in local elections. There was not much possibility for the revolutionary alliance to realize electoral successes in the Colonial Council, for the electorate for that body was less than forty-five thousand, and did not as a rule include elements in Saigon, where those sympathetic to the aims of the group at *La Lutte* were most in evidence. Elections for the Saigon municipal council, however, were based on universal suffrage, and here the revolutionaries might be expected to have a better chance of success. In May of 1933, the group submitted its own list for the municipal elections and two of its nominees were elected.[8] In 1935, a combined slate of Trotskyites and members of the ICP ran in the March elections. This time four candidates were elected.[9] They appealed primarily to workers

6. I. Milton Sacks, "Marxism in Vietnam," in Frank Trager, ed., *Marxism in Southeast Asia* (Stanford, 1959), and Daniel Hemery's soon-to-be-published *Révolutionnaires légaux et pouvoir colonial à Saigon de 1932 à 1937: Le Groupe et le journal "La Lutte"* (Maspero, forthcoming), are the best sources for Trotskyite activity in French Indochina.

7. Most important were Trotskyites Ta Thu Thau, Phan Van Hum, ICP members Nguyen Van Tao and Duong Bach Mai, and the independent Nguyen An Ninh.

8. Elected were ICP member Nguyen Van Tao and independent Tran Van Thach. Nguyen Van Tao came from a gentry family in Cochin China fallen on hard times. He was dismissed from the lycée Chasseloup-Laubat in 1926 for fomenting disorder. Escaping to Paris, he later went to the Stalin School and attended the Comintern Congress. Back in France, he was expelled for instigating riots in 1930, and returned to Saigon the same year to become a journalist. See the report of governor-general, Oct. 3, 1936, in AOM Carton 330, Dossier 2665. Tran Van Thach later became a Trotskyite.

9. Tran Van Thach, Nguyen Van Tao, Ta Thu Thau, and Duong Bach Mai. They were disqualified on a technicality, and then, after an appeal to Paris, ran again and were victorious. Duong Bach Mai, born in Cochin China in 1904, also spent two years in Moscow. Briefly a Trotskyite, he later recanted and became a loyal member of the ICP.

in the Saigon-Cholon area, but also considered middle class concerns.[10]

Although it attempted to attract the votes of the urban bourgeoisie, the group at *La Lutte* did not try to achieve an alliance with moderates. Rather, it criticized such parties as the Constitutionalists and labeled them as collaborators, and enemies of the masses.[11] When some in the party questioned the necessity of antagonizing the Constitutionalists, *La Lutte* quoted Comintern directives to the effect that the best strategy was to isolate collaborationist elements by winning middle class support away from them.[12] If such was the aim, the group was reasonably successful, for in the 1935 municipal elections they wrested control of the Vietnamese section of the council away from the Constitutionalists, who had dominated the lists ever since the mid-1920s.

In the meantime, ICP leaders elsewhere in Vietnam and in South China continued their efforts to revive the party apparatus. A party congress was finally scheduled for March 1935. Originally set for Hong Kong, the location was changed to Macao after the original site was leaked.[13] In attendance at the congress were representatives from all five areas of Indochina, plus representatives from the two directing committees in Thailand and South China.[14] The major work of the congress concerned the problems of rebuilding the party apparatus, of reestablishing it as a major political force in the country, and of strengthening the party's mass organizations, which had substantially deteriorated after the Nghe-Tinh period. At the apex of the party, a Central Committee of nine members was chosen with a Standing Committee set at Saigon.

10. *La Lutte,* Feb. 19, 1935, has their platform. According to Governor Pagès, the group at *La Lutte* was masterful in the local councils, and became the "entitled counsellors" of the workers and petit bourgeoisie in the Saigon-Cholon area. See AOM Carton 329, Dossier 2654, report of Governor Pagès.

11. By this time, with Bui Quang Chieu in Paris, Nguyen Phan Long had become the leader of the Constitutionalist Party.

12. *La Lutte,* Dec. 6, 1934.

13. SLOTFOM, Series III, Carton 54, *Note périodique,* no. 35 (second trimester 1935), pp. 60–65.

14. Ho Chi Minh and Le Hong Phong were both in Moscow and did not attend. The French estimated that because of their harassment, no formal meeting took place. See SLOTFOM, Series III, Carton 54, *Note périodique,* no. 35 (second trimester 1935).

Above the Central Committee, however, a Directing Bureau was established at Shanghai to maintain liaison with the Comintern in Moscow.[15] The program issued by the congress called for the establishment of an anti-imperialist front, but its limits continued to be narrowly defined: among the forces to be opposed were Sun Yat-sen's Three People's Principles, Trotskyism, national reformism and petit bourgeois revisionism. In effect, the ICP's concept of the united front in 1935 did not differ substantially from that of 1930.

But the Macao conference was held on the eve of a new era in the history of the world communist movement. With the growth of National Socialism in Germany and the rise to power of Adolph Hitler in 1933, Soviet policy became more concerned with the need to build up antifascist popular fronts in countries around the world. The anti-imperialist struggle that had dominated communist policy since World War I was thus to be replaced in part by an antifascist one. The Seventh Congress of the Comintern held in the summer of 1935 provided the major platform for the declaration of this new policy. Returning delegates from the Seventh Congress were expected, of course, to transmit the results of the meeting to their own parties so that appropriate changes could be made in domestic strategies.

When Le Hong Phong returned from the Comintern congress to report to the ICP, he found that the program formulated by the party leadership in March was already out of date. What was now needed was not a narrow "united front from below" but a broad democratic front composed of all those elements in Indochina opposed to the spread of fascism, not only workers and peasants, but the urban bourgeoisie, local landowners, and all the minority peoples. The new slogans should call for peace, freedom, clothes and food, not independence and antifeudalism. Le Hong Phong set to work to bring the local party program abreast of the developments in Moscow, and in July of 1936 he convened a

15. SLOTFOM, Series III, Carton 54, *Note périodique*, no. 37 (fourth trimester 1935). It is interesting to note the degree of Comintern control over the ICP at this time. The Directing Bureau was placed under the Comintern. Of its members, a majority were to be selected by the Comintern, and of its three-member Permanent Bureau, two were to be selected from delegates chosen by Moscow.

plenary meeting of the Central Committee to revise the party's program of action. The party was no longer to oppose the moderates, but to cooperate with them and encourage their progressive tendencies, in order to build a wide alliance of all peace-loving and democratic forces.[16]

For the Vietnamese, the first concrete manifestation of the new mood came from France, with the formation in May 1936 of the Popular Front government led by the French Socialist Party under Leon Blum. Although the FCP was not a part of the Front, it supported the new government, which entered office with a clear program to oppose fascism, to support the Soviet Union, to end restrictive laws in France limiting free speech and association, to improve the economy, and to reduce unemployment. The program of the new government made only one reference to the colonial problem: it created a commission of inquiry to look into conditions and suggest reforms.[17]

The Popular Front government received a favorable welcome from most sectors of opinion in Vietnam. Judging from the reaction at *La Lutte*, the events in Paris received tentative approval from the ICP as well. Nguyen Van Tao, in an article in the June 5, 1936, issue of *La Lutte*, called the appointment of Moutet a "relatively happy choice." The FCP was not in the Popular Front government, he noted, but Moutet was sympathetic to the needs of the colonies; he had been a friend of Phan Chu Trinh and had opposed colonial brutality in Indochina.[18]

The new government in France immediately took action to improve conditions in Vietnam. The right to form political parties was recognized in Cochin China, and hundreds of political prisoners, including a number of prominent communists, were released from prison. Restrictions on the publication of journals and newspapers in Vietnamese were eased, and a committee was appointed to inspect labor conditions in Vietnam. The communists

16. See the confidential letter sent by the Central Committee to lower echelons, in SLOTFOM, Series III Carton 54, *Note périodique*, no. 44 (Sept. 1936), annex 1.

17. Tran Van Giau, *Giai Cap Cong Nhan Viet Nam, 1936–1939* [The Working Class of Vietnam, 1936–1939] (Hanoi, 1962), p. 10. Hereafter *Giai Cap (1936–1939)*.

18. *La Lutte*, May 5, 1936.

were dubious about the prospects for improved labor conditions because they considered many members of the new commission unsympathetic to working class interests, but in October 1936 a new labor law was issued calling for some major improvements for workers: (1) the working day would be gradually reduced over a two-year period to eight hours per day in industrial and commercial establishments, (2) women would not be permitted to do night work in factories and mines, (3) a six-day work week was established for workers in factories and mines, and (4) the annual paid vacations for workers should be increased gradually to ten days a year.[19] Finally, in a gesture to the colonies, the new government announced that a colonial inspection commission would be set up to obtain "an open expression" of opinion from French subjects abroad.

As the Popular Front government struggled to realize its program in Paris, the ICP adjusted its own policy to the new requirements from Moscow. Reacting to the decision by Paris to permit Vietnamese to found political parties in Cochin China, the Central Committee determined to prepare for the establishment of a legal party organization in the South. Second, the Committee called for the founding of a new Indochinese Democratic Front to appeal to all parties and classes in Indochina opposed to fascism and reactionary colonial forces. Since the main enemy was no longer French imperialism in general, but fascism (in Asia, the main representative of fascism, of course, was Japan) and its allies in Indochina, the party should abandon its narrow interpretation of the united front and form a wide alliance to include the urban bourgeoisie and patriotic landowning elements, as well as progressive elements of the French community. Attacks on the moderate reformists and the "wavering" petit bourgeoisie should immediately cease.[20] As Ho Chi Minh wrote from abroad:

At the present time the ICP should not make excessive demands (independence, parliament, etc.) so as not to fall into a snare prepared by the Japanese fascists. The party must limit itself to demanding democratic rights, freedom of organization, assembly and press, general

19. *Giai Cap (1936–1939)*, p. 144.
20. *TLTK*, VII, 56–58; and SLOTFOM, Series III, Carton 54, *Note périodique*, no. 44 (Sept. 1936), annex 1.

amnesty for political prisoners—struggle for the right of legal activities. To realize these goals the party must successfully form a wide national-democratic front which would unite not only the local population of Indochina, but progressive French forces, not only of the working class, but also representatives of the national bourgeoisie.[21]

At the July 1936 plenum, the party formulated a list of specific demands to be presented to the government, and which would become the demands of the proposed Indochinese Democratic Front itself: (1) transform the Grand Council of Financial and Economic Interests into a popularly elected assembly empowered to discuss political as well as economic questions, (2) universal suffrage for all over 18 years of age, (3) freedom of speech, assembly, organization and movement, (4) establish a local labor law, including provisions for an eight-hour day, social insurance, and better working conditions, (5) amnesty for political prisoners, (6) lower taxes, (7) unemployment insurance, (8) abolition of the monopolies, (9) abolition of the policy of seizing the land of debtors, (10) fire corrupt and reactionary officials, (11) broaden educational opportunities, and (12) sexual equality.[22]

With its plenum of July 1936 the ICP had moved clearly into a new, semilegal stage in its short history. The party was rapidly reviving from its long years in the shadow of French repression; provincial committees formed and became active in all three areas of Vietnam.[23] As another indication of party growth, the membership allegedly quadrupled in size during 1936.[24] In the South, the party existed at both open and covert levels, while in the Center and the North, it operated semilegally through the new front group, the Indochinese Democratic Front. One obvious

21. Quoted in I. A. Ognetov, "Komintern i revoliutsionnoe dvizhenie vo Vietname" [The Comintern and the Revolutionary Movement in Vietnam], in *Komintern i Vostok* [The Comintern and the East] (Moscow, 1969), pp. 440–441.

22. Tran Van Giau, "Dang cong san dong duong trong giai doan lich su 1936–1939" [The ICP in the historical period 1936–1939], *Hoc Tap*, Feb. 1959, p. 65.

23. The formation of these regional committees is documented in SLOT-FOM, Series III, Carton 59, *Note périodique,* no. 55 (Aug.-Sept. 1937).

24. French estimates are in SLOTFOM, Series III, Carton 55, *Notes périodiques,* no. 55 (Aug-Sept. 1937), no. 65 (Dec. 1938), and no. 67 (Feb. 1939). The problem with this rapid growth was that many fellow-travelers joined, and had to be weeded out later. Ognetov, p. 441.

manifestation of the new stage was the open publication of communist newspapers and journals. In the South, a communist paper *Dan Chung* (The People) became the first newspaper to receive formal permission to publish in Vietnamese.[25] When it was not harassed or censored by the government, other publications began to appear elsewhere in Vietnam, even though no formal permission to publish in *quoc ngu* had been issued. In addition, books and journals on Marxism were openly published, and communists began to discuss in cultural publications issues such as art for art's sake versus art for life's sake, and materialism versus idealism.[26] For the first time, the Vietnamese populace was learning about socialism without fear of arrest.

The Indochinese Congress

When the Popular Front government in early August 1936 announced the establishment of a Colonial Inspection Commission, it unleashed a new series of demands from nationalist groups in Vietnam. The first suggestion from a radical source came through an article by Nguyen An Ninh in *La Lutte* entitled "Toward an Indochinese Congress." In Nguyen's view:

For too long, the working masses of this country have been unable to raise their voices to cry out their distress and demand of those responsible some measures to alleviate their miserable existence. The Constitutionalists, in their successive lists of demands, have defended bourgeois interests with ardor and talent. But they have not even had the decency to claim the elementary rights for the working classes, of whom they claim to be the representatives.[27]

A simple list of demands submitted by a few people close to the Constitutionalists will do the workers no good, he said. What is needed is a congress to represent the wishes of all classes of the population, and to elaborate a "cahier des voeux" to be presented to the government in the name of the entire Vietnamese people. The idea of presenting demands, of course, was not new, and had been done on previous occasions. But this was the first time that an organized movement to formulate demands was suggested. The

25. *Giai Cap (1936–1939)*, p. 303.
26. *TLTK*, VII, 58.
27. *La Lutte*, July 29, 1936.

probable origin of Nguyen's idea is easy to find. In France's North African colonies similar plans which were well-publicized in Vietnamese newspapers during the mid-1930s, had already been formulated.

With Nguyen An Ninh's suggestion the dam broke in Vietnam. Representatives of the middle classes—Nguyen Van Sam, an editor of the Vietnamese newspaper *Duoc Nha Nam* and chairman of the local Cochin Chinese press association, and Nguyen Phan Long, vice-chairman of the Colonial Council and editor of the *Tribune indochinoise*—both came forward with proposals to convene a preliminary meeting to discuss the question.[28] On August 13, 1936, the meeting took place, with five hundred people in attendance. Of the total, however, the majority were apparently workers brought in by the communists. Many of the moderate journalists and intellectuals invited did not dare appear, and there were no representatives from the Center or the North, although some had been invited.[29]

The original intention of the planners had apparently been to arrange for a group to meet the inspection team on its arrival in Saigon, but at the meeting of August 13, Nguyen An Ninh and other radicals in attendance brought up the question of selecting a temporary committee composed of all classes to ascertain the wishes of the population, and ultimately to elect representatives to an all-Indochina Congress, which would then submit the list of demands to the French inspection team. Many of the moderates, attempted to head off this proposal, probably sensing that they would lose control of the meeting, but they were outvoted. In the end, Nguyen An Ninh's proposals were approved, and a temporary committee of thirty-five was formed, composed of all factions, including Trotskyites and communists.[30]

But it was at the local level where ICP activity in promoting the Indochinese Congress was most evident. In factories, streets, offices, and villages, committees of action (*uy ban hanh dong*) were formed under ICP encouragement to stimulate the drawing up of people's demands to be presented to the inspection team. Over

28. *La Lutte*, Aug. 5, 1936. SLOTFOM, Series III, Carton 48, *Note périodique*, no. 43 (Aug. 1936).

29. *Giai Cap (1936–1939)*, pp. 74–75.

30. *Ibid.*, p. 78.

six hundred committees were formed throughout Cochin China during a period of two months in late summer of 1936. Most were run and controlled by the ICP although in some areas around Saigon the Trotskyites were also active.[31]

The promotion of the Indochinese Congress was quite uneven in the various areas of Indochina. In the South the movement was active, but in the Center and the North less so, prompting Nguyen An Ninh to wonder in print what had happened to all of the patriotic youth in the rest of the country. In the Center, the imperial court prohibited the holding of meetings to consider demands, and conservative elements in the regional Chamber of Representatives claimed that that body alone was the proper conduit for the submission of demands. In consequence, progressive elements took action in Annam, feeling perhaps, as a later communist expressed it, that the water was far, but the fire was near.[32] Ultimately, the Chamber drew up a list of demands of its own for submission to the government.

In the North, the communist journal *Hon Tre* (Soul of Youth) had already submitted its own list of demands in July 1936, calling for workers' laws, freedom to form labor unions, and other democratic rights similar to those mentioned by the first plenum of the ICP. But there, as in the Center, conservative elements in the Chamber of Representatives managed to set up their own committee to formulate requests. Workers under ICP direction held a meeting of their own on September 27 and formulated their own list, but communist sources admit that the movement for a congress was weak throughout Tonkin, with only a few workers joining.[33]

Understandably, the Indochinese Congress movement made the

31. *Ibid.*, p. 80. Committees of two types were formed: (1) those based on area, such as village or street, and (2) those based on vocation, such as plantation or factory. An earlier ICP circular stated that these committees would be transformed into "struggle committees" at the appropriate time.

32. One prominent nationalist said that the Congress was "in the land of dreams." *Ibid.*, p. 82. Activity in the Center is discussed in "Ve dong chi Phan Dang Luu, mot tri thuc cach mang kien cuong" [On comrade Phan Dang Luu, a dedicated revolutionary intellectual], *NCLS*, no. 147 (Nov.–Dec. 1972), p. 18.

33. Tran Huy Lieu, *Lich Su Thu Do Ha Noi* [A History of the City of Hanoi] (Hanoi, 1960), p. 184.

government nervous, since it had the potential to develop into something much more explosive, and by early September the French began to take action to discourage the formation of committees of action and lists of demands. Journals were closed, and arrests were made for inciting riots; management fired workers who participated in the movement. In Cochin China, Governor-general Pagès prohibited meetings in the Saigon area and sent a telegram to Paris claiming that a danger to the social order existed. Minister of Colonies Moutet, who was vainly attempting to straddle the issue, responded by asking him to keep order but by peaceful means. Pagès did not dare close the temporary committee down entirely, but in mid-September he demanded that all lists be submitted between September 21 and 25, after which "all agitation should cease." The communist leadership rejected the request. Nguyen An Ninh wrote in *La Lutte* that submission in such a short time was clearly impossible and contended that the ultimatum showed that the government had no intention of responding to the demands.[34] In early October, Pagès moved again, and arrested Nguyen An Ninh, Nguyen Van Tao, and Ta Thu Thau—all of the Lutte group—on the charge of undertaking "subversive maneuvers." At the same time he managed to persuade some members of the temporary committee who belonged to the Colonial Council to abandon it and, as in the Center and North, submit their own list of demands. The arrest of the three members of the Lutte group strongly antagonized some moderate elements.[35] So while the movement for a congress temporarily died down in the fall, three radicals won some unexpected sympathy for their cause from bourgeois quarters. After a hunger strike that lasted several days, the three were set free.[36]

The Visit of Justin Godard

The Popular Front government in France did not schedule a visit of the proposed inspection team to Indochina in 1936, and nationalist opinion in Vietnam grew restive. Presumably to ward off criticism of its dilatory attitude, the government dispatched Minis-

34. *La Lutte,* Sept. 24, 1936.
35. Nguyen Phan Long sent a telegram to Moutet which is reproduced in *La Lutte,* Nov. 1, 1936.
36. For a discussion, see *Giai Cap (1936–1939),* pp. 99–125.

ter of Labor Justin Godard to observe conditions in Indochina while the inspection team was being prepared for its duties. Upon his arrival on the first day of 1937 the "labor ambassador," as he was called by the Vietnamese press, was immediately greeted by mammoth crowds convened by the ICP and other radical groups to demonstrate to him (and to the government in Paris) the strength and determination of the workers' movement in Vietnam. Wherever he went he was met by demonstrations and slogans. They welcomed the Popular Front government, but demanded a free press and permission to form labor unions, and expressed opposition to high taxes.

From the Vietnamese point of view, Godard's visit left ambivalent feelings. Although he was a minister from the Popular Front government in Paris, he appeared at times to favor French colonial interests (for example, he commented soon after his arrival that an eight-hour day meant eight *working* hours, not just eight hours in the plant). He praised the French *mission civilisatrice,* and one observer complained that he seemed to have a special affection for the owners of the big rubber plantations. On the other hand, he tried to appear sympathetic to the problems of the working man. Before his departure he asserted that a conflict between labor and management was dangerous and that "only if there are unions can the proletariat be educated to take responsibility to protect the interests of industry."[37]

Although the people in Indochina were not aware of it at the time, the departure of Godard meant the end of the proposal for an inspection team to visit Indochina. Colonial circles in Vietnam, nervous about the explosive potential of the Congress movement, contended that Godard's tour had demonstrated that a visit by an inspection team from France would only cause greater difficulties for the Indochinese government in its attempt to maintain public order. At the same time, ICP member Duong Bach Mai went to pains to persuade Minister of Colonies Moutet that a visit by an inspection team was necessary to quiet tensions in Vietnam. Moutet, manifestly nervous about the possible consequences of either course of action, suggested to his visitor a new formula for the proposed Indochinese Congress. Instead of the free-

37. *Ibid.,* p. 185.

wheeling committees of action that had been formed in the last months of 1936, he proposed that an Indochinese Congress be formed on the basis of the administrative and economic units already existing in society, with a representative from each unit to form an Indochinese Congress. These representatives would then compile a list of demands to be presented to the authorities.

It is hard to say at this point whether there was a misunderstanding between Moutet and his visitor from Vietnam. Duong Bach Mai wired back to Saigon on 7 January that the Minister had agreed to permit the formation of committees, and the party immediately began to form them again. The newly arrived governor-general, Auguste Brevié, attempted to stall for time, and while awaiting a fixed policy from Paris, shut down the revived action committees. In an article in *La Lutte,* Duong Bach Mai accused Brevié of "not wanting to see or hear anything" and encouraged the people to continue forming committees as before, but in as orderly and legal a manner as possible.[38]

In Paris, an inspection team was finally formed on January 30, and four days later thirty delegates were appointed, including a subcommittee composed of two writers long critical of French policies in Indochina—Andrée Viollis and Louis Roubaud. The appointment of the latter to the team enraged conservative colonial opinion and led some to predict a "bloody conflict" if they came. As was so often the case with French policy toward Indochina, the Popular Front government then caved in to colonial opinion and cancelled the inspection trip.[39] For the radicals, it was a further sign that the Popular Front government, from whom so much had been expected, was another of those creatures with the tail of a mouse. In November, a mass meeting under the chairmanship of Duong Bach Mai met to finish drawing up a list of demands to send to the inspection team, which was "studying the question" in Paris. Thus ended the Indochinese Congress movement.

38. La Lutte, Feb. 28, 1937, and SLOTFOM, Series III, Carton 59, *Note périodique,* no. 48 (Jan. 1937), p. 32. Committees of Action were formed through March, despite Brevié's attempts to prevent them. Nguyen An Ninh estimated that at their height there were over one thousand committees. AOM Carton 330, Dossier 266, Report of Governor-general, March 13, 1937.

39. *Giai Cap (1936–1939),* p. 196.

The congress movement, however, was not a total loss for the ICP, for it did provide the momentum for the building up of the party's Indochinese Democratic Front. At the second plenary meeting of the Central Committee in March 1937, action was taken to put a democratic front of all progressive forces formally into effect, and the party sent out letters to other political factions and groups asking for their cooperation in the common endeavor. The new posture of the party was not a total and immediate success. Many within the party, particularly those who had suffered through the long years of police suppression, were reluctant to move their activities into the open, and many were openly critical, calling the party's open workers "politicians" (*chinh khach*) and asserting that such individuals had no capability to make revolution. In addition, resentment against the party's new and broader version of the United Front also inspired mistrust and suspicion among many members who evidently could not bring themselves to make a serious effort to cooperate with middle class intellectuals and groups.

This ambiguous attitude of members toward the changing policies of the ICP was the subject of comment by the French communist Honel, who visited Indochina in August and September of 1937 on an inspection visit. He voiced his criticism of the ICP's dilatory advance into the open.[40] Le Hong Phong was of the same opinion, and another plenary meeting of the party was convened in September 1937 to clarify the position of the movement on the question of open and covert work. The party leadership agreed that maintenance of the secret apparatus of the party was vital, in order to protect the party against the possibility of a return to suppression by the colonial authorities. But where open work was called for, the party membership was told to move unhesitatingly into the open. As for the Indochinese Democratic Front, it would obviously operate in the open, since it was designed to appeal to wide segments of the populace who could not be reached by secret activities. The covert aspect of the party's work would be continued, of course, and the secret apparatus would in all instances be the directing body of the party, but members were categorically

40. *TLTK*, VII, 107.

told to use every opportunity to operate legally in order to obtain maximum support.[41]

The Democratic Front in Action

As the communists began to move into a new stage in the history of their movement, they were assisted by two factors—the continued existence of social unrest because of economic conditions, and the lack of serious competition from other political forces. The reforms of the Popular Front period did not appreciably change economic or social conditions in Vietnam. Despite the new labor laws, salary levels were still abysmally low and working conditions did not markedly improve. For the peasantry, high taxes and rents, and the continued confiscations of communal land—all normal aspects of rural life in colonial Vietnam—were compounded by floods in both the South and the North.

As for the nature of the communists' competition, the middle 1930s witnessed a further decline in the only organized political force among the Vietnamese bourgeoisie—the Constitutionalist Party. Not only was the party deprived of forceful leadership because of the frequent absence of Bui Quang Chieu (who spent more and more time in Paris), but it became increasingly factionalized. Even before the rise of the Indochinese Congress movement some of the younger members of the party wanted more progressive policies. Then, a split had taken place within the traditional leadership of the party when Nguyen Phan Long had attempted to establish meaningful cooperation with the elements associated with *La Lutte* who were on the temporary committee. (The move was opposed by Bui Quang Chieu and Le Quang Liem.) The gradual weakening of the Constitutionalists did not, however, result in the emergence of more radical urban nationalists.[42]

With no unity within the nationalist camp, the ICP became by

41. Materials on the plenum are in SLOTFOM, Series III, Carton 59, *Note périodique*, no. 55 (Aug.–Sept. 1937). Apparently the matter was not entirely settled, for another plenum on the question was held the following March.

42. Nguyen An Ninh, noting the weakness of progressive forces among the Cochin Chinese intellectuals, asked plaintively, "where are all the indigenous liberal intellectuals?" *La Lutte,* Feb. 11, 1936.

default the major party to attempt to knit together the disparate groups that made up the resistance movement of prewar Vietnam. Because of the varied conditions in the three regions, the nature of the front varied considerably in each area. In Tonkin, the basic nucleus of communist strength was built around the party's journals *Tin Tuc* and *Le Travail*.[43] Noncommunist target groups to be attracted into the front in Tonkin were the Hanoi branch of the French Socialist Party and the Ngay Nay (These Days) group. On several occasions, notably on the first of May, 1938, when over twenty thousand workers turned out to sing the Internationale, chant slogans, and press demands on the government, the ICP and its allies produced large crowds to demonstrate their collective will.[44] Cooperation was also attempted in a meeting of two hundred delegates representing eighteen different journals which met on April 24, 1937, to demand freedom of the press, amnesty for political prisoners, and the right to form an all-Indochina Press Association. The group was dispersed by the French, however.

A more specific area of coordination was in the Tonkin Chamber of Representatives, where the Tin Tuc group established cooperation with the French Socialist Party and others in support of the election of front members to the chamber.[45] All in all, however, front activity in the North was limited in scope. Moderate elements were relatively more hostile to the ICP than in the South, and there is evidence that communist leaders in the region were less effective in promoting front work.

In the Center, the major source of cooperation among progressives was in the Chamber of Representatives. In 1937, Popular Front candidates were strikingly successful and won several seats, including chairman, deputy chairman, and general secretary of the assembly. Within the chamber, the alliance group presented a minimum program of demands calling for an all-Indochina representative parliament with the right to pass laws, increase democratic freedom, and reform the Central Vietnamese criminal law

43. Party members in the latter included Nguyen The Duc, Vo Nguyen Giap, Tran Huy Lieu, Dang Thai Mai, and Truong Chinh. *Lich Su*, p. 119.
44. *Ibid.*, pp. 143–144.
45. *Giai Cap (1936–1939)*, p. 415. Because of bickering, the front was not very successful.

and tax system. Social reforms and an end to the monopolies were also demanded.[46] Outside the chamber, however, the democratic front alliance was not clearly drawn, partly because of a lack of organized progressive parties in the area.

Communist activity had been most pronounced in the South since the beginning of the front movement in 1936, and the ICP's efforts to achieve cooperation were the most concentrated there. As the congress movement developed, the party joined with other progressive groups in Saigon to demonstrate for social reforms.[47] Most significant, however, was the policy of informal cooperation with members of the Constitutionalist Party such as Nguyen Phan Long and Nguyen Van Sam. Since the early days of the League, the Constitutionalists had been considered too collaborationist to be considered as a potential ally. In the Popular Front period, for the first time the paths of communists and Constitutionalists briefly converged. The phenomenon was momentary, however. The bulk of the Constitutionalists remained aloof from the Congress movement and only a few such as Nguyen Phan Long broke loose to cooperate with radicals.[48] A united front with all major factions in the Vietnamese middle class was still only a partial reality.

Another problem for the ICP was closer to home. Since the early 1930s the ICP had informally cooperated with Trotskyites at *La Lutte,* and in municipal elections in Saigon-Cholon. In 1937, however, with the Trotsky trials in Moscow and the growth of the Democratic Front alliance in Indochina, ideological and tactical disagreements began to surface, leading to a final split in midyear. The Trotskyites began to oppose ICP tactics in late 1936, calling the Popular Front policy of cooperation with nonproletarian elements in Vietnam useless and harmful to working class interests. By early 1937, when ICP members at *La Lutte* began making attempts to achieve cooperation from some elements of the Constitutionalist Party, the Trotskyites refused further cooperation in the Democratic Front and advocated a strictly defined proletarian-

46. *Lich Su,* p. 143.
47. *Ibid.,* p. 128.
48. In late 1936, the ICP unsuccessfully supported Nguyen Phan Long against Bui Quang Chieu for election as delegate to the Conseil Superieur des Colonies.

peasant alliance.[49] The ICP initially responded with moderation. A message from the External Directing Bureau in South China suggested that the ICP could cooperate with the Trotskyites if they "sincerely joined" the Popular Front movement.[50] By mid-1937, however, cooperation had come to an end. Disagreement between the two factions on the editorial staff at *La Lutte* surfaced in bitter editorials in the pages of the journal.[51] The climax came on May 15, 1937, when Ta Thu Thau published a famous article calling support of the Popular Front treasonous.[52] By mid-summer the Trotskyites had taken over the journal completely and transformed it into a mouthpiece for their own views. The ICP launched a bitter series of denunciations against the Trotskyites for their failure to join in the struggle against fascism.

The growing friction with the Trotskyites hindered the ICP's effort to form a cohesive united front in Cochin China during the late 1930s. With the bulk of their own strength coming from workers and urban petit bourgeoisie in the Saigon-Cholon area, the Trotskyites were a formidable rival to the communists. During the congress period, they formed their own committees of action in Saigon which competed actively with those formed by the ICP Until mid-June of 1937, some of the communists hoped that cooperation could be restored. They were criticized in the ICP's journal *Avant Garde:* "Some members of the ICP and the Socialist Party here still believe that because of special conditions the Trotskyites in Indochina still have an anti-imperialist character."[53] By summer, competition began to intensify. Through 1939, the Trotskyites seemed to have the best of it in Saigon. In that year a Trotskyite slate of Ta Thu Thau and Tran Van Thach triumphed over an ICP list in elections for the Colonial Council.[54]

49. *Giai Cap (1936–1939)*, p. 376.
50. SLOTFOM, Series III, Carton 59, *Note périodique*, no. 55 (Aug.-Sept. 1936), annex 2.
51. This controversy can be followed in the pages of *La Lutte*. See in particular the issues of March 18 and 25; May 13 and 20, 1937. The major participants were Nguyen An Ninh, Ha Huy Tap, and Ta Thu Thau.
52. *La Lutte*, May 15, 1937. For that outburst, he earned two years in prison.
53. *Avant Garde*, May 29, 1937.
54. Anh Van and Jacqueline Roussel, *Mouvements nationaux et lutte des classes au Vietnam* (Paris, 1947), p. 57.

In summary, the overall performance of the ICP in its attempt to form an Indochinese Democratic Front during the years immediately following 1936 was mixed. On the positive side, the party had begun to move for the first time beyond its covert origins into the glare of open struggle, and in the process had begun to play a major role as a cohesive force in the nationalist movement. This process was most advanced in Cochin China, where the French allowed a greater latitude for indigenous political activities. Elsewhere, the party's activities were less effective, but so too were those of its rivals.

But if the ICP was beginning to take the lead in the resistance movement during the Popular Front period, its ability to do so effectively was still questionable. Urban middle class nationalism was still badly divided and the general performance of the congress movement was spotty. This is not all the fault of the communists, of course. Moderate nationalism in general gives an image during these years of both timidity and incompetence. Until the party could gain the confidence of vacillating elements, it would not be able to forge a united movement under its general leadership.[55]

Still, the communists themselves sometimes seemed unsure how to handle the new role assigned to them. Many party members were evidently uncomfortable with the new open posture. Party journals only perfunctorily appealed to middle class interests, and often found it difficult to distinguish between collaborator elements and potential allies within the urban bourgeoisie. Moreover, the antinationalist bias of the early 1930s had not entirely dissipated, and some members disdained the use of patriotic appeals to the populace. A similar ambivalence was noticeable in the party's attitude toward the peasantry. Rural issues began to be given more prominent attention by the party in the late 1930s, particularly in Cochin China, where communists led an active and broad-based peasant movement against the unpopular capitation tax. This was an in-

55. An example of ICP difficulties can be seen in the efforts it made to forge an alliance with VNQDD elements in South China in the late 1930s. A representative from the ICP was able to achieve agreement for an alliance with the VNQDD, but personal rivalries within the latter and the hostility of some to the communists caused the union to break down. See SLOTFOM, Series III, *Notes périodiques* of 1937, *passim*.

dication that some elements in the ICP leadership were beginning to focus on the countryside as an area of revolutionary potential, but priority was still given to the cities. The effects of Comintern strategy during the early 1930s had not yet worn off.

In effect, the ICP found itself during the Popular Front period in a state of transition. A full consciousness of the vital role of nationalism, of the need for a Vietnamese way to revolution had not yet formed, but the strands of the future revolutionary effort were beginning to come together. With a new world crisis approaching, it was none too soon.

Chapter 14

The Coming of War

The year 1938 saw a brief decline in the resistance movement. In that year the Popular Front government in Paris gradually lost its strength as Blum was replaced by Chautemps and then by Daladier. Although the Popular Front still lived in name, it had died in spirit, and the decline of the Popular Front in France in 1938 had a perceptible effect on Vietnam. Government suppression of open political activities increased throughout the year. Party journals and newspapers were closed, a number of radicals were arrested, and restrictive legislation limiting open political activity was enacted.[1] The Daladier government was less concerned with nationalist activity in Vietnam, however, than with the rising danger of war in Europe. In an effort to build up French strength in the event of hostilities, Paris turned to Indochina as a source of funds and manpower. Bonds were issued to buy munitions, and were viewed by many Vietnamese as a war tax. Then, the Minister of Colonies called for the dispatch of twenty thousand Vietnamese troops to France to strengthen the military position of the *metropole* against the possibility of German attack. The Indochinese budget went up, and defense expenditures increased; that resulted in still higher taxes.

In Vietnam, the crisis in Europe could hardly take priority over the rising danger in Asia from Japan. Japanese actions in South China, and Japan's increasingly obvious ambitions for regional domination in Southeast Asia, made more real the Vietnamese nationalists' fear of Japanese domination, a fear that had existed since the days of Phan Boi Chau. Some elements in the nationalist

1. Among those arrested was Le Hong Phong.

movement, believing that Japanese expansion into Southeast Asia would mean Vietnamese independence, took the Japanese side. Most prominent was the old Restoration Society now under the leadership of Phan Boi Chau's old colleague, Cuong De. The exiled prince had for many years been living in Japan and when the Sino-Japanese war began in 1937 he went to Hong Kong to organize anti-French activity for an eventual attack on Indochina. By early 1939, he was able to gather together a few scattered elements into a new organization Viet Nam Phuc Quoc Dong Menh Hoi (the Alliance to Restore Vietnam), which he viewed as a broad front group allying all parties in Vietnam to evict the French with Japanese support.[2] A few political groups in Vietnam were attracted to the idea—notably the Cao Dai and a few members of the Constitutionalist party—but such an attitude did not really represent nationalist feeling as a whole. Most nationalists did not trust Japan, and considered a Japanese conquest simply an exchange of one tyrant for another. For those Vietnamese who held this view, the French policy of draining Indochina in order to bolster her European defense was a gross abandonment of France's most basic obligation to her colonial subjects, that of providing for their security from external attack.

The ICP, still adhering to Comintern policy, which until the Russo-German Pact in the summer of 1939, required the alliance of all democratic forces against the preeminent danger of fascism, played a leading role in declaring Vietnamese nationalist hostility to Japanese expansion in Southeast Asia and the necessity for a strong defense in Indochina. Official communist policy is illustrated by an editorial in *Dan Chung:*

In the present situation in Asia, we approve the policy of defending Indochina against fascist aggression. We maintain that the methods utilized by the government have been definitely inadequate, and that we must have the support of the masses in both the spiritual and the material sense. If the government is of the same view, it should grant increased freedom and raise the standard of living in order to increase the power of the masses to defend themselves. At the same time it should organize the masses into defensive units, so that when war

2. Cuong De, *Cuoc Doi Cach Mang Cuong De* [The Revolutionary Career of Cuong De] (Saigon, 1957), pp. 129–130.

comes, they can be armed and have sufficient strength to defend themselves.[3]

This apparent support of the French and their slogan of "defend Indochina," even if coupled with criticism of the inadequacy of governmental efforts, was costly to the communists in terms of local popularity, for many nationalists at the time could not accept the logic of supporting the French simply to keep the Japanese wolf out the back door. In particular, the Trotskyites took advantage of the ICP's delicate position by accusing it of subordinating Vietnamese interests to those of the Soviet Union, and were able to make inroads into communist strength among workers and intellectuals, particularly in Saigon. The ICP, on the defensive, attempted to salvage its credibility as a nationalist force by publicly complaining that French policies were taxing the poor, and not the rich. Said *Dan Chung:* "We cannot deny that we do not want to fall into the hands of the Japanese fascists, but we cannot, just on the basis of the two words 'anti-fascism,' ask the people to sacrifice in order to support the interests of financial and capitalist reactionaries in the colonies." If we are to be asked to provide support, the editorial concluded, we must be given freedoms in return.[4]

In August of 1939, the Soviet Union concluded a nonaggression pact with Nazi Germany. That act not only led to the attack of Germany on Poland and the beginning of the Second World War, but it also signalled the end of Moscow's attempt to promote her own security through a broad alliance with the Western democracies. And it had two consequences that immediately affected the communist movement in Vietnam. First, general mobilization was ordered throughout the French colonies on September 3, 1939, the day of the German invasion of Poland. Second, the government moved to tighten its control in order to maintain peace and stability in Indochina. Therefore, all political parties, not only the ICP but also such pro-French groups as the Constitutionalists and the Democratic Party lost their legal right to exist and were forced to disband by a decree issued by the colonial government. The government was determined, in particular, to root out the communist movement, now that the Soviet Union was no longer deemed a

3. *Dan Chung,* Oct. 29, 1938, as cited in *Giai Cap (1936–1939),* p. 384.
4. *Ibid.,* p. 389, citing *Dan Chung,* Aug. 30, 1939.

potential ally of France against Germany. The new governor-general, Catroux, declared that only when the communist party was totally destroyed would tranquillity come to Indochina and loyalty to France develop among the native population. Declaring a "total and rapid" attack on the ICP, he declared the party illegal on September 26, and two days later issued a directive (1) prohibiting all propaganda activities directly or indirectly under Comintern control, (2) scattering all of the communist mass associations, (3) prohibiting all communist publishing activities, and (4) threatening all members of the party with imprisonment and the payment of a heavy fine.[5] The open publications of the party, *Dan Chung* and *Tin Tuc,* were immediately closed down, and hundreds of members of the party were arrested. Throughout Vietnam over two thousand people were arrested, with eight hundred in the South alone.[6] The party's urban leadership was literally decimated, and a gradual shift to rural areas took place. Those who were able to evade arrest fled into exile as the Central Committee in a replay of the early 1930s tried to relocate itself in South China or in a remote area north of Hanoi.

The party attempted to retreat back into illegality with a maximum of dignity and order. The party's official journal, *Dan Chung,* put out a final issue. In November, in need of a new strategy, the Central Committee convened its sixth plenary meeting in the village of Ba Diem near Saigon. Attending were some new faces and a variety of representatives from the regional committees.[7] Following the line established by the Comintern since the signing of the Russo-German pact in August, the Committee declared the conflict in Europe to be a capitalist war between fascist and democratic capital. Declaring that "we won't help the French imperialists with a single soldier, with a single piaster," the party leadership

5. *Ibid.,* pp. 11–12.
6. Tran Van Giau, "Trong giai doan chien tranh the gioi lan thu hai va cach mang thang tam" [During the stage of World War II and the August Revolution], *Hoc Tap,* March 1959, p. 37.
7. Attending were Nguyen Van Cu, Phan Dang Luu, Vo Van Tan, and Le Duan, among others. Nguyen Van Cu, born of a scholar-gentry family related to Nguyen Trai in Bac Ninh province in 1912, became general secretary of the ICP from 1938 to 1940, at which time he was arrested at a house in Saigon. He was executed in August 1941. See *NCLS,* no. 145 (July-Aug. 1972), pp. 7–18, for biographical information on him.

opposed conscription, requisition, and taxes, and the sending of Vietnamese troops to France. Helping France, it declared, "would be like exchanging fetters of iron for those of steel."[8] Few of the Central Committee's decisions at the plenum have survived, but, according to one source, the resolution drafted by chairman Nguyen Van Cu stated that the period of political struggle was coming to an end, and called for preparations for a general uprising to come.[9]

With the outbreak of war and the new policies declared in Paris, Hanoi, and Moscow, the Democratic Front as constituted had clearly outlived its usefulness, and the Sixth Plenum declared its intention to form a new National United Anti-Imperialist Front to struggle for independence and national liberation for all five areas of Indochina. Surviving resolutions of regional committees indicate that the changes from the old Indochinese Democratic Front were not extensive. The new front was still aimed at the capitalist class, as well as at the national minorities and the peoples of Laos and Cambodia.[10] It did not, however, make any attempt to approach the French government or its supporters in Indochina. It also appeared to place less emphasis on winning support from so-called "national reformists." Only those landowning elements and urban bourgeoisie who were sincerely anti-imperialists would be considered candidates for the new organization. While the difference is not large, it appears that the new front was going to place more emphasis on the "national" struggle, while at the same time attempting to avoid isolation.[11]

By early 1940, the threat of Japan to French Indochina was more clearly defined. Japanese military activities had extended southward to the region around Canton, Hainan, and the Paracel Islands in the Tonkin Gulf. Japanese diplomatic pressure on France to discontinue the traffic of war materiel up the Red River

8. *Giai Cap* (*1936–1939*), p. 29.

9. Trung Chinh, "Nguyen Van Cu: mot can bo lanh dao dang trong thoi ky 1938–1940" [Nguyen Van Cu: a leading cadre of the party in the period 1938–1939], *NCLS*, no. 145 (July-Aug. 1972), p. 16. Because the plenum marked the revival of the struggle for independence as a matter of high priority, it is considered one of the landmark conferences of the ICP in Hanoi today.

10. Tran Van Giau, "Trong giai doan," p. 41.

11. See the discussion in *Giai Cap* (*1936–1939*), p. 38.

Valley into South China was increasing. In response, Governor-general Catroux attempted to put Indochina on a war footing. All political activity was suppressed and, in order to tighten efficiency, many of the reforms that had been granted during the Popular Front period were annulled. "Police villages" and "volunteer groups" were formed for self-defense, and an Indochinese Order Party (Dang Trat Tu Dong Duong) was established.[12]

The crisis in Indochina came to a head in the summer of 1940, when Japan demanded the closing of the Sino-Vietnamese border and a cessation of the transport of war materiel to the beleaguered Chinese government at Chungking. Governor-general Catroux attempted to buy time, but the Japanese soon made further demands, for permission to transport troops across North Vietnam to South China, to build airports, and to station six thousand Japanese troops in Tonkin. The Japanese threat coincided with the German invasion of France, the capitulation of the French government in Paris, and the establishment of the puppet Vichy regime. Catroux was replaced with another military man, Admiral Decoux. The new government was reluctant to consent to Japanese demands, but felt as powerless to prevent gains in Indochina as had its predecessor. While Decoux consented to the Japanese demands in September, Japanese troops crossed the border from China—whether or not by order from Tokyo is unknown—and attacked French border posts near Lang Son. The incident was quickly settled, but the French now seemed reconciled to tolerating a considerable measure of Japanese influence in Indochina. By the time of the opening of the general Asian war in December of 1941, Japanese military forces were present in force throughout much of Indochina. Vietnam became a virtual colony of Japan for the duration of the war.

The reaction of the Vietnamese population to Japanese advances in the North was mixed. Some wanted to resist the Japanese, and demonstrations of loyalty to France took place in Hanoi and Saigon with Vietnamese subjects demanding resistance to Japanese demands and promising to contribute financial support to the war effort. Pro-Japanese elements, of course, welcomed the recent developments; and a variety of nationalists attempted to

12. Tran Van Giau, "Trong giai doan," p. 44.

form pro-Japanese political parties.[13] For the communists, there was no question of supporting the Japanese, even against the French. The Sixth Plenum of November 1939 had set the tone by declaring Japanese fascism and French imperialism the joint enemies of the oppressed masses of Indochina.

The Communist Uprisings

In late September, Japanese troops crossed the border near Lang Son to punctuate their demands for troop movements and airfield rights in Indochina. They were assisted by Vietnamese military units, organized and directed by Cuong De's Restoration Society, which attempted to launch an uprising of its own in the mountainous areas along the Chinese frontier. The uprising was not successful (in part because the Japanese soon ceased their own attacks and withdrew into South China), but the social unrest unleashed by the attacks soon led to a more extensive revolt among the local population, and that more extensive revolt was directed by elements of the communist party in the area.[14] Although the communist uprising probably was not decreed by the party leadership, it quite likely was launched in response to the Sixth Plenum's call for military uprisings. At a September 1940 meeting of the Tonkinese regional committee, secretary-general Nguyen Van Cu had directed that cadres be trained in the mountainous areas in the North in preparation for an uprising.[15]

Communist strength had long been evident in the mountainous area of the Viet Bac, inhabited by such minority peoples as the Tay, the Nung, and the Black and White Tai.[16] In the late 1920s, the League had established cells there and in April 1930, the ICP had set up the first communist cell in Hoa An district of Cao Bang province.[17] By the middle 1930s, this area had become the base headquarters for communist activity throughout Tonkin.

13. *Ibid.*, p. 46.

14. This uprising is discussed in *TLTK*, X, 10–16.

15. Trung Chinh, "Hoi nghi trung uong lan thu sau va hai cuoc khoi nghia dau tien do dang ta lanh dao" [The Sixth Plenum and the two first uprisings led by the party], *NCLS,* no. 146 (Sept.-Oct. 1972), p. 6.

16. Most of the population in the Viet Bac area are Nung or Tay (also known as Tho). There are over 500,000 Tay in the Democratic Republic of Vietnam and 313,000 Nung, according to 1960 estimates.

17. Phan Ngoc Lien, "Cong tac van dong giao duc quan chung cua Ho

There were problems for the communists in exploiting the natural grievances in the area, for although the mountain peoples had long been exposed to exploitation by the colonial government, they also felt a sense of hostility toward the Vietnamese, whose own behavior was not beyond question. A Vietnamese political party, whatever its ideological persuasion, would not necessarily receive a hearty welcome in the Viet Bac.[18]

The ICP was conscious of the problem, and its program of October 1930 had promised self-determination for all minority groups in Vietnam. Later programs and resolutions consistently referred to the minority question and called for social and political benefits as well as the opportunity for self-determination.[19] To provide its promises with substance, the party attempted to set up an active policy in minority areas, and to include representatives from non-Vietnamese groups in the party leadership. In 1935, Tay leader Hoang Dinh Giong was elected to the Central Committee at the Macao Conference, while a certain Tu Huu allegedly represented the minority peoples at the Seventh Congress of the Comintern the same year.[20] Conscious of the "hearts and minds" aspect of the problem, the ICP worked hard to dispel the natural suspicions of the mountain peoples against the lowland Vietnamese. Party cadres active in the area learned the local languages and adapted to local ways. While there is little indication that the mountain peoples were converted en masse to communism, the party evidently achieved considerable support in areas of the Viet Bac.

The minority work done by the party began to pay dividends in 1940. The Japanese invasion at Lang Son took place in an area

Chu Tich trong thoi gian Nguoi o Pac Bo" [Agitprop work of Ho Chi Minh during his stay at Pac Bo], NCLS, no. 149 (March-April 1973), p. 20.

18. This would be less true of the Tay, who were relatively more exposed to Vietnamese influence—possible because they are valley rice farmers—than most other national minorities in Vietnam. McAlister contends that the Tho-ti, the mixed Tay-Vietnamese elite group of the Tay peoples, were particularly attracted to communist influence because of their loss of status under the French. See John T. McAlister, "Mountain Minorities and the Vietminh," in Peter Kunstadter, ed., Southeast Asian Tribes, Minorities, and Nations (Princeton, 1967), II, 794.

19. Le Van Lo, "Ba muoi nam thuc hien chinh sach dan toc cua dang" [Thirty years of creating a nationality policy for the party], NCLS, no. 10 (Jan. 1960), pp. 69–71.

20. Phan Ngoc Lien, p. 20.

inhibited primarily by Tay tribesmen. Hostile to the French, the Tay rose against the government in response to the Japanese invasion. They took advantage of the confusion and the flight of local authorities to seize weapons and control of several areas of Bac Son district, a few miles southwest of Lang Son.[21] The local ICP leadership managed by the end of September to assume the direction of the spontaneous uprising, and it continued the attacks, evidently hoping to spark the nationwide general uprising forecast by the Sixth Plenum in late 1939. Revolutionary tribunals were set up to punish class enemies in the area, while local paramilitary units with both propaganda and military responsibilities were organized to destroy French power at the village level, seize the property of reactionary landlords, and spur armed revolt. For a brief period the guerrilla movement appeared to have considerable momentum. With high spirits guerrilla leaders under the direction of the regional committee's secretary-general, Luong Van Tri, launched an attack on the French-controlled fort in the mountain valley of Bac Son.[22] By mid-October, however, the French were able to regain the offensive. The guerrillas, lacking organization and training, were defeated, and the area was pacified.

The leaders of the Bac Son revolt, however, were better prepared for the possibility of defeat than those of the Nghe-Tinh uprising. As their position weakened they broke up into small units and retreated into the mountains to await further orders from the party leadership. In the history of the communist movement this would be a historic moment, for with the formation of rebel guerrilla units in the Bac Son area, and their preservation in the aftermath of defeat, the party was on the verge of forming the revolutionary base area from which the war of national liberation would ultimately be launched.

While the Bac Son uprising was taking place, the Seventh Plenum of the ICP convened in the village of Dinh Bang, near Hanoi in Bac Ninh province, in order to determine party policy in the face of changing conditions.[23] The Bac Son revolt had broken

21. The main attacks were in the villages of Mo Nhai and Binh Gia. After they were suppressed, the unrest spread elsewhere in the province.
22. Trung Chinh, "Hoi nghi," p. 9.
23. Attending were Truong Chinh, Phan Dang Luu, Hoang Van Thu,

Map 3. Tonkin

out without any specific direction from the Central Committee
and, lacking any contact at this point with the Comintern, the
party leadership was probably not certain what tack to take. In

Hoang Quoc Viet, and Tran Dang Ninh. *Histoire de la Révolution d'Août*
(Hanoi, 1972), p. 20.

the view of the leadership, however, certain things were obvious. The Bac Son revolt was premature; although party units were present in the immediate area, the party itself was clearly unprepared to launch a major nationwide uprising against colonial authority. Nor was the country as a whole ready for a general uprising to evict the French and install revolutionary leadership.

On the other hand, there were certain advantages to the Bac Son uprising. After many years of placing primary emphasis on revolutionary work in urban areas, the party was becoming aware of the success of guerrilla techniques utilized by the communists in China, and of the importance of a base area from which to launch a war of national independence. In consequence, the plenum determined that the guerrilla forces organized at Bac Son were to be preserved if at all possible in order to establish a base area for further operations in the region near the border. A representative from the plenum, Hoang Van Thu, was sent to transmit these directions to the rebels. To provide maximum support for the Bac Son revolt itself, uprisings were to be launched elsewhere, where appropriate.[24]

With the defeat at Bac Son, the defeated guerrilla units broke into two main groups, one heading toward Cao Bang in the West, the other remaining in the area of Bac Son-Dinh Ca where it would soon become engaged in further conflict with French military units, and would eventually become the nucleus for the Cuu Quoc Quan (National Salvation Army).[25]

The Bac Son uprising was only part of the ICP's problem of establishing a national strategy. Still faced with the difficulty of coordinating political and military activities throughout all areas of Vietnam, much of the party's apparatus remained isolated from local leadership because of French security measures. As the Bac Son revolt in the North was coming to a close, and the Seventh Plenum was worrying about how to react to that problem, the

24. Trung Chinh, "Hoi nghi," p. 9.
25. The group in Bac Son split up, with Phung Chi Kien leading one, and Chu Van Tan leading the other further south. Phung Chi Kien, who replaced Hoang Van Thu as a leader of the northern group, was a long-time member of the Chinese Peoples' Liberation Army and had participated in the Long March. He was born in Nghe An. Nguyen Khac Vien, p. 69. Chu Van Tan became a party member in 1934, and a member of the Tonkin regional committee about 1940. *Ibid.*, p. 63.

ICP's regional leadership in Cochin China was launching an uprising of its own against French colonial rule.

Throughout the 1930s, the communist movement in the South had seemed stronger and better led than elsewhere in Vietnam. Economic conditions in Cochin China were unsatisfactory by local standards (although probably not as bad as in the Center), taxes were higher, and the price of rice was falling.[26] Also there was a strong movement in the South against the draft and the dispatch of Vietnamese troops to Europe. Even after the French surrender to Japan the movement continued as troops were disbanded without their clothing, and others were ordered to go to the Thai border as war with Thailand over Cambodia became imminent. The ICP took an active part in organizing discontent among indigenous troops in the army, popularizing slogans such as "Don't die for the *colons* along the Thai border," and uprisings took place in several provinces throughout Cochin China.[27] There was allegedly some support from the peasantry as well—one source claims that a full 30 per cent of the population in the South supported the ICP.[28]

In July 1940, the regional committee for Cochin China met at My Tho in the delta to consider how the party should react to local conditions. According to some sources, it had received directives referring to the need to prepare for uprisings (this was in line with the decisions taken by the Sixth Plenum in 1939). There was apparently much support for launching an uprising, and the possible formation of a provisional government was discussed. In March 1940, the regional committee issued a directive to local units to train soldiers, obtain weapons, and to propagandize among Vietnamese troops in the French army. After a meeting in July, Phan Dang Luu was sent north to discuss the possibilities of a nationwide general uprising with the Central Committee.[29]

By mid-fall, conditions seemed even more appropriate for a revolt. In November, troops were ordered by the French government to the Thai border and in Saigon fifteen thousand soldiers rioted in

26. Tran Van Giau, *Giai Cap Cong Nhan Viet Nam, 1939–1941*, p. 67.
27. *TLTK*, X, 18.
28. *Ibid.*
29. *Ibid.*, p. 69. Trung Chinh, "Hoi nghi," p. 8, says there was another meeting on August 10, 1940, to discuss the uprising plans, and that Phan departed after this meeting in October to attend the Seventh Plenum.

protest. Others responded at Cap St. Jacques and My Tho, and, a communist source asserts, two-thirds of the Vietnamese troops in Cochin China supported the rioters.[30] With fifteen thousand enrolled to support an uprising, and five thousand weapons (the remainder possessed knives or spears), the Cochin China regional committee under secretary-general Ta Uyen decided to launch a revolt, despite the lack of word from the Central Committee in the North.[31]

The request for a general uprising caused a dilemma for the Seventh Plenum meeting near Hanoi. Aware of the uprising in the Viet Bac, the leadership was prepared to call for military activity elsewhere in Vietnam to demonstrate support for the rebels in Bac Son; but the Bac Son revolt was ending in defeat, and the plenum felt that conditions in Vietnam as a whole were not ripe for a general uprising. In addition they suspected that the revolutionary forces in the South were too small and were unprepared for the possibility of defeat. The plenum therefore determined that the uprising in Cochin China should be postponed until the national leadership of the party had an opportunity to make a further evaluation of the possibilities of success.[32] Any insurgency should be planned and led by the Central Committee. Phan Dang Luu and an unspecified number of military experts were sent south to order a postponement. Unfortunately for the ICP, Phan and his entourage were arrested on November 22, 1940, by French authorities in Saigon, without being able to contact the local party leadership.[33]

One day later, the uprising broke out on schedule, with attacks taking place in a number of areas—around Gia Dinh, My Tho, Can Tho, Bien Hoa, Cholon, and Tan An. French military posts were attacked and communications were cut. In some areas in the delta, such as Soc Trang and Bac Lieu, power went to the revolu-

30. *TLTK*, X, 20.
31. The involvement of the plenum in the uprising is not clear. Many sources indicate that the regional committee of Cochin China went ahead on its own, and that appears to be the case. Certainly Phan Dang Luu had not been able to return with the plenum's decision. Yet Trung Chinh, "Hoi nghi," p. 9, says that the plenum sent word to launch uprisings in support of Bac son, and that the Southern uprising was in response. Most likely the South was aware of the general directive to prepare for uprisings, but was not cleared for a specific major revolt in the fall of 1940.
32. *Révolution d'Août*, p. 22.
33. *TLTK*, X, 20–21.

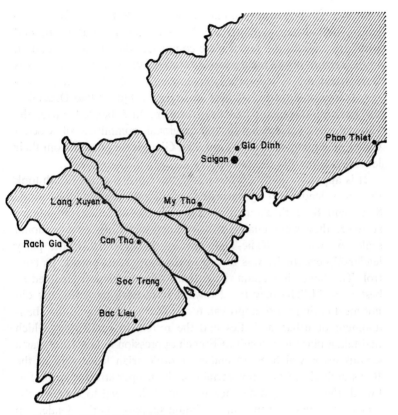

Map 4. The Mekong Delta

tionary forces for a brief time, and tribunals were established. Unfortunately for the revolutionaries, however, the French had been sufficiently forewarned of the planned revolt by informers. Martial law was declared, much of the party's local leadership was seized, and many Vietnamese troops were disarmed.[34] The party's hopes for substantial troop participation were dashed in most areas, and the uprising became more a jacquerie than an organized military

34. Arrested were Ha Huy Tap, Vo Van Tan, Nguyen Van Cu, and regional committee members from Cochin China. Trung Chinh, "Hoi nghi," p. 10. They were executed in August 1941. Phan Dang Luu was executed on May 24, 1941. Regional committee secretary Ta Uyen was seized and died in prison in late 1940.

offensive. Despite a last-minute effort by the ICP leadership to organize nationwide support, the French response was swift, and within two weeks the rebels were completely dispersed. In addition to the seizure of the leadership, a total of over five thousand rebels were arrested.[35] A few days later uprisings took place among military troops stationed elsewhere in Vietnam, but by late December the back of the revolt had been broken. In a belated move, the "adventuristic" elements in the regional committee of Cochin China, including its leader Tran Van Giau, were purged from their leading positions in the party.[36]

It is apparent that the uprisings in the North and the South took the party leadership by surprise, and despite the attempts of the Sixth and Seventh Plenum to move in the direction of military struggle, they were unable to coordinate activities on a national scale. As with the Nghe-Tinh uprising in 1930–1931, the party leadership eventually was forced to react to events outside its control. The Seventh Plenum, faced with difficult choices, reacted as best it could. The new trend toward rural uprisings evidently did not meet entirely with approval, for as the plenum saw it, the abandonment of urban activities and the retreat to rural areas which had taken place as a result of French oppression in late 1939 was a serious error which could endanger proletarian leadership of the ICP's activities.[37] Still not certain of the proper strategy to be followed, the plenary conference reasserted the need to broaden the united front in order to gain maximum support. Worker leadership in the party was strongly reaffirmed, and the danger of bourgeois leadership was emphasized.

35. *TLTK*, X, 23–25.

36. I. Milton Sacks, "Marxism in Vietnam," in Frank Trager, ed., *Marxism in Southeast Asia* (Stanford, 1959), p. 145. Communist sources available to me do not mention this.

37. *TLTK*, X, 16.

Chapter 15

Before the Dawn

If the Indochinese Communist Party leadership appeared some-what confused and leaderless in the fall of 1940, new conditions were at work which were to result in a heightened sense of order and purpose in the communist movement during the years of World War II. Sometime in 1940, after an absence of nearly a decade, Ho Chi Minh returned to South China and restored contact with his comrades within Vietnam. In the ten years since his previous appearance in South China as Comintern representative (when he presided over the original founding of the ICP), Ho had undergone a variety of experiences.

In June of 1931, he had been arrested by Hong Kong police and put in jail. The French requested his extradition to Indochina, but his case came to the attention of the public in Great Britain. The Labor Party and the Red Cross started a campaign for his liberation and he was defended in court by a British lawyer who successfully protested against his extradition to Vietnam. Released and sent to Singapore (from whence the Singapore authorities returned him to Hong Kong), he eventually escaped to South China, where he lived briefly in disguise as a rich capitalist while regaining the health he had lost in prison.[1] In Shanghai he made contact with the Chinese Communist Party (CCP) through a letterbox drop at the home of Sun Yat-sen's widow Soong Ch'ing-ling. With Chinese aid he managed to obtain passage on a ship from Shanghai to Vladivostok in 1933 and from there he went by train to Moscow. He spent about five years in the Soviet Union, studying first at the Lenin Institute and then teaching at the Institute.

1. SLOTFOM, Series III, Carton 48, Dossier 20, periodic report of the first trimester 1933.

Late in 1938, he returned to China and went to CCP head-quarters in Yenan, where he is believed to have become a radio operator and the manager of an Eighth Route Army club.[2] Eventually he was sent to Hanyang as an envoy to the New Fourth Army and then taught guerrilla tactics to Kuomintang troops somewhere in South China. Finally, in February 1940, he arrived in Kunming in Yunnan province where he got in touch with communist units in the border areas under the leadership of Phung Chi Kien and Trinh Dong Khai (Vu Anh).[3]

Upon his arrival, he initiated cooperation between ICP units in Yunnan and local elements of other nationalist groups, such as the Vietnam Quoc Dan Dang (VNQDD). He soon became aware, however, that opportunities were brighter to the east, in Kwangsi province, where Chinese military leaders had been attempting to utilize local Vietnamese nationalist groups against the Japanese in Indochina. The VNQDD had long been active in the area, and a number of their members had joined the Chinese army. Among those who did so were Truong Boi Cong and Ho Ngoc Lam, both of whom had been directed by local Kuomintang military commanders to initiate a training program among local Vietnamese in preparation for a possible Chinese invasion of North Vietnam.[4] Shifting his base to Kweilin in Central Kwangsi province, Ho Chi Minh attempted to promote cooperative efforts between local ICP elements—some were refugees from the recently defeated Bac Son uprising—and nationalist groups active in the area. He also got in touch with Li Chi-shen, head of the Kuomintang's Southeast Bureau, and with Fourth Army Commander Chang Fa-kuei. General Li, apparently unaware of Ho's connection with the ICP (or possibly he was indifferent), encouraged the latter and any of his followers to participate in the training program under Kuomintang auspices.[5] Under the umbrella of Kuomintang activities, then, a broad united front that included all nationalist groups in the area (the ICP among them) began to take shape. With the active promotion of Ho, a front organization was created under the name

2. King Chen, *Vietnam and China, 1938–1954* (Princeton, 1969), p. 35.
3. *Nash President Ho Chi Minh* (Hanoi, 1967), p. 188.
4. King Chen, p. 43.
5. Li was not a hard-line anticommunist and after the Civil War remained on the mainland.

Viet Nam Doc Lap Dong Menh Hoi (Association for Vietnam Independence League).[6] Headquarters was placed in the sleepy border town of Chinghsi, and the leadership was appropriately mixed—with the pro-VNQDD nationalist Ho Ngoc Lam as director, and communist Pham Van Dong as his deputy. Eventually, the front was broadened to include other groups and changed its name to *Viet Nam Giai Phong Dong Minh* (Vietnam Liberation League).[7]

Informal cooperation between communists and noncommunists lasted for several months in the border areas under the general aegis of the Kuomintang. Eventually, however, internal conflict broke out, allegedly because communists such as Pham Van Dong and Vo Nguyen Giap were attempting to take over the front movement. In early 1942, Nguyen Hai Than, a member of the VNQDD and former follower of Phan Boi Chau, went to Kuomintang headquarters to complain about ICP activities, and the local Chinese military commander, in reprisal, shut down the front's activities.[8] In the meantime, however, the ICP had won over many of the local groups hostile to the Japanese. With the front organization disbanded, communists in the area were forced to go underground or flee across the border to Vietnam.[9]

These tentative attempts to achieve cooperation with Kuomintang authorities and noncommunist nationalist elements in South China were only a part of Ho's preparations in gearing up the communist movement for the coming struggle of liberation. A keystone of his strategy was to initiate cooperation with noncommunist elements in a wide united front to oppose all foreign authority in Vietnam. He reached the conviction that many social classes formerly indifferent to the revolution—such as patriotic landlords and the national bourgeoisie—had come to detest the French and

6. According to King Chen, the name was originally used by a noncommunist organization started in Nanking in 1935. In 1940, it was revived as a front between the original founders in South China and ICP members in the area.

7. King Chen, pp. 60–61. This is the predecessor of the later noncommunist front, the Viet Nam Cach Menh Dong Menh Hoi (Vietnamese Revolution League) founded in 1943.

8. *Ibid.*, pp. 50–51.

9. Vo Nguyen Giap, *Du Nhan Dan Ma Ra* [From the People] (Hanoi, 1964), pp. 30–31.

Japanese conquerors and could be brought to support a war of national liberation. At the same time he demonstrated what he had learned from his years of experience with the Chinese communist movement in Yenan and Central China: the second aspect of his grand design was to make use of the guerrilla bases in the mountain regions as staging areas from which to launch a general uprising at the end of the war.[10]

In his efforts, Ho was assisted by two young communist leaders who had been sent to South China in May 1940 by the Central Committee, presumably on orders to make contact with party leaders in exile. The two, Vo Nguyen Giap and Pham Van Dong, made contact with Ho in June, and Ho immediately decided to send them to Yenan to study guerrilla tactics with the experienced leaders of the CCP.[11] The two never arrived in Yenan, however. In the summer of 1940, while they were awaiting transportation to the North at Kweiyang, Paris fell and France surrendered to Germany. For Ho, this meant that possibilities for insurrection in Indochina were improved, and he cancelled their orders and directed them to join him at Kweilin, where with Vu Anh they began to expand united front activities in the border area.

By late fall, the communist leadership in exile, now committed to the foundation of a new front under its direction, decided to infiltrate back into Cao Bang province with the aid of the troops and cadres who had fled to South China after the Bac Son uprising. The aim was to establish a revolutionary base area in North Vietnam and to reestablish contact with the Central Committee.

10. Presumably, however, he was unaware of the Bac Son uprising before it erupted.

11. Vo Nguyen Giap was born of a poor scholar-gentry family in Quang Binh in 1912. After studying at the National Academy in Hué, earlier attended by Ho Chi Minh, he got a law degree in Hanoi and became a history teacher. At one time a member of the Revolutionary Party, he was active in leading riots in Hué during the Nghe-Tinh period and was arrested. He became a communist at an unspecified time—probably in the early 1930s—and worked for the journals *Tin Tuc* and *Nhan Dan*, while engaging in front work in Annam. See Vo Nguyen Giap, *Military Art of People's War* (New York, 1970), p. 14. His colleague Pham Van Dong was born in 1906 of a mandarin family in Quang Ngai province and became a member of the League in Canton in the late 1920s. From 1926 to 1932 he was in jail. He became a journalist at *Nhan Dan* in the late 1930s. *Ibid.*, pp. 13–17 and 39–43; Phillipe Devillers, *Histoire du Vietnam* (Paris, 1952), p. 70.

By late 1940, the new revolutionary leadership at Chinghsi decided to prepare for a plenary meeting of the Central Committee to take place in the mountains not far from the border town of Cao Bang. After a preliminary meeting at Chinghsi in the fall of 1940, and exploratory trips to the village of Pac Bo in Ha Quang district, Cao Bang province, to make advance arrangements for the plenary meeting, Ho returned to Vietnam in early February. On May 10, 1941, the Eighth Plenum was convened at Pac Bo. Chaired by Ho for the first time since the official founding of the party, the plenum was concerned with establishing a new and more effective united front to struggle for national independence.[12]

Without question, the most important result of the plenum was the establishment of the new front organization, to be entitled Viet Nam Doc Lap Dong Minh (Vietnam Independence League, or Vietminh).[13] According to the plenum's resolution:

The landlords, rich peasants, native bourgeoisie, have all greatly changed their attitude. Before, they had an antipathy to the revolution and wanted to destroy it or were indifferent. Now it is different, and with the exception of a few running dogs who flatter and fawn on the Japanese enemy, the majority have sympathy with the revolution or are neutral. . . . If previously the landlords and the native bourgeoisie were the reserve forces of the anti-revolutionary imperialists, they have now become the reserve army of the revolution. With these changes, our strength is on the rise and the reserves of the enemy are dwindling rapidly.[14]

In effect, the Eighth Plenum extended the widest possible net to capture allies in the struggle against the French and the Japanese. All, in their words, should be united, "whether workers, peasants, rich peasants, landlord, or native bourgeoisie, to work for the seizure of independence." The resolution warned that this does not mean

that our party is abandoning the concept of class struggle in the Indochinese revolution. No, the problem of class struggle will con-

---

12. In attendance were Hoang Van Thu, Phung Chi Kien, Truong Chinh, Hoang Quoc Viet, Hoang Van Hoan, Vu Anh, Nguyen Ai Quoc (Ho Chi Minh) and two unnamed representatives from the Center. *Révolution d'Août*, p. 25. The new central committee included Hoang Quoc Viet, Hoang Van Thu, and Truong Chinh.

13. For a discussion, see Vo Nguyen Giap, pp. 32–33.

14. *Lich Su*, II, 70.

tinue to exist. But in the present stage, nation is above all; thus all demands of party which would be beneficial to a particular class but would be harmful to the nation should be postponed in order to be resolved at a later date. At this moment, the interests of a particular class must be subordinated to the survival of the nation and race. At this moment, if we do not resolve the problem of national liberation, and do not demand independence and freedom for the entire people, then not only will the entire people of our nation continue to live as beasts, but also the particular interests of individual classes will not be achieved for thousands of years either.[15]

The working class, in other words, was to take a short step now in order to take a longer step later. Here was the clearest possible statement of the party's claim to represent Vietnamese nationalism. For the first time, nationalism and communism were completely joined, and the emphasis was clearly on the former. Inevitably, the land revolution would have to be postponed. Slogans calling for the confiscation of landlord land were abandoned, and only the land of French imperialists and their Vietnamese collaborators was to be seized: "If we raise the slogan of crushing the landlords, confiscating their land and distributing it to the tiller, not only would we be abandoning an ally and a supporting force in the revolution to overthrow the French and the Japanese, but we should also be pushing their strength over to the side of the enemy, and to make it the enemy's reserve force."[16]

To achieve the goal of the united front, all nationalist parties and groups, even such erstwhile pro-Japanese elements as the Cao Dai, were to be attracted into the movement. Moreover, new mass organizations were to be established as conduits for the integration of the population into the movement. These new mass organizations, called Cuu Quoc, or National Salvation associations, were simply adaptations of the organizations already established, with the label Cuu Quoc attached to them. The Cong Nhan Hoi (Workers' Associations) became Cong Nhan Cuu Quoc, the Thanh Nien Hoi (Youth Associations) became Thanh Nien Cuu Quoc, and so forth.[17] There were four main groupings—for workers, peasants,

15. *Ibid.*
16. *Ibid.*
17. *TLTK,* X, 39. The Cuu Quoc were thus not "entirely new" as McAlister said. See John T. McAlister, *Vietnam: The Origins of Revolution* (New York, 1971).

youth, and women, but in recognition of the broader nature of the Vietminh alliance, others were to be established for landlords and urban intellectuals. The new Cuu Quoc were to be organized within the body of the Vietminh League on the basis of democratic centralism, with local units at the village level led by locally elected executive committees, and then up through district and province levels to a central executive committee.[18]

The second aspect of the plenum's work was concerned with developing the new guerrilla strategy patterned after the experience of the communist movement in China. In the eyes of Ho, the Japanese occupation of key parts of Indochina, and the gradual diminution of French colonial authority because of the war, provided the communists with an unparalleled opportunity to launch a national insurrection aimed at achieving total independence. In 1941, the time was not yet ripe, but preparations should be immediately undertaken in order that the Vietnamese revolutionaries could take power before the French were able to return in force after the end of the war. In furtherance of the new strategy two revolutionary base areas were built in the mountainous zone of the Viet Bac, in the area of Bac Son, and in the province of Cao Bang. Leadership in Cao Bang was to be in the hands of Ho, and he was to be assisted to Pham Van Dong, Vo Nguyen Giap, Vu Anh, and Hoang Van Hoan. Leadership in the Bac Son area was to be under the regional committee of Tonkin, with Phung Chi Kien as head, assisted by Luong Van Tri and Chu Van Tan.[19] The two areas were to be freed of colonial control and organized by the revolutionary forces before the end of the war. The basic unit would be at the village level, with militia organized to arrange for local self-defense, and higher echelons would be established in cantons, districts, and finally the province itself. It would be from these areas along the Sino-Vietnamese border that the war of national liberation would be launched.[20]

Cadres were sent at the direction of the plenum to the various

18. *TLTK*, X, 54.
19. *Révolution d'Août*, p. 34.
20. For Ho Chi Minh's activity during this period, see Phan Ngoc Lien, "Cong tac van dong, giao duc quan chung cua Ho Chu Tich trong thoi gian Nguoi o Pac Bo" [Agitprop work of Chairman Ho Chi Minh during his stay at Pac Bo], *NCLS*, no. 149 (March–April 1973).

base areas being established in the Viet Bac in order to undertake the process of organization. Because of the nature of the area, care was to be taken to attract minority support for the cause.[21] Throughout 1941, the base areas functioned with increasing effectiveness. One-third of the districts in Cao Bang province were totally organized and taken over by the revolutionaries, with Vietminh organizations replacing those of the colonial government. A headquarters was established, and a training base for cadres turning out forty participants every ten days.[22]

In Bac Son, however, the revolutionaries met with greater resistance. French attacks intensified in late 1941 and early 1942, and in a major battle in Na Ri village the communist leader Phung Chi Kien was killed; Luong Van Tri was captured and later died in prison. After the defeat at Na Ri in northern Bac Can province, the remaining communists dispersed or fled to Vo Nhai where Chu Van Tan was building up the new National Liberation Army.[23] Despite French pressure, therefore, the two base areas were able to survive and become the headquarters for the communist-led revolt after the war.[24]

The events of 1941 were destined to have fateful consequences for the future, and to cause the Vietnamese communists to look back on the Eighth Plenum in that isolated mountain area of Pac Bo as a landmark in the history of their movement, and of their nation. For out of the conference had come the strategy that was to carry communism to its partial victory over the French in the postwar period, culminating in the settlement at Geneva in the summer of 1954.

The strategy of victory forged at Pac Bo was not an immediate success. The united front with moderate and conservative elements was more easily talked of than realized. In the first place, some nationalist elements continued to place their trust in the Japanese, and right up to the end of the war in 1945 many preferred cooperation with Japan to alliance with France or the communists in the Vietminh. (A specific indication of this attitude is the so-

21. *Ibid.*, pp. 13–22.
22. *TLTK*, X, 64–65; Vo Nguyen Giap, pp. 39–42.
23. Vo Nguyen Giap, p. 60; *Révolution d'Août*, p. 35.
24. McAlister, p. 116, says that communist success among the minorities was vital to their overall success in their war against the French.

called independent Bao Dai government formed under prime minister Tran Trong Kim by the Japanese in March 1945.) In the second place, many nationalists were suspicious of the communists and their new front organization, and had no desire to join with them even against a common enemy. This was particularly true among the exile groups in South China, where awareness that the Vietminh was a fundamentally communist organization was highest. It is notable that Ho Chi Minh was unable to win over many of the VNQDDs and other noncommunist nationalists in South China during the early years of World War II. Only in 1944, when he was released after two years in jail were the Vietminh able to establish informal cooperation with noncommunist groups in the area, under the sponsorship and constant prodding of the local Kuomintang military leader Chang Fa-kuei.

As the war closed, the problem of developing the united front became a matter of even greater urgency as the party attempted to forge an alliance of all classes of the Vietnamese people against the colonial authority. The problem was complicated, however, by the continuing hostility to communism of a number of major nationalist figures and parties. Such major political figures as Pham Quynh, Bui Quang Chieu, Ngo Dinh Diem, and even the Trotskyite Ta Thu Thau looked with disfavor on the aims of the Vietminh. With the exception of Ngo Dinh Diem, all would pay dearly for their opposition. All were executed, presumably on orders of the communists, before the end of 1945.[25]

As the war drew to a close in the late summer of that year, the Vietminh had some partial success in winning over hesitant individuals and groups to their side. Having abolished the ICP (in name only, for a covert organization continued to exist until the formation of the Lao Dong Party in 1951) in order to minimize the visual signs of communism in the Vietminh movement, Ho Chi Minh proclaimed the establishment of a Provisional Government in Hanoi in August 1945.[26]

25. Joseph Buttinger, *Viet-Nam: A Dragon Embattled* (New York, 1967), II, 553. In Vietminh eyes, of course, the common denominator was collaboration with Japan.
26. It was this time that he openly took the pseudonym of Ho Chi Minh. Until this point he was known in the revolutionary movement by a variety of aliases, but to the public as a whole as Nguyen Ai Quoc.

The declaration was made in the name of the nationalist alliance that had been formed under the aegis of Chang Fa-kuei in South China in 1944, but in actuality the dominant force behind the new government was that of the communists in the Vietminh. While lower-level cadres were spreading out through the villages in the mountain and delta areas in North and Central Vietnam, the government, under the leadership of Ho Chi Minh, began to attract noncommunist nationalist figures and parties in preparation for the coming struggle against the returning French. While some moderates refused their cooperation, it is apparent that many—often not aware of the communist character of the leadership—agreed to participate, and the Provisional Government became by 1946 reasonably representative of the major political forces in Tonkin and Annam in the postwar period. Even Emperor Bao Dai, who had accepted a spurious independence from the Japanese in March, was compelled with some reluctance to abdicate the throne and transfer legitimacy to the new government in Hanoi, in return for the sinecure position as Supreme High Adviser.

In the South, the communists were less fortunate. Although the communist movement had been stronger in the South during the 1930s than elsewhere in Vietnam, moderate parties were also better organized there. As the war ended, radical and pro-French forces jockeyed for position to take advantage of the confusion in Saigon. Hindered by distance, the Vietminh were only slowly beginning to construct their political and military base at the village level in the South. Further resistance to the spread of Vietminh influence came from religious sects like the Cao Dai and the Hoa Hao who resented outside control—whether from the communists or from the government. Finally, the communists were disadvantaged by the attitude of General Douglas Gracey, commander of the British Expeditionary Force assigned to accept Japanese surrender and maintain law and order south of the 16th parallel until a political solution could be realized. Gracey was sympathetic to the return of the French and refused to deal seriously with radical nationalist elements. The French were, therefore, able to return with ease to the South, whereas in the North, Chinese occupation authorities, while not openly favoring the Vietminh, permitted their consolidation of power. Local communist leaders in Cochin China were able to achieve a position of influence in the Committee of the South, a temporary body of nationalists formed to negotiate with the British forces and the returning French. But when Gracey proved unsympathetic, the communists and all other anti-French elements were forced to abandon Saigon and retreat to the rural areas, where they were attacked and driven to cover by Gracey's forces. By early 1946, the South was securely in French control. The division that ensued—with Ho Chi Minh at the head of the Provisional Government in the North and the French returned to power in Saigon—was an indicator of things to come.

Whatever the immediate limitations of their position, however, the communists had emerged from the war in a strong position. They were the dominant political force in Vietnam, and had begun to be recognized by the majority of the population and through the medium of the Vietminh as the chief spokesmen for Vietnamese independence.

By the time hostilities broke out with the French in December 1946, the Vietminh had won the support or sympathy of wide sections of the populace. No other party was able to rival the Vietminh as an anticolonial force in the country. Some moderates, fearing communism more than continued colonial control, joined Bao Dai in establishing an "associated state" under French control to support the French in the war against the Vietminh movement. Many of the old figures were gone, but Nguyen Phan Long was prominent in the so-called "Bao Dai solution." Others, like Ngo Dinh Diem, refused to join forces with either side and waited for other opportunities. As events developed, the communists, through the Vietminh alliance, took over the mantle of nationalism in Vietnam.

Conclusions

With the formation of the Vietminh League at the party's Eighth Plenum in 1941 the communist movement entered its sixteenth year of active existence. During that period it had endured a number of major setbacks which would undoubtedly have annihilated an organization of lesser skill and determination. But despite the attempts of the French to eliminate it, it had become a major political force in Vietnam, and certainly the most dynamic and effective organization within the Vietnamese nationalist movement.

Who were these men, and what drew them to communism? We

have at this point relatively few sources of information on the backgrounds of the communist party leadership, but such evidence as is available demonstrates that the leadership of the communist movement in the interwar years was composed primarily of intellectuals. While there were undoubtedly workers and peasants in the movement—and particularly in the party's mass associations—few seem to have become professional revolutionaries, and even fewer reached a position of leadership in the party.

From their background it is fairly clear that the founding generation of the communist movement was made up of basically modern men—Vietnamese who had been exposed to Western culture and political ideology. Most of the party's leadership had at one time or another been educated in the Franco-Vietnamese school system and many had received a degree and entered such careers as teaching and journalism.[27] As such, they had become members of the emerging middle class, and were of the same general social stratum as the young Vietnamese who formed the nucleus of the urban nationalist parties that arose in Vietnam after World War I. Why some of these educated young Vietnamese became revolutionaries while others were satisfied to expend their energies in moderate reformism is not an easy question to answer. From the evidence available, however, it appears that moderates tended to come from the relatively affluent section of the bourgeoisie. They were somewhat more likely to have gone to the prestigious schools in the Franco-Vietnamese system and on to France for their higher education, and they were more likely to have joined such lucrative vocations as law, commerce, and medicine, than those who became members of radical parties. It would probably be wrong to view the founding members of the communist movement as totally deprived of opportunities to rise within the system. Many of the leaders of the movement, by their education and background, could have expected to achieve reasonable success in a number of careers open to them—in teaching, government, or journalism. Yet it is probably true that, as John T. McAlister states in his study, *Vietnam: The Origins of Revolution,*

27. Many who had gone to France for their education, of course, later went on to the Stalin School in Moscow. Of those educated in Moscow, however, remarkably few emerged from World War II in leading positions in the party.

many young Vietnamese were drawn to revolution by a sense of being denied access to the status in society they deserved.[28] Many of the careers to which these young men would have aspired were relatively low-paying and did not open the doors to either wealth or political power.

Yet it is not really enough to say that many became revolutionaries simply because reality did not accord with their personal aspirations, for in many cases, they seem to have become radicalized before entering the job market. It is interesting to note that of the top leadership of the communist movement during this period, the vast majority for whom we have biographical information came from scholar-gentry backgrounds. And, where we have information, it often appears that members of their immediate family were active in, or least in sympathy with, the nationalist or protonational organizations opposed to French rule—the Can Vuong, Phan Boi Chau's Exodus to the East, or the Hanoi Free School. If this is the case for the bulk of the early communist leadership, then it is likely that many acquired their resentment of French rule and their activist proclivities from their families even before entering the larger society. From this point of view, the leaders of the communist movement in the 1920s and 1930s can be viewed as direct heirs of the Phan Boi Chau scholar-patriot generation. They were a generation removed, to be sure, and more modern in their outlook and in their solutions, but essentially carried on the tradition of resistance established by their elders.

Eventually the communist movement became more than just the home of the offspring of scholar-gentry families, of course, but it is wise to keep in mind how small and how socially limited the party leadership was in its early years. The Comintern was critical of the petit bourgeois character of the League, and in the 1920s and early 1930s had emphasized the need to build up worker participation in the movement.[29] There is not much indication, however, that this had much effect, at least prior to World War II.

28. McAlister, pp. 302–303. That should not be taken to imply that their decision to join the revolutionary cause reflected selfish interests only. Revolutionary work opened serious risks of death and imprisonment.

29. Comintern communications with the ICP in the early 1930s were often preoccupied with the problem of increasing worker influence in the party.

Party work in rural areas was similarly plagued with problems. The movement had begun to make inroads among the peasantry in some areas, notably in Annam and in parts of the Mekong delta, but Comintern distrust of the peasantry prevented the communists from following up immediately on the experience in Nghe-Tinh and it could hardly be said that before the anti-Japanese war the ICP had deep roots in the villages.[30]

This early failure to broaden the base of the movement is not the only limitation of the party in the prewar period. Like its predecessors, it suffered from adventurism and factionalism, particularly in the early years. To a degree, such problems were the consequence of inadequate communications, ambiguous Comintern directives, and the zealous activities of the French Sûreté-Général. In retrospect, it is striking to observe how little regional sentiment surfaced in the first decade of the communist movement.[31] In this respect the party had gone beyond its predecessors.

Whatever their early weaknesses, the uniqueness of the communists in the history of Vietnamese nationalism was that, unlike their rivals, they were able to eliminate or minimize obstacles to the ultimate seizure of power. For by the late 1930s, the ICP had begun to formulate a positive strategy which would eventually carry it to victory in the postwar period. And in the process many of the old errors would be eliminated. Some of the major elements of that strategy had already been laid out—by Lenin's theory of a nationalist alliance designed to ally all progressive and anti-imperialist forces in a colonial or semicolonial area in opposition to imperialist control; and by Mao Tse-tung's application of Marxist-Leninist strategy to a specifically Asian setting, involving the deliberate use of the peasantry as a major force in the revolution, and the adoption of guerrilla tactics in an attempt to utilize

30. This is a matter of some disagreement. Jean Chesneaux, in his *tradition et révolution au Vietnam* (Paris, 1971), p. 220, contends that the shift to a rural strategy occurred only in the late 1930s. Tran Van Giau disagrees, and asserts that the ICP always had a "rural strategy." See his discussion in *NCLS*, no. 142 (Jan.–Feb. 1972), p. 26. Without further evidence to the contrary, I am inclined to agree with Chesneaux' conclusions on this point. The ICP worked among the peasantry, but appeared to have no concerted strategy involving rural areas.

31. There are some indications of regionalism during the life of the League, but few examples in the history of the ICP after 1930.

the strength of the rural population to surround the cities peopled by the bourgeoisie and controlled by the colonial power. The strategy began to become apparent in the years immediately prior to the World War II, with the Bac Son uprising and the establishment of the Vietminh front. The new emphasis, the establishment of guerrilla bases along the border, reflected a shift away from the cities and the orthodox, Stalinist-style urban insurrection.[32]

But perhaps the major significance of the formation of the Vietminh League was its solidification of the party's determination to utilize the role of nationalism in the struggle to evict the French. As the brief biographies of the countless communist figures in this study seem to show, communism in Vietnam was born out of the nationalist movement. Communist leaders commonly started their revolutionary careers as members of more manifestly nationalist groups—the VNQDD, the Youth Party, the Tam Tam Xa, or the Revolutionary Party—and then turned to Marxist-Leninist doctrine because it seemed like the most effective way to achieve independence.

Communism and nationalism were not always so easily matched, of course. Zealous party members occasionally puristically rejected the emotional appeals of patriotism. Slogans calling for national independence and self-determination, which appealed to the urban bourgeoisie, often had little meaning in rural communities, where

32. McAlister contends, p. 132, that the new strategy was probably a consequence of Truong Chinh's emergence as a major political figure in the party leadership. Dang Xuan Khu, whose pseudonym Truong Chinh means "Long March" in Chinese, has long been presumed to be a member of the pro-Maoist faction in the party. It is not improbable that his growing influence in the party is one cause of the shift to a Maoist strategy, but it is more likely that the shift to a new approach in 1940 and 1941 was at the urging of Ho Chi Minh himself, who was clearly in charge after his arrival in the border area in 1940. While there are some indications that communist leaders in Vietnam were thinking along the same lines, the most direct link between the Vietnamese communist movement and the Maoist movement in China was Ho and, for lack of contrary evidence, the new approach can be viewed as a direct consequence of his own exposure to Chinese strategy during the late 1930s when he spent considerable time with the CCP in Yenan. There is certainly nothing to make one doubt his ideological ascendancy in the party. It might thus be said that his experience in China represented a weaning away from the Soviet training of his earlier career, and that he saw greater utility in the "Maoist model" for Vietnam.

a sense of nationalism was only beginning to emerge. On the other hand, as the communists found out in 1930–1931, policies that could win the support of the rural poor risked alienating the middle class in the towns. The challenge for the communists was to tailor their message to the particular target group—national concerns in the cities, economic issues in the rural areas—without destroying the effectiveness of the front as a whole. And, with the formation of the Vietminh, the party had taken a major step towards achieving their goal of building a mass-based movement of national proportions. It had reached the apex of a period of self-education. It was now prepared to commence the struggle to grasp political power in Vietnam.

Chapter 16

The Character of
Nationalism in Vietnam

A relatively mature consciousness of nationalism existed in Vietnam at the beginning of World War II. But the roots of modern nationalism are clearly discernible, well before the beginning of the present century, in Vietnam's historically strong sense of ethnic awareness, an awareness that was tempered by her age-old struggle to resist conquest from the north. Western colonialism, then, did not "create" a sense of separate national or ethnic identity in Vietnam as it did in other societies in Asia; it merely channeled Vietnam's traditional self-awareness along more modern lines.

The protonationalism of the precolonial period met its end in the protracted but undirected struggle against the French in the late nineteenth century. The failure of the Can Vuong illustrated the basic weakness of the traditionalist approach in the face of an invading force endowed with modern weapons, and the next generation of Vietnamese patriots was quick to interpret the French conquest as a sign that the old ways would not work against the new enemy. That Confucian figures such as Phan Boi Chau and Phan Chu Trinh concluded so rapidly that tradition had ceased to have relevance is indicative of the degree to which the Vietnamese gave precedence to national survival over cultural purity.[1] The image of the new society they spun in their dreams was perhaps superficial and naive, but theirs was a sincere attempt to bring Vietnam abreast of the modern world; they took the first step toward modern nationalist movement in Vietnam.

1. In China, by contrast, the transitional generation of Confucian-trained reformist intellectuals found it relatively difficult to abandon their emotional commitment to traditional values.

The weakness of the scholar-patriots was inadvertent, but nonetheless fatal. Lacking experience, they did not see all the implications of the changes taking place in the world, and their techniques and actions were heavily laden with traditionalist assumptions and attitudes. Their simple slogans and isolated feats of derring-do were no match for the sophisticated colonial administration. Clearly it took more to build a modern nationalist movement in Vietnam.

The generation that grew to maturity in the wake of World War I was highly conscious of the weakness of its predecessor. With this generation Vietnamese nationalism moved into the cities. Exposed from childhood to French culture, these modern patriots deliberately brought a new Western flavor to Vietnamese nationalism and were often openly contemptuous of traditional institutions. The urbanization of Vietnamese nationalism did not represent a complete break with the past, however. Many of the leading elements in the new nationalist parties which sprang up in Saigon, Hanoi, and Hué were direct offspring of the scholar-patriots and the Can Vuong, and they felt strongly an emotional responsibility to follow the examples of their elders.

The movement into the cities was a necessary phase in the evolution of nationalism in Vietnam, for only urban Vietnamese were truly conscious of the nature of the Western challenge and were capable of devising a strategy to cope with it. But urbanization created a number of new problems. Nationalist activities in urban areas were relatively easily controlled by the authorities, and clandestine operations were more difficult to carry on than in the countryside. Also, the diversity of the urban class structure exposed the resistance movement to the possibility of increased fractionalization and a lack of unity so necessary to the success of their efforts. Intellectuals, of course, are habitually prone to ideological theorizing and the urban nationalist movement seemed to spend more time in inner controversy than in opposing the colonial regime.

Most important, perhaps, the movement into the cities isolated the nationalists intellectually as well as physically from the traditional roots of Vietnamese society in the village. The modern urban Vietnamese, in absorbing Western values and habits, and in seeking a Western vocation, and perhaps even in speaking a Western language in preference to his own, became an alien force in the countryside, where traditional forms still retained considerable vitality. Although members of the scholar-patriot generation were by their education and, frequently, their family background, distinct from the average peasant, they generally had been raised in the village, had absorbed the traditional Sino-Vietnamese heritage, and, in a word, could speak the villager's language. The modern nationalist, by contrast, often grew up in the city, went through the Franco-Vietnamese school system, and frequently spent several years working or studying in Paris. In the process he lost his link with the villagers, who often viewed him with considerable suspicion. The break in communication, of course, frequently worked both ways, for urban nationalists had little comprehension of the problems of peasants, and the urbanite's concern for constitutional democracy and individual liberty, and his desire for more exposure to Western culture, often had little meaning outside the confines of Saigon and Hanoi.

In abandoning Confucianism as a symbol of Vietnamese nationalism, urban nationalists lost the vital emotional link with the village that a religion could provide. Where urban movements elsewhere in South and Southeast Asia maintained the essential link between elites and peasants by relying heavily on an indigenous religious tradition such as Hinduism, Islam, or Buddhism, Vietnamese intellectuals could go to the peasant only with the still alien values of Western science and democracy. The urbanization of Vietnamese nationalism, then, solved some old problems, but created some uncomfortable new ones, and risked putting modern nationalism in a position of permanent weakness. There were few indications that by the beginning of the Pacific War in 1940 the nationalist movement as a whole was on the road to finding a solution.

Out of this social milieu the Vietnamese communist movement arose. As has been contended above, communism in Vietnam began as one answer to the "national" problem, and it was seen as such by much of its early membership, including Ho Chi Minh. As a primarily urban movement it was subject to the problems created by the urbanization of Vietnamese nationalism. Indeed, by the time a formal party was created in 1930, the urban orientation of the movement was deliberately encouraged by Comintern strategy devised in Moscow. During these formative years, the communist movement did relatively well in competing with pure nationalist organizations for support among the workers and urban petty bourgeoisie. If they suffered to a degree for their dependence on a foreign ideology, they made up for this disadvantage by their determination and ability. By the late 1930s they had become the most vital force in Vietnamese nationalism. The striking success of the communists among educated Vietnamese was somewhat unusual in Southeast Asia and deserves further comment. One advantage for the Indochinese Communist Party perhaps, was the colonial tie with France. A large number of Vietnamese intellectuals received their education (and their Marxist beliefs) in Paris, and it is likely that the attraction of the French intellectual to Marxism rubbed off on many French-trained Vietnamese.

Another advantage of Marxism in Vietnam lay in its attractiveness to intellectuals who were in the midst of an identity crisis. As has been observed earlier, nationalists in Vietnam could not build their movement around native religious symbols because Confucianism, closely linked with the reactionary court, never took hold as a symbol of Vietnamese identity within the nationalist movement. The decline of Confucianism in the cities left an emotional and intellectual void in the minds of patriotic intellectuals, and many obviously found Marxist doctrine an attractive modern alternative to the discredited Sino-Vietnamese tradition. As an intricate and sophisticated philosophy, with a universal dogma and a comprehensive explanation of history that was optimistic, scientific, impregnated with moral fervor, and staunchly anti-imperialist, Marxism could be accepted without great difficulty as a modern equivalent of Confucianism.[2]

Still, without a broader base than the urban areas could provide, Vietnamese communism was in the same leaky boat as its nationalist rivals, and it was first and foremost the communists who made the effort to transform nationalism into a mass phenomenon. The experience of the Nghe-Tinh soviets showed, albeit briefly,

2. This phenomenon has been discussed in its Chinese context by a number of authors. For an analysis of the relationship between Confucianism and Marxism in modern Vietnam, see Nguyen Khac Vien, "Confucianisme et Marxisme," in Jean Chesneaux, ed., *Tradition et révolution en Vietnam* (Paris, 1971).

the potential force of the peasant, but the destruction of the Central Vietnamese apparatus and the emergence into leadership of Stalin School graduates trained in Moscow nipped the early indications of a rural strategy in the bud. By the late 1930s, however, changes were in the wind. The Popular Front showed that the party could work with all classes. The Comintern showed less interest in Indochina and allowed the Indochinese Communist Party greater freedom to design its own strategy. By 1938, two young Communists, Vo Nguyen Giap and Truong Chinh, had written a study of the peasant question which, though unspecific about the peasant's role in the Vietnamese revolution, called him an "invincible force" and intimated that the party should pay more attention to his problems.[3] Then, in 1939–1940, the Indonesian Communist Party was driven from the cities and a new strategy was discovered at Bac Son. In 1941 the leadership caught up with events and at the Eighth Plenum at Pac Bo, put the final touches on the new strategy.

As the Pacific War began, then, the communists had begun the process of building a mass movement for national liberation on the basis of an alliance between the peasantry and the urban intellectuals. The fusing of intellectuals and peasants, if effective, would combine the leadership ability of the former with the tempestuous force of rural discontent. If the Vietminh could successfully attain the pose of an essentially nationalist movement, if it could become the most effective force opposed to French rule in Vietnam, with a finger on the pulse of the discontents of all major strata of Vietnamese society, it would be able to establish itself in the minds of millions of Vietnamese as the legitimate heir to French rule in Vietnam, and the new recipient of the Mandate of Heaven.

Victory would not be rapid or easy, as Ho Chi Minh continually reminded his colleagues. It would take discipline, organization, patience, and willingness to sacrifice. Whether the communists would be able to sustain their momentum after the war was a question only the future could decide, for new times would call for new solutions, new policies. Would the peasant follow the communists? Would the party be able to convince the peasant that it

3. Vo Nguyen Giap and Truong Chinh, *The Peasant Question (1937–1938)*, trans. and with an introduction by Christine Pelzer White (Data Paper no. 94, Southeast Asia Program, Cornell University, Jan. 1974).

was the heir to the Heavenly Mandate? Would it be able to reconcile the sometimes conflicting demands of city and country, of national self-determination and social reform, in a hard, bitter struggle against its rivals as well as against the French?

In 1941, there were no answers to these questions. Yet the potential for growth was there. The party was small, but it was dedicated and its members were steeled in adversity; their revolutionary zeal was undeniable. And, of course, they were blessed with a leader of singular capacity, for over two decades Ho Chi Minh had shown a striking ability to steer the party from the shoals of factionalism, regionalism, and adventurism. In 1941, the movement, the man, and the moment converged. The communists stood on the brink of grasping victory. They had demonstrated that they alone possessed the understanding, and that indefinable sense of will so necessary to the achievement of victory in human affairs.

Bibliography

Documentary and Archival Sources

Archives Nationales de France, Section Outre-Mer. Paris.

Gouvernement Générale de l'Indochine. "Direction des Affaires Politiques et de la Sûreté Générale." *Contribution à l'histoire des mouvements politiques de l'Indochine Française*. 6 vols. Hanoi: Imprimerie d'Extrême Orient, 1930–1933.

Sources in Western Languages

Ajalbert, Jean. *Les Destinées de l'Indochine*. Paris: Michaud, n.d.

———. *L'Indochine en peril*. Paris: Stock, 1906.

Anh Van and Jacqueline Roussel. *Mouvements nationaux et lutte des classes au Vietnam*. Paris: Reamur, n.d.

Beau, Paul. *Situation de l'Indochine, 1902–1907*. Saigon: Marcellin Rey, 1908.

Boudarel, George. "Bibliographie des oeuvres relatives à Phan Boi Chau editées en quoc ngu à Hanoi depuis 1954," *Bulletin de l'Ecole Française d'Extrême Orient*, 56 (1969).

———, trans. "Phan Boi Chau: Memoires," *France-Asie*, 22, third and fourth trimesters, 1968.

Buttinger, Joseph. *Viet-Nam: A Dragon Embattled*. 2 vols. New York: Praeger, 1967.

Cahier des voeux annamites. Saigon: Imprimerie de l'Echo Annamite, 1926.

Castex, Raoul. *Jaunes contre blancs*. Paris: Lavauzell, n.d.

Chack, Paul. *Hoang Tham: Pirate*. Paris: Editions de France, 1933.

Chautemps, Maurice. "Le Vagabondage en pays annamite." Thesis, Université de Paris, 1908.

Chesneaux, Jean, ed. *Tradition et révolution au Vietnam*. Paris: Anthropos, 1971.

Coulet, Georges. *Les Sociétés secretes en terre d'Annam*. Paris: Ardin, 1926.

Dabezies, Pierre. "Forces politiques au Vietnam." Thesis, Université de Bordeaux, 1955.

Degras, Jane, ed. *The Communist International: Documents*. 3 vols. London: Oxford University Press, 1960–1963.

Demanaux, Jean-Claude. *Les Secrets des Iles Poulo Condore*. Paris: Peyronnet, 1956.

Devillers, Phillipe. *Histoire du Vietnam du 1940 à 1952*. Paris: Editions du Seuil, 1952.

Dorgelès, Roland. *Sur la route mandarine*. Paris, 1929.

Dorsenne, Jean. *Faudra-t'il évacuer l'Indochine?* Paris: Nouvelles Sociétés d'Editions, 1932.

Doumer, Paul. *Situation de l'Indochine, 1897–1901*. Hanoi: Schneider, 1902.

Duiker, William J. "Hanoi Scrutinizes the Past: The Marxist Evaluation of Phan Boi Chau and Phan Chu Trinh," *Southeast Asia: An International Quarterly*, 1 (Summer 1971).

——. "The Red Soviets of Nghe-Tinh: An Early Communist Rebellion in Vietnam," *Journal of Southeast Asian Studies*, 4 (Sept. 1973).

——. "The Revolutionary Youth League: Cradle of Communism in Vietnam," *China Quarterly*, no. 53 (July-Sept. 1972).

Duong Van Giao. "L'Indochine pendant la guerre de 1914–1918." Thesis, Université de Paris, 1925.

Fall, Bernard, ed. *On Revolution*. New York: Praeger, 1967.

Garros, Georges. *Forceries humaines*. Paris: André Delpeuch, 1926.

Hemery, Daniel. *Révolutionnaires légaux et pouvoir colonial à Saigon de 1932 a 1937: Le Groupe et le journal "La Lutte."* Paris: Maspéro, forthcoming.

Histoire de la Révolution d'Août. Hanoi, 1972.

Ho Chi Minh: Notre camarade. Paris: Editions Sociales, 1970.

Hoang Ngoc Thanh. "The Social and Political Development of Vietnam as seen through the Modern Novel." Ph.D. Dissertation, University of Hawaii, 1969.

Isoart, Paul. *Le Phénomène nationale vietnamien*. Paris, 1961.

King Chen. *Vietnam and China, 1938–1954*. Princeton: Princeton University Press, 1969.

Lacouture, Jean. *Ho Chi Minh*. New York: Random House, 1968.

Langlois, Walter G. *Indochina Adventure*. New York: Praeger, 1966.

Lebel, Guy. *Deux aspects de l'évolution du Protectorat Français en Annam-Tonkin*. Paris: Mecheline, 1932.

Le Thanh Khoi. *Le Vietnam*. Paris: Editions du Minuit, 1955.

Lewis, John Wilson. *Peasant Rebellion and Communist Revolution in Asia*. Stanford: Stanford University Press, 1974.

Marquet, Jean. *L'Avenir du pays d'Annam*. Qui Nhon, 1926.

Marr, David. *Vietnamese Anticolonialism, 1885–1925*. Berkeley: University of California Press, 1971.

McAlister, John T. "Mountain Minorities and the Vietminh," in Peter Kunstadter, ed., *Southeast Asian Tribes, Minorities, and Nations*. 2 vols. Princeton: Princeton University Press, 1967.

——. *Vietnam: The Origins of Revolution*. New York: Doubleday, 1971.

McKenzie, Kermit. *Comintern and World Revolution, 1928–1943*. New York: Columbia University Press, 1964.

McLane, Charles B. *Soviet Strategies in Southeast Asia*. Princeton: Princeton University Press, 1966.

Mkhitarian, Suren A. "O formirovanii rabochevo klassa vo Vietname" [On the formation of the working class in Vietnam], in *Narody Afriky i Asii* [The Peoples of Africa and Asia], no. 2 (1965).

——. *Rabochii Klass i Natsional'no-Osvoboditel'noe Dvizhenie vo Vietname* [The Working Class and the National Liberation Movement in Vietnam]. Moscow, 1967.

Monet, Paul. *Français et Annamites: Entre deux feux*. Paris: Rieder, 1928.

Nash President Ho Shi Minh [Our President Ho Chi Minh]. Hanoi, 1967.

Ognetov, I. A. "Komintern i Revoliutsionnoe Dvizhenie vo Vietname" [The Comintern and the Revolutionary Movement in Vietnam], in *Komintern i Vostok* [The Comintern and the East]. Moscow, 1969.

Orgwald [pseud.]. *Tactical and Organizational Questions of the Communist Parties in Indochina and India*. New York: no publisher, 1932.

Osborne, Milton. *The French Presence in Cochinchina and Cambodia*. Ithaca: Cornell University Press, 1969.

Outline History of the Vietnam Workers' Party. Hanoi: Foreign Languages Press, 1970.

Peroz, Lt. Colonel. *France et Japon en Indochine*. Paris: Chapelot, 1906.

Pham Quynh. Charles Maurras: *Penseur politique*. Hué, 1942.

——. *Lettre ouverte à son Excellence le Ministre des Colonies*. No publisher, n.d.

——. *Nouveaux essais franco-annamites*. Hué, 1937.

——. *Quelques conférences à Paris*. Hanoi, 1923.

Phan Thien Chau. "Transitional Nationalism in Vietnam, 1903–1931." Ph.D. dissertation, University of Denver, 1965.

Pinto, Roger. *Aspects de l'évolution gouvernementale de l'Indochine Française*. Saigon and Paris, 1946.

Pouvoirville, Albert de. *L'Annam sanglante*. Paris: Figuere, 1935.

——. *L'Asie française: La garder ou la perdre*. Paris, 1911.

Récits de la résistance vietnamienne. Paris: Maspero, 1966.

Roubaud, Louis. Vietnam: *La Tragédie indochinoise*. Paris: Valois, 1931.

Sacks, I. Milton. "Communism and Nationalism in Vietnam, 1918–1946." Ph.D. dissertation, Yale University, 1960.

——. "Marxism in Vietnam," in Frank Trager, ed., *Marxism in Southeast Asia*. Stanford: Stanford University Press, 1959.

Scott, James C. *The Political Economy of the Peasant Subsistence Ethic in Southeast Asia*. New Haven: Yale University Press, forthcoming.

Smith, Ralph B. "Bui Quang Chieu and the Constitutionalist Party in French Cochin China," *Modern Asian Studies*, 3 (April 1969).

——. "Some Vietnamese Elites in Cochin China, 1943," *Modern Asian Studies*, 6 (Oct. 1972).

Tessan, Francois de. *Dans l'Asie qui s'éveille*. Paris: Renaissance du Livre, n.d.

Thai Van Kiem. "Un Grand Patriote: Le Prince Cuong De," in *France-Asie*, no. 106 (March 1955).

Thompson, Virginia. *French Indochina*. New York: Macmillan, 1937.

Tikhvinskii, C. L. *Syn Yat-sen: Vneshnepoliticheskiie Vozzreniya i Praktika* [Sun Yat-sen: International Views and Policies]. Moscow, 1964.

——. "Vneshnepoliticheskiie vzgliady i deiatel'nost' Syn Yat-sena v 1905–1912 godu" [The international views and activities of Sun Yat-sen from 1905 to 1912], in *Sin'khaiskaya Revoliutsia v Kitae* [The Hsin-hai Revolution in China]. Moscow, 1962.

Tran Huy Lieu. *Les Soviéts du Nghe Tinh*. Hanoi: Foreign Languages Press, 1960.

Truong Buu Lam. *Patterns of Vietnamese Response to Foreign Intervention, 1858–1900*. New Haven: Yale University Press, 1967.

Truong Chinh. *President Ho Chi Minh*. Hanoi: Foreign Languages Press, 1966.

——. *Primer for Revolt*. New York: Praeger, 1963.

Truong Chinh and Vo Nguyen Giap. *The Peasant Question (1937–1938)*. Christine Pelzer White trans. Southeast Asia Program, Cornell University, Data Paper no. 94, Jan. 1974.

Van Lande, Rene. *Sous la menace communiste indochinoise*. Paris: Payronnet, 1930.

Vella, Walter, ed. *Aspects of Vietnamese History*. Honolulu: University of Hawaii, 1973.

Viollis, Andrée. *Indochine S.O.S.* Paris: Gallimard, 1935.

Vo Nguyen Giap. *Military Art of People's War*. New York: Monthly Review, 1970.

———. *People's War, People's Army*. New York: Praeger, 1962.

Werth, Leon. *Cochinchine*. Paris: Rieder, 1926.

Sources in Vietnamese and Chinese

Bui Huu Khanh. "Mot vai y kien ve van de phan phong trong phong trao xo viet Nghe Tinh" [A few opinions on the problem of anti-feudalism in the Nghe-Tinh Soviet movement], *NCLS*, no. 34 (Jan. 1962).

———. "Tu con duong di tim chan ly cuu nuoc cua Ho chu tich den viec thanh lap dang cua giai cap cong nhan Viet Nam" [From the time chairman Ho began the search for the road to national salvation to the founding of the workers' party in Vietnam], *NCLS*, no. 149 (March-April 1973).

Buoc Ngoat Vi Dai cua Lich Su Cach Mang Viet Nam [A Great Step Forward in the History of the Vietnamese Revolution]. Hanoi, n.d.

"Cac co so bi mat cua co quan lanh dao dang cong san dong duong" [The secret basis of the leading organs of the ICP], *NCLS*, no. 37 (April 1962).

Chu Dang Son and Tran Viet Son. *Luan De ve Nhom Nam Phong Tap Chi* [Essays on the Group Connected with Nam Phong Magazine]. Saigon: Thang Long, 1960.

Chu Quang Tru. "Tim hieu Phan Chu Trinh trong lich su can dai Viet Nam" [Searching for Phan Chu Trinh in the modern history of Vietnam], *NCLS*, no. 72 (March 1965).

Chuong Thau. "Anh huong cach mang Trung quoc ve Phan Boi Chau" [The influence of the Chinese revolution on Phan Boi Chau], *NCLS*, no. 43 (Oct. 1962).

———. "Anh huong cua Phan Boi Chau doi voi mot so to chuc cach mang Trung quoc" [Phan Boi Chau's influence on Chinese revolutionary organizations], *NCLS*, no. 56 (Nov. 1963).

———. "Hai van kien ngoai giao dau tien cua Phan Boi Chau" [The first diplomatic documents of Phan Boi Chau], *NCLS*, no. 90 (Sept. 1966).

———. "Moi quan he giua Phan Boi Chau va Cuong De" [The relationship between Phan Boi Chau and Cuong De], *NCLS*, no. 45 (Dec. 1962).

———. "Moi quan he giua Ton Truong Son va Phan Boi Chau" [The relationship between Sun Yat-sen and Phan Boi Chau], *NCLS*, no. 91 (Oct. 1966).

———. Nguon goc chu nghia yeu nuoc cua Phan Boi Chau" [The origins of Phan Boi Chau's patriotism], *NCLS*, no. 88 (July 1966).

——. "Nha yeu nuoc va nha van Phan Boi Chau" [Phan Boi Chau: Patriot and writer], *NCLS,* no. 136 (April 1971).

——. "Phan Boi Chau qua mot so sach bao mien nam hien nay" [Phan Boi Chau through a number of articles and books published in contemporary South Vietnam], *NCLS,* no. 67 (Oct. 1964).

——. "Qua trinh hinh thanh cua giai cap Viet Nam" [The process of formation of the working class of Vietnam], *NCLS,* no. 13 (April 1960).

——. "Tinh hinh nghien cuu Phan Boi Chau tu truoc den nay" [The situation concerning research on Phan Boi Chau from past to present], *NCLS,* no. 104 (Nov. 1967).

——. "Ve hai tap tu chuyen cua Sao Nam: *Nguc Trung Thu* va *Phan Boi Chau Nien Bieu*" [Concerning the two autobiographies of Sao Nam: Nguc Trung Thu and Phan Boi Chau Nien Bao], *NCLS,* no. 75 (June 1965).

Cuong De. *Cuoc Doi Cach Mang Cuong De* [The Revolutionary Career of Cuong De]. Saigon, 1957.

Dang Huy Van. "Cuoc dau tranh giua phai 'chu chien' va nhung phai 'chu hoa' trong cuoc khang chien chong Phap o cuoi the ky XIX" [The struggle between the "hawk" and "dove" factions in the anti-French war at the end of the 19th century], *NCLS,* no. 94 (Jan. 1967).

——. "Them mot so vai y kien ve cong tac su hoc cua Phan Boi Chau" [Some new opinions on the historical work of Phan Boi Chau], *NCLS,* no. 109 (April 1968).

Dang Thai Mai. *Van Tho Cach Mang Viet Nam Dau The Ky XX* [Revolutionary Essays and Poetry in the Early 19th Century]. Hanoi: Van Hoc, 1964.

——. *Van Tho Phan Boi Chau* [The Essays and Poetry of Phan Boi Chau]. Hanoi: Van Hoa, 1960.

Dang Viet Thanh. "Danh gia quan diem luan ly dao duc cua cu Phan Chu Trinh" [An estimate of the moral and ethical concepts of Phan Chu Trinh], *NCLS,* no. 68 (Nov. 1964).

——. "Phong trao Dong Kinh Nghia Thuc" [The Dong Kinh Nghia Thuc movement], *NCLS,* no. 25 (April 1961).

"Dia vi cu Phan o quoc dan ta" [The place of Uncle Phan in the hearts of our countrymen], *Dong Phap Thoi Bao,* 1926. Undated publication, Bibliothèque Nationale, Paris.

Duy Minh. "Danh gia Phan Chu Trinh" [An assessment of Phan Chu Trinh], *NCLS,* no. 69 (Dec. 1964).

Ho Song. "Phan Chu Trinh voi thoi dai cua ong" [Phan Chu Trinh and his times], *NCLS,* no. 73 (April 1965).

Hoa Bang. "Phan Chu Trinh, 1872–1926" [Phan Chu Trinh, 1872–1926], *NCLS*, no. 72 (March 1965).

Hoang Trung Thuc. "Ba muoi lam nam dau tranh cua dang" [Thirty-five years of struggle of the party], *NCLS*, no. 91 (Oct. 1966).

Hoang Van Dao. *Viet Nam Quoc Dan Dang*. [Vietnamese Nationalist Party]. Saigon: Khai Tri, 1970.

Hong Han. "Su thong nhat ve tinh chat phan dong cua Pham Quynh trong linh vuc chinh tri va van hoc" [The unity in the reactionary nature of Pham Quynh's thought in the political and literary spheres], *Van Su Dia*, no. 48 (Jan. 1959).

Hong Quang. "May y nghi ve van de nghien cuu y nghia va tai dung lich su cua xo viet Nghe Tinh" [A few ideas on the problem of studying the meaning and significance of the Nghe Tinh Soviets], *NCLS*, no. 35 (Feb. 1962).

Hung Ha. "Tu tuong quoc gia cai luong cua Phan Chu Trinh" [The national reformist thought of Phan Chu Trinh], *NCLS*, no. 68 (Nov. 1964).

Huong Pho. "Gop phan danh gia tu tuong cua Phan Boi Chau" [A contribution to the evaluation of the thought of Phan Boi Chau], *NCLS*, no. 94 (Dec. 1967).

Huynh Thuc Khang. *Buc Thu Bi Mat cua cu Huynh Thuc Khang Tra loi cu Ky Ngoai Hao Cuong De* [Secret Letter of Huynh Thuc Khang in Reply to Ky Ngoai Hao Cuong De]. Hué: Anh-minh, 1957.

Huynh Van Tong. *Lich Su Bao Chi Viet Nam* [A History of Vietnamese Journalism]. Saigon: Tri dong, 1973.

Le Duan. *Chu Nghia Le Nin va Cach Mang Viet Nam* [Leninism and the Vietnamese Revolution]. Hanoi: Su That, 1960.

Le Huu Muc. *Luan De ve Hoang Dao* [Essays on Hoang Dao]. Hué: Nhan Thuc, 1957.

Le Sy Thang. "Thu neu len mot so nhan xet ve tu tuong triet hoc cua Phan Boi Chau" [An attempt to add some views on the philosophical thought of Phan Boi Chau], *NCLS*, no. 104 (Nov. 1967).

Le Van Lo, "Ba muoi nam thuc hien chinh sach dan toc cua dang" [Thirty years of realizing the nationality policy of the party], *NCLS*, no. 10 (Jan. 1960).

Luong Khe, "Gop may y kien danh gia Phan Chu Trinh" [A few more opinions evaluating Phan Chu Trinh], *NCLS*, no. 69 (Dec. 1964).

Luu Tran Thien. *Phan Boi Chau, Tieu Su va Van Tho* [Phan Boi Chau: A Short History and Selected Writings]. Ngay-mai, 1940.

Minh Tranh. "Dong chi Nguyen Ai Quoc va van de nong dan Viet Nam" [Comrade Nguyen Ai Quoc and the problem of the Vietnamese peasant], *NCLS*, no. 12 (March 1960).

Nguoi Truoc Nga, Nguoi Sau Tien [From Stagnation to Advance]. Hanoi, 1960.

Nguyen Anh. "Dong Kinh Nghia Thuc" [The Dong Kinh Nghia Thuc], *NCLS*, no. 32 (Nov. 1962).

——. "Vai net ve giao duc o Viet Nam tu khi Phap xam luoc den cuoi chien tranh the gioi lan thu nhat" [A few figures on education in Vietnam from the time of the French conquest until the First World War], *NCLS*, no. 98 (May 1967).

——. "Vai net ve giao duc o Viet Nam tu sau dai chien the gioi lan thu nhat den truoc cach mang thang tam" [A few figures on education in Vietnam from the First World War to just prior to the August Revolution], *NCLS*, no. 102 (Sept. 1967).

Nguyen Dinh Chu. "Thuc chat cuoc dau tranh giua Ngo Duc Khe va Pham Quynh chung quanh van de Truyen Kieu" [The truth about the struggle between Ngo Duc Khe and Pham Quynh about Kim Van Kieu], *Nghien Cuu Van Hoc* [Literary Research] (Dec. 1960).

Nguyen Duc Su. "Chu nghia yeu nuoc cua Phan Boi Chau" [The patriotism of Phan Boi Chau], *NCLS*, no. 83 (Feb. 1966).

——. "Phan Chu Trinh voi nhiem vu chong de quoc trong cach mang Viet Nam" [Phan Chu Trinh and the duty of anti-imperialism in the Vietnamese revolution], *NCLS*, no. 69 (Dec. 1964).

Nguyen Duy Dien. *Luan De ve Nam Phong Tap Chi* [Essays on the Nam Phong Journal]. Saigon: Khai Tri, 1960.

Nguyen Hien Le. *Dong Kinh Nghia Thuc* [The Hanoi Free School]. Saigon: La Boi, 1968.

Nguyen Khanh Toan. *Van De Dan Toc trong Cach Mang Vo San* [The National Problem in the Proletarian Revolution]. Hanoi: Su That, 1962.

Nguyen Kien Giang. "Nhung tac pham mo dau mot thoi dai cach mang moi o Viet Nam" [The opening works in a new stage in the Vietnamese revolution], *Hoc Tap*, May 1960.

Nguyen Nghia. "Cong cuoc hop nhat cac to chuc cong sau trong nuoc sau hoi nghi Huong Cang va viec to chuc ban trung uong lam thoi dau tien" [The unification of all communist organizations in the country after the Hong Kong conference and the organization of the first provisional central committee], *NCLS*, no. 62 (May 1964).

——. "Gop them mot it tai lieu ve cong cuoc hop nhat cac to chuc cong san dau tien o Viet Nam va vai tro cua dong chi Nguyen Ai Quoc" [Few additional materials on the unification of all communist organizations in Vietnam and the role of Nguyen Ai Quoc], *NCLS*, no. 59 (Feb. 1964).

Nguyen Thanh Nam. "May nhan xet ve Phan Chu Trinh" [A few observations about Phan Chu Trinh], *NCLS*, no. 71 (Feb. 1965).

Nguyen Trong Hoang. "Chinh sach giao duc cua thuc dan Phap o
Viet Nam" [The educational policy of the French colonialists in
Vietnam], *NCLS*, no. 96 (March 1967).

Nguyen Truong. "Nhan thuc cua Phan Boi Chau ve vai tro quan
chung trong su nghiep dau tranh giai phong dan toc" [The truth
about Phan Boi Chau's thoughts on the role of the masses in the
national liberation struggle], *NCLS*, no. 143 (March–April 1972).

Nguyen Van Trung. *Chu Nghia Thuc Dan Phap o Viet Nam* [The
French Ideology in Vietnam]. Saigon: Nam Son, 1963.

"Nguyen Van Vinh," *Bach Khoa*, no. 32 (May 1958).

Nhan Dan Ta Rat Anh Hung [Our People Are Very Heroic]. Hanoi:
Van Hoc, 1960.

Pham Quynh. *Thuong Chi Van Tap* [The Essays of Thuong Chi]. 5
vols. Saigon, 1962.

Pham Quynh va Nguyen Van Vinh [Pham Quynh and Nguyen Van
Vinh]. Saigon, 1958.

Pham The Ngu. *Lich Su Van Hoc Viet Nam* [A History of Vietnamese Literature]. Saigon: Quoc Hoc, 1961.

Phan Boi Chau. "Ai Viet Dieu Dien" [Lament for Vietnam and Yun-
nan], *NCLS*, no. 56 (Nov. 1963).

——. *Cao Dang Quoc Dan* [A People of Quality]. Hué: Anh minh,
1957.

——. *Khong Hoc Dang* [The Light of Confucius], Hué: Anh minh,
1957.

——. *Nguc Trung Thu* [A Letter from Prison]. Saigon: Mai-linh, n.d.

——. *Phan Boi Chau Nien Bieu* [A Chronological Biography of
Phan Boi Chau]. Hanoi, 1957.

——. *Phap-Viet De-Hue Chinh-kien Thu* [A Letter on Franco–Vietnamese Harmony]. Hanoi: Tan-dan, n.d.

——. *Tan Viet Nam* [New Vietnam], *NCLS*, no. 78 (Sept. 1965).

——. *Truyen Pham Hong Thai* [The Story of Pham Hong Thai].
Hanoi: Van Hoc, 1967.

——. *Van Tho Phan Boi Chau Chon Loc* [Selected Writings of Phan
Boi Chau]. Hanoi: Van Hoc, 1967.

Phan Chu Trinh. "Dao duc va luan ly Dong Tay" [Morality and
ethics of East and West], *NCLS*, no. 66 (Sept. 1964).

——. "Quan tri chu nghia va dan tri chu nghia" [Monarch and
democracy], *NCLS*, no. 67 (Oct. 1964).

——. "That dieu tran" [Seven-point letter], *NCLS*, no. 66 (Sept.
1964).

——. "Thu gui toan quyen Beau" [A letter for Governor-general
Beau], *NCLS*, no. 66 (Sept. 1964).

Phan Ngoc Lien. "Cong tac van dong, giao duc quan chung cua Ho chu tich trong thoi gian nguoi o Pac bo" [Agitprop work of Ho Chi Minh during his stay at Pac Bo], *NCLS*, no. 149 (March-April 1973).

Phan Van Ban. "Dang cong san Phap doi voi cach mang Viet Nam" [The FCP and the Vietnamese revolution], *NCLS*, no. 23 (Feb. 1961).

Phuong Huu. *Phong Trao Dai Dong Du* [The Exodus to the East Movement]. Saigon: Nam Viet, 1950.

Phuong Lan. *Nha Cach Mang Nguyen An Ninh* [The Revolutionary Nguyen An Ninh]. Saigon, 1971.

Quynh Cu. "Tai lieu ve tinh hinh dau tranh cua nong dan trong thoi ky mat tran binh dan" [Materials on the peasant struggle during the period of the Popular Front], *NCLS*, no. 57 (Dec. 1963).

Thanh Le. "Phan Chu Trinh: mot si phu phong kien tu san hoa gian long yeu nuoc" [Phan Chu Trinh: a feudal literatus who became a patriotic bourgeois], *NCLS*, no. 71 (Feb. 1965).

The Nguyen. *Phan Chu Trinh*. Saigon: Tan Viet, 1956.

To Minh Trung. "Ban ve chu nghia cai luong Phan Chu Trinh" [Discussion of Phan Chu Trinh's reformism], *NCLS*, no. 67 (Oct. 1964).

To Trung. "Phong trao Dong Kinh Nghia Thuc" [The Dong Kinh Nghia Thuc Movement], *NCLS*, no. 29 (Aug. 1961).

Ton Quang Duyet. "Mot vai y kien bo sung ve lich su hai dong chi Tran Phu va Nguyen Thi-minh Khai" [A few additional opinions on the history of the two comrades Tran Phu and Nguyen Thi-minh Khai], *NCLS*, no. 139 (July-Aug. 1971).

Ton Quang Phiet. *Phan Boi Chau va Phan Chu Trinh* [Phan Boi Chau and Phan Chu Trinh]. Hanoi: Van Su Dia, 1956.

——. "Phan Chu Trinh: tu cach con nguoi va chu truong chinh tri" (Phan Chu Trinh: his character and his political views), *NCLS*, no. 70 (Jan. 1965).

Ton That Le. *Cuoc Doi Cach Mang Cuong De* [The Revolutionary Career of Cuong De]. Saigon, 1957.

Tran Dan Tien. *Nhung Mao Chuyen ve Doi Hoat Dong cua Ho Chu Tich* [Glimpses of the Life of Ho Chi Minh]. Hanoi: Van Hoc, 1960.

Tran Huy Lieu. *Dang Thanh Nien* [The Youth Party]. Hanoi: Su Hoc, 1961.

——. "Gioi thieu lich su bao chi Viet Nam" [Introduction to the history of Vietnamese journalism], *NCLS*, no. 1 (March 1959).

——. "Gioi thieu mot vai y kien cua cu Phan Boi Chau ve su hoc"

[Introducing a few opinions of Phan Boi Chau on history], *NCLS*, no. 104 (Nov. 1967).

——. *Lich Su Tam Muoi Nam Chong Phap* [A History of 80 Years of Resistance to the French]. 2 vols. Hanoi: Van Su Dia, 1958.

——. *Lich Su Thu Do Ha Noi* [A History of the City of Hanoi]. Hanoi: Su Hoc, 1960.

——. "Nho lai ong gia Ben Ngu" [In memory of Phan Boi Chau], *NCLS*, no. 47 (Feb. 1963).

——. "Phan Boi Chau, tieu bieu cho nhung cuoc van dong yeu nuoc o Viet Nam dau the ky XX" [Phan Boi Chau: the model for all patriotic movements in Vietnam in the early 20th century], *NCLS*, no. 105 (Dec. 1967).

——. "Phan dau de tro nen mot dang vien cong san" [How I became a member of the communist party], *NCLS*, no. 10 (Jan. 1960).

——. *Tai Lieu Tham Khao Lich Su Cach Mang Can Dai Viet Nam* [Historical Research Materials Concerning the Modern Revolution in Vietnam]. 12 vols. Hanoi, 1958.

——. "Van de chinh quyen xo viet" [The problem of Soviet power], *NCLS*, no. 33 (Dec. 1961).

Tran Minh Thu. "Tu *Nguc Trung Thu* den *Phan Boi Chau Nien Bieu*" [From Nguc Trung Thu to Phan Boi Chau Nien Bieu], *NCLS*, no. 69 (Dec. 1964).

Tran Van Giau. "Dang cong san dong duong trong giai doan lich su 1936–1939" [The ICP during the historical period 1936–1939], *Hoc Tap*, Jan. 1959.

——. *Giai Cap Cong Nhan Viet Nam* [The Working Class of Vietnam]. Hanoi: Su That, 1961.

——. *Giai Cap Cong Nhan Viet Nam, 1930–1935* [The Working Class of Vietnam, 1930–1935]. Hanoi: Su Hoc, 1962.

——. *Giai Cap Cong Nhan Viet Nam, 1936–1941* [The Working Class of Vietnam, 1936–1941]. 2 vols. Hanoi: Su Hoc, 1962.

Trung Chinh. "Hoi nghi trung uong lan thu sau va hai cuoc khoi nghia dau tien do dang ta lanh dao" [The Sixth Plenum and the first two uprisings led by our party], *NCLS*, no. 146 (Sept.-Oct. 1972).

——. "Nguyen Van Cu: mot can bo lanh dao dang trong thoi ky 1938–1940" [Nguyen Van Cu: a leading cadre of the party in the period 1938–1940], *NCLS*, no. 145 (July-Aug. 1972).

——. "Tinh chat doc dao cua xo viet Nghe Tinh" [The unique character of the Nghe-Tinh Soviets], *NCLS*, no. 32 (Nov. 1961).

——. "Tinh chat hien thuc cua xo viet Nghe Tinh" [The reality of the Nghe-Tinh Soviets], *NCLS*, no. 30 (Sept. 1961).

——. "Tinh chat tu phat cua xo viet Nghe Tinh" [The spontaneous character of the Nghe-Tinh Soviets], *NCLS*, no. 32 (Nov. 1961).

Truong Giang. "Nhung quan diem triet hoc ve lich su cua Phan Chu Trinh" [All of Phan Chu Trinh's views on the philosophy of history], *NCLS*, no. 73 (April 1965).

Truong Huu Ky. "Them mot so tai lieu ve cu Phan Chu Trinh" [Some additional material on uncle Phan Chu Trinh], *NCLS*, no. 70 (Jan. 1965).

Van Tan. "Nguyen Truong To va nhung de nghi cai cach cua ong" [Nguyen Truong To and his reformist proposals], *NCLS*, no. 23 (Feb. 1961).

——. "Qua trinh tien hanh cong tac mat tran cua dang ta" [The process of building a united front by our party], *NCLS*, no. 139 (July-Aug. 1971).

Van Tao. "Ban ve lien minh giai cap trong cach mang Viet Nam sau 1930" [Discussion of the class alliance in the Vietnamese revolution after 1930], no. 10 (Jan. 1960).

——. "Tim hieu qua trinh hinh thanh va phat trien cua mat tran dan toc thong nhat Viet Nam" [Search for the process of formation and development of the Vietnamese national united front], *NCLS*, no. 1 (March 1959).

Van Than. "Lanh tu cua dang" [The party leadership], *NCLS*, no. 10 (Jan. 1960).

Vo Duc Phuc. "May nhan xet ve qua trinh phat trien cua cach khuynh huong thuoc trao luu van hoc lang man, 1930–1945" [Some observations on the process of development of the romantic school of literature in 1930–1945], *Nghien Cuu Van Hoc*, March 1963.

Vo Nguyen Giap. *Tu Nhan Dan Ma Ra* [From the People]. Hanoi: Quan doi Nhan dan, 1964.

Vu Tho. "Mot so van de lich su dang thoi ky 1936–1939" [A few problems concerning the party in the period 1936–1939], *NCLS*, no. 85 (April 1966).

——. "Qua trinh thanh lap dang vo san o Viet Nam da duoc dien ra nhu the nao" [How did the process of forming a proletarian party in Vietnam take place?], *NCLS*, no. 71 (Feb. 1965).

——. "Tu *Duong Cach Menh* den *Luon Cuong Chinh Tri* cua dang cong san dong duong" [From the Duong Cach Menh to the Luon Cuong Chinh Tri of the ICP], *NCLS*, no. 72 (March 1965).

"Y nghi lich su hoi nghi lan thu sau cua ban chap hanh trung uong dang doi voi cach mang thang tam va cac phong trao dau tranh chong ngoai xam tu 1945 cho den ngay nay" [The historical significance of the Sixth Plenum of the party with regard to the August

Revolution and the struggle against foreign aggression from 1945 to the present], *NCLS,* no. 146 (Sept.-Oct. 1972).

Newspapers and Journals

Asie Française
Avant garde
Cloche fêlée
Ecolier annamite
Effort
Hoc Tap
Jeune Annam
La Lutte
Nam Phong
Nghien Cuu Lich Su
Nghien Cuu Van Hoc
Tribune indigène
Tribune indochinoise

Index

*The Rise of Nationalism
in Vietnam, 1900–1941*

Designed by R. E. Rosenbaum.
Composed by York Composition Company, Inc.,
in 10 point linotype Times Roman, 2 points leaded,
with display lines in monotype Deepdene.
Printed letterpress from type by York Composition Company
on Warren's Number 66 text, 50 pound basis.
Bound by John H. Dekker and Sons, Inc.
in Columbia book cloth
and stamped in All Purpose foil.